Julie Cairnie,
Dobrota Pucherova (Eds.)

Moving Spirit

African Languages – African Literatures
Langues Africaines – Littératures Africaines

Volume 4

LIT

MOVING SPIRIT

The Legacy of Dambudzo Marechera
in the 21ˢᵗ Century

edited by

Julie Cairnie and Dobrota Pucherova

LIT

Cover art: Victor Mavedzenge, *Dambudzo*, 2009. Oil on canvas.

Publikácia je súčasťou grantového projektu VEGA 2/0167/11
This book has been peer-reviewed by two anonymous reviewers.

Layout: Margareta Kontrišová

Bibliographic information published by the Deutsche Nationalbibliothek
The Deutsche Nationalbibliothek lists this publication in the Deutsche
Nationalbibliografie; detailed bibliographic data are available in the Internet at
http://dnb.d-nb.de.

ISBN 978-3-643-90215-3

A catalogue record for this book is available from the British Library

©LIT VERLAG GmbH & Co. KG Wien,   LIT VERLAG Dr. W. Hopf
Zweigniederlassung Zürich 2012   Berlin 2012
Klosbachstr. 107   Fresnostr. 2
CH-8032 Zürich   D-48159 Münster
Tel. +41 (0) 44-251 75 05   Tel. +49 (0) 2 51-620 320
Fax +41 (0) 44-251 75 06   Fax +49 (0) 2 51-23 19 72
e-Mail: zuerich@lit-verlag.ch   e-Mail: lit@lit-verlag.de
http://www.lit-verlag.ch   http://www.lit-verlag.de

Distribution:
In Germany: LIT Verlag Fresnostr. 2, D-48159 Münster
Tel. +49 (0) 2 51-620 32 22, Fax +49 (0) 2 51-922 60 99, e-mail: vertrieb@lit-verlag.de

In Austria: Medienlogistik Pichler-ÖBZ, e-mail: mlo@medien-logistik.at

In Switzerland: B + M Buch- und Medienvertrieb, e-mail: order@buch-medien.ch

In the UK: Global Book Marketing, e-mail: mo@centralbooks.com

ACKNOWLEDGMENTS

This book emerged from the symposium *Dambudzo Marechera: A Celebration*, held on May 15-17, 2009 at Trinity College, Oxford, which was generously funded by Oxford University's Fell Fund and other sponsors, including *Journal of Southern African Studies* and *Wasafiri*. We also wish to thank New College, Oxford, which gave permission for archival photographs of Dambudzo Marechera to be reprinted here, and other artists whose work appears here: Ernst Schade and Victor Mavedzenge. The book was published with the financial and collegial support of Humboldt University, Berlin; University of Guelph, Canada; and Research Grant Agency (VEGA) of Slovak Ministry of Education and Slovak Academy of Sciences. Special thanks go to the anonymous reviewers of the book for their constructive criticism. Above all, we want to express gratitude to Flora Veit-Wild, whose involvement with this book on many levels has been invaluable.

CONTENTS

CONTRIBUTORS

Jennifer Armstrong was born in Harare in 1968. When she was a teen, her parents decided to emigrate to Australia where she would later attend the Ph.D. programme at the University of Western Australia. The title of her 2011 doctoral dissertation at UWA is: "Dambudzo Marechera as Shamanistic 'Doppelgänger': His Shamanistic Sensibility in His Life and Works." Dr. Armstrong's memoir, *Minus the Morning*, is available from Amazon. She currently teaches ESL for a Japanese-based company. She is also a founding director of the Break Free self-defence school of martial arts in Zimbabwe. Jennifer holds a brown belt; working toward a black belt.

Chris Austin is a South African filmmaker who divides his time between Cape Town and London. He left South Africa at the age of 23 and over his years abroad returned secretly to film documentaries and feature films. His films typically combine drama, documentary and performance and include *Not a Bad Girl, Keita! Destiny of a Noble Outcast, A Brother with Perfect Timing, Awake from Mourning, I Talk About Me, I Am Africa, South Africa Belongs to Us, The Rhythm of Resistance* and *The House of Hunger* (1984). www.christopheraustin.com

heeten bhagat is a Zimbabwean. Trained primarily as a pattern cutter, he entered the film industry in Zimbabwe as a costume designer. This afforded on-the-job training in filmmaking. He makes short experimental fiction films and documentaries both in Zimbabwe and in the Southern African region. Having completed an MA in Audio-Visual Production in London, he took up the position of Curator in The National Gallery of Zimbabwe for a short while. Currently, he is involved in a series of educational and cultural projects that are aimed at building peace and stability in post-conflict, post-surreal Zimbabwe.

Elleke Boehmer is internationally known for her research in international and postcolonial writing. Her books include *Colonial and Postcolonial Literature: Migrant Metaphors* (1995, 2005), *Empire, the National and the Postcolonial, 1890-1920* (2002), *Stories of Women* (2005), *Nelson Mandela* (2008) and the acclaimed edition of Robert Baden-Powell's *Scouting for Boys* (2004). In 2009 she co-edited essay collections on J.M. Coetzee and on "postcolonial terror." Boehmer has published four widely praised novels and a collection of short stories. She is the Professor of World Literature in English at the University of Oxford.

Jane Bryce is Professor of African Literature and Cinema at the University of the West Indies, Cave Hill. Born in Tanzania, she was educated there and in the United Kingdom and Nigeria. She has been a freelance journalist and fiction editor and has published in a range of academic journals and essay collections, specializing in popular fiction, contemporary African fiction, representations of gender and visual culture. She also writes creatively and is working on a memoir of colonial Tanzania.

Julie Cairnie is Associate Professor of Postcolonial Literature in the School of English and Theatre Studies at the University of Guelph in Canada. She has presented and published widely on Southern African literature, including *"Imperialists in broken boots": Poor Whites and Philanthropy in Southern Africa* (2010), and is currently working on several linked projects, including a study of narratives of childhood in Zimbabwe and a novel for young adult readers.

Memory Chirere is a Zimbabwean short story writer and University of Zimbabwe lecturer. His stories have appeared in *No More Plastic Balls* (1999), *A Roof to Repair* (2000), *Writing Still* (2003) and *Creatures Great and Small* (2005). He has published three short story collections: *Somewhere in this Country* (2006), *Tudikidiki* (2007) and *Toriro and his Goats* (2010). He compiled and edited (with Maurice Vambe) *Charles Mungoshi: A Critical Reader* (2006).

James Currey added over 250 titles to the African Writers Series for Heinemann between 1967 and 1984. He then founded James Currey Publishers which has become an outstanding imprint for academic studies of Africa. He is now also an adviser to Pearson Heinemann about new publishing in the African Writers Series, which includes reissues of books by Dambudzo Marechera. His book *Africa Writes Back* concludes with his consideration on "Publishing Dambudzo Marechera."

Comrade Fatso is one of Zimbabwe's most innovative spoken word artists. His radical poetry is street, urban, hip hop and African. It is studied at universities in Africa, Europe and North America and has appeared in print and broadcast media in over fifty countries around the world. Comrade Fatso and his band Chabvondoka are an explosive, genre-busting, insurgent act that defies musical boxes, blending rock, hip hop, chimurenga, jiti, kwaito and reggae. Their 2008 album, *House of Hunger*, was praised internationally but banned in Zimbabwe due to its "political content." They have performed all over the world from Europe to the USA, from Africa to the Caribbean.

Robert Fraser is Professor of English at the Open University. He has taught at the universities of London, Leeds and Cambridge. He is the author of books about Proust, Sir James Frazer and Ben Okri, and is a Fellow of the Royal Society of Literature. He has published full-length biographies of the poets George Barker (2002) and David Gascoyne (2012). His latest stage play, depicting the relationship between D.H. Lawrence and Katherine Mansfield, was published in 2010. His copy of *The House of Hunger* is inscribed "To Robert Fraser, all the best, Dambudzo Marechera."

Gerald Gaylard is a Professor in the Department of English at the University of the Witwatersrand, Johannesburg. He writes broadly on postcolonial aesthetics and his publications include *After Colonialism: African Postmodernism and Magical Realism* (Wits Press, 2006) and *Marginal Spaces: Reading Ivan Vladislavić* (Wits Press, 2011).

Carolyn Hart is the author of five books in various stages of production. Her experimental novel *Into the Silence the fishing story* is forthcoming with Red Hen Press. She is completing a historical novel entitled *Waiting in the Rain: The Blood Notebook* and a monograph, *Transgressive Texts: Production and Reception of African and Diasporic Literatures.* She received her PhD from SOAS, University of London. Recent publications include excerpts from her novel *Aurora* in *Blackbox Manifold, Shearsman Magazine,* and *Stride,* as well as an article in *The Journal of African Cultural Studies.* She is Convenor of the MA Creative Writing Programme at London Metropolitan University.

Ilpo Jauhiainen (1977, Finland) is a composer, music producer and sound artist. He works collaboratively and globally across the arts, from music production to art installations, from dance and performance to film and theatre. His song, based on Marechera's poem "A Shred of Identity," is included on Ilpo's new album called *Shimmer & Bloom* (2011).

Katja Kellerer was born in Germany and obtained a Bachelor's degree in Politics and African Studies at the University of San Francisco in 2009. Currently, she is studying at the Department of African Studies at Humboldt University in Berlin and is writing her M.A. thesis on hip hop and urban youth culture in Harare, Zimbabwe.

Alle Lansu (1954, The Netherlands) is a freelance literary journalist. He has reviewed world literature for Dutch and Belgian newspapers and magazines, worked as an editor for literary programmes on Dutch television and radio and interviewed some famous writers such as Paul Bowles, Pascal Mercier, João Ubaldo Ribeiro, and Dambudzo Marechera, among others.

Fiona Lloyd is a Zimbabwean arts journalist and media trainer. She co-founded Zimbabwe Women Writers (ZWW) and the Zimbabwe Women in Culture Trust (ZWICCT). In the early years of Zimbabwe's independence she presented "Spectrum," a weekly radio show which highlighted new writers, artists and musicians, including Dambudzo Marechera. Her work was also broadcast on BBC Africa Service. After Marechera's death, Fiona Lloyd produced a cabaret show based on his writing that was staged in Harare's Gallery Delta and assisted Flora Veit-Wild in compiling *Cemetery of Mind*, an anthology of Marechera's poetry.

Olley Maruma (1952-2010) was a Zimbabwean pioneer filmmaker, journalist, broadcaster, socio-political commentator and novelist. Among a few Zimbabweans to own a production company, Moonlight Productions, Maruma produced the films *The Big Time* (2003), *Consequences* (1983), and the documentary about Zimbabwean writers, *After the Hunger and the Drought* (1985).

Victor Mavedzenge is a Zimbabwean artist currently living and practising in Oakland, California. He holds an M.F.A. from the Slade School of Art. His art is inspired by Victor's personal journey, contemplating from afar the cultural and political turmoil of his native Zimbabwe, commenting on living abroad and the meaning of home and belonging. His work is characterized by vivid color, broken surfaces and movement. Victor is also an art teacher, poet, actor and comedian. www.mavedzenge.com

Nhamo Anthony Mhiripiri is Senior Lecturer in Media and Society Studies at Midlands State University in Gweru, Zimbabwe. He has published critical works in *Emerging Perspectives on Dambudzo Marechera* and in *The Hidden Dimensions of Operation Murambatsvina*. He has short stories in the anthologies *No More Plastic Balls*, *A Roof to Repair*, *Creatures Great and Small*, and *Dreams, Miracles and Jazz: New Adventures in African Writing* as well as poems in the anthologies *State of the Nation* and *Ghetto Diary and Other Poems*. His recent articles appear in *Journal of African Media Studies*, *Radio Journal*, and *Muziki: Journal of Music Research in Africa*.

Tinashe Mushakavanhu is a "born free" Zimbabwean who came into the world in 1983. He graduated with a First Class honors degree in English from Midlands State University and became the first African to receive an MA in Creative Writing from Trinity College, Carmarthen in Wales. He recently completed a PhD in English from University of Kent. He has co-edited *State of the Nation: Contemporary Zimbabwean Poetry* (2009) and *Emerging Perspectives on Chenjerai Hove* (Africa World Press, forthcoming). He is currently producing a series of audio documentaries on Zimbabwean literature.

Ery Nzaramba is a UK-based actor who has written and directed 5 short films (*Annex*, *G54*, *Train Trip*, *Disillusioned* and *Dambudzo*) and performed on radio, in theatre and on television. He also writes poetry and gives poetry workshops. He is currently writing an English adaptation of the play *Fama* by Koffi Kwahulé, developing a short film based on Shakespeare's *Othello*, and a feature film based on Marechera's life. In 2012 he stars in *The Bacchae* and *Blood Wedding*, both plays produced by Royal & Derngate Theatres in London.

Nana Oforiatta-Ayim is a writer and filmmaker based in Accra and London. She founded the platform A-N-O in 2002, which integrates film, writing, curating, publication and research in projects that explore the construction of narratives and meaning, as well as the play of power. She has created books and films for exhibitions such the Generational Triennial, New Museum, New York; Neue Gesellschaft für Bildende Kunst, Berlin (2012), Vela Gallery, London (2011) and The Museum of African Diaspora, San Francisco (2008). She also writes for publications such as *The National Geographic, frieze,* and *The Statesman*.

Dobrota Pucherova is a researcher at the Institute of World Literature, Slovak Academy of Sciences, Bratislava, and a lecturer in African literature at the University of Vienna. Her book, *The Ethics of Dissident Desire in Southern African Writing* (Wissenschaftlicher Verlag Trier, 2011), analyzes South African and Zimbabwean literature in the context of existentialism, French feminism and ethics. Her current research is on African writers living in Europe and the USA. She received her PhD from Oxford University in 2009.

Ernst Schade (1949, The Netherlands) received training in tropical agriculture. For 16 years he worked in Zambia, Zimbabwe and Mozambique with governmental institutions and non-governmental organizations in rural development programmes. Self-taught in photography, this is now his main activity. Since 1995 he has lived in Lisbon, Portugal. He is the co-author (with Flora Veit-Wild) of *Dambudzo Marechera 1952-1987*. He is represented by the photo agencies Panos Pictures (UK) and Hollandse Hoogte (The Netherlands). www.ernstschade.com

Anna-Leena Toivanen is a post-doctoral researcher at the University of Eastern Finland. In her doctoral thesis (2010), she discussed Yvonne Vera's and Dambudzo Marechera's work and authorial images against the backdrop of the Zimbabwe crisis. Some of her recent essays have been published in *Research in African Literatures*, *Postcolonial Text* and *RELIEF*. In her current research project, she is studying the tensions between globalization and nationhood in African women's writing.

Norman Vance was born in Belfast and read English at Wadham College, Oxford. He was Salvesen Research Fellow at New College, Oxford, 1974-6, before moving to the University of Sussex where he is now Professor of English Literature and Intellectual History. His books include *The Victorians and Ancient Rome* (1997) and *Irish Literature since 1800* (2002).

Flora Veit-Wild is Professor of African Literatures and Cultures at Humboldt University, Berlin. Her research interests include Anglophone writing of Southern Africa, Francophone writing of Central Africa, surrealism, body concepts, urban language and literature as well as writing in African languages. Her major publications include *Teachers, Preachers, Non-Believers: A Social History of Zimbabwean Literature* (1992), *Dambudzo Marechera: A Source Book on his Life and Work* (1992), and *Writing Madness: Borderlines of the Body in African Literature* (2006).

PROLOGUE
Dambudzo Marechera—Long Live!

Elleke Boehmer

The free-wheeling verbal energies of Dambudzo Marechera were never to be contained within the moment of history he inhabited, as this collection of tributes amply demonstrates. His posthumous future was already being generated, even as, in Britain and then Zimbabwe, he sprayed out upon ears and pages the poetic invective that became his trademark—an inventive, experimental, scatological and disturbing prose that would become grafted in the imaginations of the future, of the writers and readers who could not but respond to his work, having once read him.

In late 1980's Oxford I was one of those readers, then writers, who stumbled upon Marechera by chance, from a word of mouth suggestion, and was immediately captivated. Reading Marechera, not knowing he was no longer in the world, I wanted to hear him read, to meet him. I had thoughts of travelling to the Harare Book Fair in the hope of listening to him there. I found in his work, as so many others have done, the tone, the sass, the slant, of a deeply interesting successor to the important, yet also earnest, generation of Achebe, Ngugi and Soyinka—a voice that in contrast to theirs was rude, scurrilous, funny, mad, yet, when all was said and done, deadly serious about the power of the word. What could be more liberating and exciting than that, especially in a context where apartheid prevailed, and Mandela was still in prison (yet, as we later found out, reading difficult books, of which Marechera would have approved). I was astonished, impressed, even overawed, that this writer dared cite Eliot when lambasting African nepotism, that he happened upon the shaping fragments of high modernist style in the rubbish tips of Rusape township, that he risked laughing, uproariously, infectiously, even at the Manichean aspects of struggle against colonialism. And so when, many years later, my doctoral student Dobrota Pucherova came to see if I might help her organise a Marechera festival in Oxford, at Oxford University, the domain where he had possibly felt most excluded, yet which fed his first publications, there was only one answer to give: the obvious yes.

In my book *Stories of Women* I write that, the claims of social realism to the contrary, Marechera powerfully contended that "African writers cannot avoid relaying the distorted and distorting shapes of the psyche in their art" (150-1). In related terms, Ato Quayson suggests in *Calibrations* that Marechera's symbolist compulsions tend to go beyond the present moment; to gather and accrue meaning as the future unfolds (83, 86-7).

Both contentions—that writers are compelled by their writing, or that their writing writes them, and that those who are so compelled, consistently exceed the constraints of their context, of the confining forms of history—were dramatically borne out during the May 2009 Marechera Celebration in Oxford. As we listened to the presentations and reminiscences of fellow writers and critics, Marechera seemed almost to take life and walk amongst us. He appeared almost bodily to remind us that word was as powerful as world, so strongly was he remembered, respected, readdressed in that square brick built room in Trinity College. In particular, the Zimbabwean writers and artists present evoked for the audience how for them he was no writer shut away in the past, but that, at a crucial time for Zimbabwe, a time of nepotism and neo-colonialism, of Afro-pessimism and an increasingly more dominant aesthetic of the grotesque, he kept accruing meaning in the present. When he spoke of the derangements and hypocrisy of the failing postcolonial elite he spoke directly to these artists, here in the now. Though he had felt deeply alienated from his domestic context in the 1980's—or even perhaps because of that alienation—he felt close, palpably close, today.

The parochial context of Oxford itself appeared in need of Marechera's roguish and hard-hitting words that May. As the celebration unspooled, in a hall not far away, the flawed election for the Oxford Professor of Poetry was taking place. This election, with its interesting and unpredictable final denouement, ended the awkward month-long kerfuffle in which a hardnosed and ambitious woman candidate had pitted herself against the self-styled Adamic poet Walcott. It was a stand-off full of sexual drama and high-flown rhetoric, that Dambudzo would have relished, though he would have reminded all comers that what was important at the end of the day was the words on the page, not the surrounding political rumpus.

But it was not only in the benches of Convocation House, where the election result was read out, nor in Trinity College, that the ghost of Marechera could be felt, stalking, a bemused smile on his face. As befits the hurler of words he was, Marechera's spirit that May could be felt even out on the street, not far from the College he once inhabited. Here, too, I found how Marechera's shape had been grafted upon the imagination of the future; how he moved as a bemused and inspiring presence among us.

That Saturday, in my rush to cast my vote in the Professor of Poetry election, yet not miss the morning session of the Celebration, I had badly parked my car in Mansfield Road, and put on it only an hour's worth of parking ticket, as I did not have the change to hand to pay for more. At both of the morning venues, the Exam Schools, where the votes were being cast, and Trinity College, deeply involving conversations were taking place. So it was with only seconds to spare before the parking ticket (including its extra time) expired that I was able to make it back to Mansfield Road to retrieve my vehicle. Predictably, this being central Oxford, there was the inevitable parking attendant hovering close by the offending car, already making to take a photo of the car preparatory to slapping on the fine. I hared down the road, shrilling out in an ineffectual way, "Please, no." In addition to all the Professor of Poetry kerfuffle a fine was the last thing I needed.

The parking attendant turned to face me slowly, his face sceptical, curious, bemused. I could tell straightaway that he was used to extravagant pleas from middle-aged ladies accosting him in vain for a reprieve on a perfectly well-deserved parking fine. I drew up beside him and searched his eyes. Now, it is a fact well known around Oxford that many of the parking attendants are Zimbabwean. I had engaged in conversation with these men before, generally not to talk my way out of fines, I must emphasize, but because their accent intrigued me, and I was keen to hear their stories. What had brought them here? Who had they left back home?

I could not be sure this parking attendant on Mansfield Road, holding his camera up to my car, was Zimbabwean, but I was hot and flustered enough to take a chance. "Please," I said, "don't give me a fine. I'll explain why. I've been at a Dambudzo Marechera Festival. Yes, here in Oxford. It was interesting. You know, Dambudzo Marechera? It was difficult to tear myself away."

Slowly, as I spoke, the parking attendant's expression changed. He leaned slightly towards me, as if straining to hear something. Then he said: "Dambudzo Marechera? You said Marechera?"

"Yes," I said, suddenly excited, seeing he knew who I was referring to, "The great Zimbabwean writer. If you were listening to something about Marechera, could you tear yourself away?"

"Dambudzo Marechera," the man said again, without a question in his voice. "Marechera. Marechera. Marechera is here in Oxford." He paused and then at last did put a question, "Marechera is dead, but he is here in Oxford?"

"Yes," I said, "That's right."

"It is amazing, but I can believe it. Marechera is dead but with us. Marechera is great like that, always sticking with us. Celebrate Marechera. Of course we must. Please, take your car and find another parking and celebrate Marechera. Go and celebrate Marechera."

And then he turned, shaking his head as if in disbelief, even as I made to do exactly as he had said.

INTRODUCTION

Julie Cairnie and Dobrota Pucherova

Twenty-five years after his death, Dambudzo Marechera's spirit continues to haunt us. Known as the *"enfant terrible* of African literature," Dambudzo Marechera (1952-1987) has become something of a cult figure in his native Zimbabwe, a country whose political developments have fulfilled his prophetic vision, and an icon of creative freedom to artists and writers world-wide. Exploding previous aesthetic and intellectual paradigms, his urgent, experimental writing gave African literature an entirely new direction. Its raw energy resists containment inside any "–ism;" subversive and iconoclastic, it creates new meanings and modes of thinking, and eagerly hurls expletives at any attempts to define it. Emerging from the pressures on a colonized individual and a black artist, it analyzes power in the postcolonial world with a liberating laughter.

The idea behind *Dambudzo Marechera: A Celebration*, held in Oxford in May 2009, was to recuperate the memory of the author in the place where his writing first emerged and that is imprinted on a number of his early texts, both topographically, as a place with its streets, landmarks, sounds and atmosphere; and also imaginatively, as an idea. From the start, the very notion posed a problem: how does one celebrate an author in an institution that to him represented everything he so detested and continually mocked: authority, "tradition," the canon, academic conceit—in short, the "establishment"? Rather than wanting to "repossess" and institutionalize Marechera through applying a particular theoretical lens to his texts, the multi-media festival proposed that the singularity of Marechera's engagement with language demands an active, inventive, performative response to do it justice. heeten bhagat articulates this challenge in his essay in this book: "How do I pay homage to his words and not lose myself in the process? How do I not fall into the trap of 'translating' but try to take this process further?" As the eclectic variety of contributions presented at the Oxford *Celebration* demonstrated, Marechera's writing invites reinvention. Performative and dissident, it plays with meaning and engenders new forms, myths and epistemologies. Embodying his art in his life, Marechera continuously reinvented himself by donning costumes, making shocking statements and creating myths about his person. Liberation from colonization, Marechera believed, could only happen by making self-reinvention a way of life, adopting a fluid chameleon identity that resisted being defined, categorized and spoken for. The performativity of the Oxford festival celebrated Marechera's ludic approach to life and death.

This was perhaps best expressed through the experimental stage production by Oxford undergraduates of Marechera's two plays, *Blitzkrieg* and *The Servants' Ball* (the first-ever production of *Blitzkrieg*), which creatively combined the two inter-related texts into a playful collage that featured a string quartet and a puppet as the central character, interrogating what national independence might mean in Zimbabwe in the historical moment of 2009 when the society found itself at the bottom of a social, economic and political crisis. Carnivalesque and subversive, with actors cast across race and gender, the play produced laughter while maintaining a sense of dangerous foreboding through its cacophonous music and chiaroscuro lighting.

This book and its audio-visual component emerge from the Oxford festival but include extra contributions not presented there. Conceived as an exploration of the relationships between Marechera and other writers, artists and scholars, the collection testifies that Marechera inspires a dangerous desire for the unknown, whether in terms of friendship, sexuality or spirituality. The volume is structurally divided into three different modes of engagement with Marechera's life and work—creative, reflective and scholarly; yet, we wish to point out that these various practices are not polarized and distinct; rather, Marechera inspires, for example, critical creativity and creative criticism.

Part 1: Inspired Creativity includes contributions from a variety of artists: poets, filmmakers, short story writers, an actor and a dramatist. Robert Fraser's short story, "Kariba's Last Stand," continues in the tradition of his piece "Kariba's Fall" from ten years before (see Veit-Wild and Chennells 105-118) by choosing parody as the appropriate genre to celebrate friendship and youth, sharing a joke with the Marechera insider while offering a strikingly intimate account of a close relationship. While Jane Bryce and Flora Veit-Wild also choose to fictionalize their relationships with the real or mythical Marechera through the short story, Pucherova's stage play, based on Marechera's fiction and poetry, works across genre to bring out the performative aspects of his writing. Special attention belongs to Austin's, bhagat's, Ayim's, and Nzaramba's essays, which are accompaniments to the videos included on the DVD and explore how Marechera's life and work can (or cannot) be transposed into film. While Comrade Fatso's songs "Dambudzo" and "House of Hunger," also included on the DVD, are a testimony that Marechera is part of the Zimbabwean popular culture, the song "A Shred of Identity" by the Finnish musician Ilpo Jauhianinen demonstrates that Marechera speaks to artists across cultures. Inspired to create a musical accompaniment to Nana Oforiatta-Ayim's film "A Shred of Identity" based on Marechera's eponymous poem, Jauhianinen says: "I found a resonance in the poem's feeling of outsiderness and quest for understanding oneself. The words inspired me to search for a new landscape in music, somewhere between Africa and Europe that would embrace the pain but at the same time strive to move toward a brighter future."

Most of the contributors in Part 2: Memory and Reflection are members of what James Currey, in his piece, refers to as the "indaba." Flora Veit-Wild simply describes herself and her fellow panellists at the *Celebration*, most of whom offer contributions here, as "elderly," but she also declares that she "feel[s] just as young as twenty-five years ago when [she] crossed paths with the ominous mindblaster." This is significant because all of the pieces here manage to balance "now" and "then," Doris Lessing's helpful terminology from *African Laughter*. All are, in large part, reflections upon the authors' personal and professional relationships with Marechera. Mhiripiri, a friend of Marechera's, also engages with a "real" person in his poem called "Letter to a Departed Buddy," but it is difficult to say how much, given Marechera's iconic and mythic status. Meanwhile, Armstrong works out her own complicated sense of self, as a "white Zimbabwean," through spiritual, indeed shamanistic connections with the dead writer. Armstrong's personal essay leads into two reflective pieces on the Marechera cult in Zimbabwe and abroad from two young Zimbabwean scholars and writers, Memory Chirere and Tinashe Mushakavanhu.

The four selected texts in the Scholarship section represent the range and complexity of academic work being produced on Marechera's canonical and lesser-known texts. All four pieces, by both established and emerging scholars, are interested in the connections that Marechera's texts explore and/or inspire. While Carolyn Hart examines Marechera's relationship with postmodern writers (especially African American), Katja Kellerer explores the inter-textualities between Marechera's *The House of Hunger* and *The Fools* (1999) by Ignatius Mabasa, a contemporary Zimbabwean writer writing in Shona. What emerges is that Marechera is not an isolated African postmodernist, but can be situated in relation to other artists, whether predecessors, contemporaries or followers. Gerald Gaylard analyzes Marechera's love poetry through the lens of the French postmodernist and psychoanalytic theorists Baudrillard, Derrida, Lacan, Kristeva and Irigaray. Exploring the risky desire to embrace otherness as a route towards a redefinition of self in Marechera's "Amelia" poems, Gaylard carefully unpacks the relationship between heterosexual love, race and colonialism. Finally, Julie Cairnie considers the ways in which Marechera's work speaks to the current crisis in Zimbabwe. She argues that Marechera's children's text, *Fuzzy Goo's Stories for Children*, underscores the relationship between children "now" and "then," and moreover explores the relationship between adult and child (a point emphasized in Veit-Wild's "Oxford Diary"). Contemporary Zimbabwe is as bleak as it was for Marechera in the early days of Independence. It is fascinating to conjecture how Marechera might have responded to the current crisis in Zimbabwe, as he always emphasized public involvement for the writer. Still, the form of that involvement might not satisfy *our* expectations.

In the Afterword Flora Veit-Wild breaks her long silence on her personal relationship with Marechera. This long-withheld story, "Me and Dambudzo," is perhaps the only extant first-hand account of an intimate relationship with him by a woman, and is complementary with her short story, "Lake McIlwaine," included in Part 1. The very unlikely bond that grew between these two very different people—a middle-class, married European woman who thought of herself as whole and in control of her life; and an African tramp writer with a deeply self-destructive attitude to life—exemplifies Marechera's life-long striving to reach across cultures, races and classes, the categories which he found at the centre of power, even as he subverted his own struggle when people tried to reach over to him.

The "irrational force" that Veit-Wild describes as drawing the two of them together might just be at the centre of this volume. What is the irrational force of art that moves us, but often cannot be explained? How do we respond to life through art, and how does art affect us? Can emotional responses to art be theorized/performed? Where is the source of artistic inspiration? How does art become timeless, appealing to audiences beyond its time—or, to use J. M. Coetzee's words, how does a work of art become a "classic"?

This volume documents that Marechera's spirit is alive among us, moving across centuries to inspire us, disturb us, provoke us, laugh at us. Will his work and accounts of his life ever satisfy our expectations for a leader, a forebear and an iconoclast? This book reflects on a moment—three cold days in Oxford in May 2009—but it also makes an important future gesture. Let's continue to think about our relationship to Dambudzo Marechera's work and life—as artists, friends, colleagues, fans and scholars.

A word remains to be said about the archival material included as bonus tracks on the DVD. Most of this material was provided by the Dambudzo Marechera Trust and has not been broadcast or published before. Most of it is unedited or only slightly edited, to provide the listener with the authentic voice. Marechera's lecture, "The African Writer's Experience of European Literature" from October 15, 1986, and his press conference in Berlin in 1979, which have been published in Flora Veit-Wild's *Source Book*, appear here in unedited expanded versions. The interview by Alle Lansu, which also appears in *Source Book*, is excerpted here by Lansu to highlight its most memorable moments. Of particular attention is the 50-minute interview with Marechera by Fiona Lloyd, which has never been made public in full. We are also particularly glad to be able to include the documentary film *After the Hunger and the Drought* (1985) by the late Olley Maruma that is a valuable archival document on Zimbabwean writing at a particular point in time.

Julie Cairnie   *Dobrota Pucherova*
Guelph, Canada   *Bratislava, Slovakia*

PART 1

INSPIRED CREATIVITY

Dambudzo[1]

Comrade Fatso

I'm the priest, the pimp, the psycho, the whore
The pick pocket, road-digger, nannie, the poor
The District Commissioner
Asian Shopkeepers
The whipping by the white school boys
The pain, betrayals, the hurts, the joys
The black, the white, the in-between
The Rho-desia, The Zimbab-weee
The Hey, everyone look at me
I'm broken mirror of society
Coz I'm Vengere and Vengere is me
Colonised my mind so now I'm free

I'm the freedom fighter fighting you and me
I'm the English language, the BSAP
The one-man demo up Second Street
I'm the stammer that startles you in your sleep
I'm the opposite of all of your beliefs
Coz I'm fuck war and I'm fuck peace

I'm the early HIV disease
I drink to plunge and not to please
I bash rotten regimes with ease
Don't teach me in your schools you see
But I'm your broken mirror—so just look at me

---

[1] This poem accompanies the music video included on the DVD.

House of Hunger[2]

Comrade Fatso

Welcome welcome to the House of Hunger
Welcome to walls of fear and anger
Listen to the cries of children raped
Hear the blood of hopes scraped
Hear activists' wrists get twisted
While life dreams get left blistered
Here those with hope in head
Are beaten, battered, left for dead
While even rest in peace is broken
Even rest in peace is broken
As sleeping coffins are dug up stolen

Yes this is the House of Hunger
I dzimba renzara[3]
This is the House of Hunger
Ndopatinogara[4]
This is the House of Hunger and we live in it
In this house you gotta make it or break it
It ain't just the president
It's a much older prison
There are foundations of famine
Built with the broken bricks of colonialism
Where property went to the whiteys and poverty went to the many
There are pillars of inequality called parliamentary democracy
Where fat chefs sit in the kitchen
Cookin' up feasts of famine
Yes this is the House of Hunger
I dzimba renzara
This is the House of Hunger
Ndopatinogara
This is the House of Hunger and we live in it
In this house you gotta make it or break it

---

[2] This poem accompanies the song included on the DVD.
[3] "house of hunger"
[4] "this is where we live"

A house built by chefs white now black
They build on the fast track
Left alone by western chefs who built towers of hunger with the IMF
Now they must build alone
Without the possibility of a World Bank loan
The western chefs have left the kitchen
Now they alone must cook the famine
So they place brick upon brick of fear and corruption
Brick upon brick of indoctrination
Brick upon brick of green bomber[5]
Brick upon brick of hunger, hunger
But the writing's on the wall and it says Zvakwana[6]
The writing's on the durawall and it says Woza[7]
Because the cement is our apathy
The cement is "we"
We're the cement and they know it
The house only stands because we support it
It's time to build a house without chefs
Without World Banks, without IMFs
Time to build a house for all
And it all starts if we stand tall!

---

[5] ZANU (PF) Youth Militia
[6] "It's enough"/underground activist organisation
[7] "Come forward"/militant women's movement

Bits and Pieces I Picked up and Pocketed

Jane Bryce

We stood in a group at the High Street end of Cornmarket, a white man with a toy AK 47, a tall skinny black man and a white woman, handing out flyers for the play. Suddenly Cheikh called out, "Dambudzo! Hey, my brother. Come here and meet my friends from the Africa Society play I told you about."

A smallish figure in dirty jeans and a short ill-fitting jacket half sidled, half swaggered up to us. Hunched against the cold, peering short-sightedly through thick-lensed spectacles, he looked insubstantial and unanchored, as though he'd forgotten where he was going and didn't know what he was doing there. He could have been a tramp if not for the bulky assemblage of books barely contained in the crook of his left arm. When he spoke, his voice was deep and peculiarly emphatic, with a stammer that might have been a deliberate ploy to keep you listening.

"*R hythm of V iolence. R* evolutionaries. How *u* nexpected among the *d* ream-ing spires." Cheikh laughed and they did that triple handshake thing by which African men signal their brotherhood. "Dambudzo," he said, "meet Liz and Mar-tin. Liz plays my girlfriend and Martin's the Boer policeman who wants to kill us. Around here, nobody wants to know us because we're too dangerous." "Inter*r* acial *r* elationships and *s* tate subversion," said Dambudzo, "are what the *c* olo-nisers tried to *s* tamp out. Has anyone got a *c* igarette?" Martin pulled out a pack and held it out saying, "It's too bloody cold and I'm bored of trying to distract people from the rituals of consumerism. Let's go and have a cup of tea."

After tea in the Market, Martin went back to college to write an essay and Cheikh, Dambudzo and I repaired to the Monk's Bar at the Mitre where Cheikh bought a round of drinks. While he was at the bar, Dambudzo spoke directly to me for the first time that afternoon. "*D* ostoevsky," he said, "understood *d* icta-torship. He understood that *f* ascism or, if you prefer, *c* ommunism, is a *d* isease of the mind and that the *b* ody politic is infested from within." I had read *Crime and Punishment* and thought I was on safe ground. "But didn't Dostoevsky," I said, "live under the tsars?" "Yes," said Dambudzo, "that's right. He lived under the *s* tars. Have you met Lewis Nkosi, the author of your play? He should read Dostoevsky to understand the *r* hythm of violence in Africa. He thinks it's all a matter of *r* evolution and *b* lack people and white people *l* oving each other. It's not. The *d* isease has no *c* olour. The *p* lague is existential and when we get rid of the dictators, we then have to *d* eal with each other. Or did you think you could *s* ave Africa by acting in a *p* lay?"

Cheikh returned with the drinks and grinned as he sat down. "I hope you're not terrorizing Liz?" he asked Dambudzo.

"*N* ot at all, old chap. We were having a *l* iterary conversation. I wanted to know if she's met the author of your play."

"He wanted to know," I said, "if I thought I was saving Africa by being in the play." Cheikh laughed loudly. "I thought so," he said. "You were terrorizing her. Liz is one of us. She grew up in Kenya."

"Ah, Ngugi, yes. Ngugi learnt from Conrad about *b* etrayal and *r* etribution. Have you read *A Grain of Wheat?*"

"Actually no," I admitted. "Medieval literature is taking up most of my time. I'm reading *Sir Gawain and the Green Knight* right now."

At the sound of the name, Dambudzo abruptly leapt up, gesticulating with his two-thirds empty beer glass. "So you are starting in the right place!" he exclaimed. "Orality, tradition, verbal formulae, the interpenetration of the natural and supernatural. These will teach you more about Africa than any number of *r* ealist novels or *r* evolutionary plays. I'd buy you a drink, but I don't have any money. We should *c* elebrate, we're both *l* abourers in the *l* iterary vineyard. Cheikh, old chap, mine's a pint of beer, and buy the white African a *h* alf of cider."

Like me, Dambudzo was in the first year of an English degree and struggling with Middle English. Unlike me, when he spoke about the Gawain poet he might have been speaking of someone he'd met the week before. Cheikh said he was a brilliant writer who'd been thrown out of Rhodesia for demonstrating against Smith's government and now had a scholarship at New College. I was impressed. If the truth be told, I grew up on a tea estate in Limuru and didn't know a thing about revolution. I'd heard of Ngugi but what I'd heard was that he was a Mau Mau sympathiser. I was in the play because I missed home and wanted to hang out with Africans, wherever they came from. Dambudzo made me feel uncomfortable because he was too clever and asked questions I couldn't answer, but occasionally I'd bump into him in the Radcliffe Camera and we'd go for a drink. He never had any money so I tried to keep it occasional, but he had a manner which was hard to resist, a mixture of ebullience and pathos, and he would start talking as soon as he saw you so it was hard to get away. Then I began to realize I was actually learning from him, and I looked for him when I was stuck with an essay. He was especially interested in the elective I was doing on medieval Italian literature and how Boccaccio's storytellers sequestered themselves from the Plague, telling each other stories. I lent him my translation of the *Decameron,* and for a while it was one of the heavy tomes he lugged to the pub in his spindly arms. He came to see the play and sat in the front row and clapped louder than anyone else, so that people looked to see who was making all the noise. Afterwards, whenever he saw me he would bow with mock formality and ask, "And how is the white African r evolutionary?" I could see he was brilliant, but talking to him was like walking in a minefield. Something could blow up in your face at any moment and you wouldn't even see it coming.

Through the Africa Society, Cheikh arranged for Dambudzo to give a poetry reading in the JCR at New College. We put notices up on all the JCR notice boards, and there was a good crowd, even people standing at the back. We had given Dambudzo the title of Revolutionary Poet, and he obliged us by looking the part. His hair had grown into small wiry spirals around his face, he was wearing fatigues and a pair of army boots he might have bought at one of those end of the line shops, and brandishing his manuscript like a weapon.

It started quietly enough, Dambudzo reading in a low voice without the hint of a stammer. At first he read poems expressing his feelings, I supposed, for Rhodesia, her granite breasts and the warmth of her arms, exile poems to which we all listened respectfully. Then he embarked on a long poem called "The Struggle," full of martial images and lines like: "Sharpen your spears for war/polish your knobkerries..." This got people's attention and they listened attentively at first, but gradually the atmosphere began to change. As modernist ambiguity began to dilute righteous anger, the images became less warlike and sounded more as if they belonged in *The Wasteland*. Then there was a section that sounded like the Senghor poem Cheikh had translated for me, about a dark continent with breasts of mountains, except that with Senghor it was all heroic and high-flown romantic like an *ubi sunt* in an Old English poem. As Dambudzo read, his language became charged with images of sexual violence, something about a frenzy of mounting and the cock mounting his hen. The Socialist Workers' Party corner became restive, and Anti-Apartheid murmured something to SWAPO.

Then he came to the final section and we were back in Eliot territory. A rat gnawing at a bone, freezing sunlight and a lost couple waiting for a bus. I was a bit lost myself by now, but when he came to the last two lines: "The feeling is always there/that I am under a microscope," I had a flash of understanding. In the pub he was always saying things like that, things I paid no attention to because they didn't seem to invite a response, but which infused his conversation with its peculiar pungency, its edge of darkness. One time I happened to look directly at him and I caught something in his eyes which took me by surprise—something childlike and vulnerable. In this company, self-confession was both audacious and risky and it opened him, I knew, to flak.

As soon as Dambudzo stopped reading, a man stood up and shouted, "Individualist bullshit! That's not about the struggle, it's about your own self-pity."

Heads turned. I recognised the man as a graduate student from St Antony's who I had seen once or twice at Africa Society meetings. There was a general murmur of agreement, and the man continued: "You can write that stuff from the safety of your Oxford room, but what's it doing for the comrades on the frontline? How will it help with decolonisation? Does it tell us anything about our history, or who we are today? It does not, my brother, and you should be ashamed."

A slightly older man, a Kenyan who had been a lecturer at the University of Nairobi until he'd had to leave in a hurry, now stood up. "Finely wrought language," he began, "cannot disguise the lack of attention to the great themes of our literature: the strength of traditional culture to withstand the assault of colonialism, the role of the artist as teacher and inspiration of his people. Pessimism and negativity are not luxuries we can afford at this stage of our development. If you continue in this direction, you will lose all clarity and disappear into the maze of western existentialism."

I was watching Dambudzo, who had rolled up his manuscript and looked ready to fling it across the room. He wasn't tall, but the intensity of his expression made him look fiercer than I had ever seen him. "I am astonished at your ignorance," he almost spat. "I did not expect such a low cultural level among you. Those who do not understand my work are simply illiterate. I will not tick all the orifices of political correctness and stimulate all the possible orgasms of brotherly love. Our so-called search for freedom has not included even the most elementary humanitarian justice. Am I supposed to *iden*tify with *Idi* Amin? To *kiss* Bokassa's *ass*, or *mas*turbate at the thought of Mo*butu*? When literature becomes a vehicle for ideology the writer is nothing but a vampire sucking his own blood. If you expect me to be a writer for a specific nation or a specific race, then *fuck you*!"

He might as well have sprayed the room with bullets and left the audience bleeding on the floor. Amidst the pandemonium, I saw him pick up a large pottery ashtray and hurl it at the plate-glass window that gave onto a smooth stretch of green quadrangle where a few gowned figures strolled with heads bent. The explosive crack that ripped across the still evening air stopped them dead in their tracks, while inside the room, glass sprayed and people screamed and fought for the exit. Cheikh and Martin more or less picked Dambudzo up by his elbows and shoving through the crowd, carried him bodily from the room. I stayed where I sat, frozen in shock, surrounded by shattered glass.

I didn't see Dambudzo for a while after that. I heard he'd been disciplined by the college authorities for smashing their window, and I presumed there'd been a fine and he had even less disposable cash than usual, so I was relieved. I was struggling to get by on my grant as it was, without the several beers I always ended up buying for him. Besides, I was preoccupied by the end of first year exams, and with trying to memorise tracts of *Beowulf*. Early in the new academic year, I was walking through Parks when I passed a crumpled figure sitting on a bench, apparently holding a conversation with the pigeons. He was dressed in an assort-ment of clothes which could have been picked at random from an Oxfam shop—a pair of jodhpurs tucked into scuffed brown leather riding boots, crumpled white shirt with worn cuffs that hung down over his wrists, an astonishingly bright silk cravate tucked into the open collar and a threadbare checked sports jacket over the narrow shoulders. Beside him on the bench lay a pile of books, and he was declaiming lines of poetry in a monotone just too low for me to catch the words. Taking him for an Oxford eccentric, I had almost passed him when I looked again and recognised him.

"Dambudzo!" I exclaimed.

As he looked at me his eyes gradually came into focus. "*N* o," he stuttered, "I am a *m* irror of the gigantic shadows which futurity casts upon the *p* resent. And now, alas, the poor Sprite is Imprison'd for some fault of his in a *b* ody like a grave."

"Dambudzo," I said again, "It's me, Liz. How are you? What are you doing here?"

Although he seemed to recognise me, his next words made little sense. "What! Alive, and so bold? Here, where black despair is thrown over the world in which I move alone? *O* bedience, *b* ane of all genius, virtue, freedom, truth, makes *s* laves of men."

I sat down next to him and said nothing for a while. We were doing the Ro-mantics that term and I realised he was quoting Shelley. I was writing an essay on the Romantic Imagination and I cast around in my memory and ventured, "A Poet is a nightingale who sits in darkness, and sings to cheer its own solitude with sweet sounds." Its effect was electrifying. Dambudzo sprang to his feet, seized me by the hand, dragged me upright and set off across the park at a trot, towing me along. "*B* eaded *b* ubbles *w* inking at the brim," he panted. "Let's *c* elebrate in the Mitre!"

So there we were again, me paying for pints of beer and halves of cider while Dambudzo expatiated on Shelley's atheism and his expulsion from Oxford. It was a free tutorial and I didn't mind. Besides, I was glad to see him and relieved he was all right. I told him about Uncle Bernie who lived in a village called Bic-knoller in Somerset, and often talked about how Keats and Wordsworth scandal-ised the locals by getting back to nature in the Quantock Hills. "Uncle Bernie," I told him, "thinks he can write poetry, maybe by association. He belongs to a local poetry group and so he has an audience."

Dambudzo was immediately interested. "Tell me more about this poetic un-cle," he demanded.

"He's actually a distant cousin of my mother's," I told him, "but he insists on acting the part of family elder and we can't shake him off. He was a Major in the British army in India and he thinks we're all his underlings. He barks orders and gets irate if we don't obey instantly. He's terribly rude and nobody likes him, but he's immovable. He's insisting on coming to visit me here next week-end, even after I told him I was too busy and had a million deadlines. A few years ago he had a crisis and was diagnosed with manic depression, but as a result of the crisis, he decided he was a homosexual. It upset his wife no end. She moved out and now he lives alone in Bicknoller and alienates all the villagers by ranting at them. He calls it telling the truth and he's proud of it, even though it means he has no friends. And that's why my parents insist we have to be kind to him, and I can't stop him from coming to Oxford."

Dambudzo looked hard at me for a minute, and then he said, "If Shelley were alive now, how would they diagnose him? He believed that 'I' and 'they' are not signs of any actual difference subsisting between people but are merely marks to denote the different modifications of the one mind. Now they might call him schizophrenic or suffering from paranoid delusions."

I suddenly had a brilliant idea. "I'll give a tea party for Uncle Bernie and you must come," I urged him. "A *t* ea party," responded Dambudzo. "I accept. To mentally strip naked all the people at a tea party and to listen attentively to their conversation and to note their gestures is a sobering lesson which ought to be done more often."

The tea party took place on a Saturday afternoon. Dambudzo made his appearance in a frilly apron and insisted on helping with the cucumber sandwiches. When people arrived, he introduced himself as the maid and held out the plate to them. Uncle Bernie, ensconced in an armchair, was tickled and asked in a loud voice, "Is your friend queer? I've always wanted to have it off with a black man."

"Sssh Uncle Bernie," I told him, "he's not gay and you're not here to pick up men."

"Oh don't be so starchy," he retorted, "He's got a lovely bottom and he's very sexy. I'd kiss him from his toes to his head."

My friend Susannah who was standing nearby saw my face and stepped in hastily. "Liz," she said, "we need more orange and lemon for the Pimms. I'll talk to your uncle." Gratefully I hurried away, as the two of them began a discussion of Oxford architecture. Though everyone else except Uncle Bernie had paper cups, Dambudzo had located a pint mug and was helping himself to Pimms as I arrived.

"So that's the family *b* ete noire. *P* lease introduce us. I believe I've come across him before in a *n* ovel and I'm trying to recall the author."

Shrinking, I led Dambudzo over to where Uncle Bernie was enthroned. "Ah," he said as we approached, "you're not as thick as you look. She thinks," he said to Dambudzo, "that because she got into an Oxford college that means she can censor me but she's met her match."

Dambudzo gave an exaggerated bow so that the frill of the apron trailed on the floor in front in him. "*C*ensorship," he pronounced, "is the resort of the *d*ictator who knows he cannot control the minds of those on whom he depends for his own survival. My own name is not *m*oney but mind."

I hurried back to the Pimms, praying that Uncle Bernie would keep his famous views on race to himself. Snatches of conversation filtered across the room to me. Delhi. Poona. Srinagar. Kashmir. Ootacamund. It was the story of The War in India and, inevitably, the story of The Colonel's Wife, which I knew by heart.

"She was twenty-five years older than me but I was quite attractive with a full head of hair and could walk without a limp. Polio, you know. My father didn't like my greasy skin which accounts for my unlined complexion and my mother said I looked 'like a Russian'. But Marjory fell in love with me. Adored me. Said I was a tender lover. Well, women were in short supply. We'd go to bed together and it was no big thing for me but I liked her sofa. I knew I was bisexual. I've read all of Gide and Spender."

From where I stood pouring Pimms for a circle of friends, I strained for Dambudzo's response. It seemed he had taken off from Gide and Spender and was enlarging the range of literary references. "Wilde, Burroughs, Bukowkski," intoned Dambudzo, waving the mug which I noticed was empty. "Mishima, Rimbaud, the Marquis de Sade..." As soon as I could I struggled across the room with the jug of Pimms.

"Oh there you are, you shrew," greeted Uncle Bernie as I arrived and refilled their glasses. "Your mother tells me she'll scrub floors if she has to to keep you at Oxford. I told her I'd have thought going on the game would have been more lucrative, if less sanitary. Pricks come in all shapes and sizes and can be smelly. Floors – well you can keep a decent distance with a modern squeegee mop, can't you? What's more, you can wring them out. Don't look so shocked, you know I always speak the truth. I don't pretend. Take my condition, now. I was labeled manic depressive by my psychiatrist in London. When I'm high I lose all inhibition and I tell it like is. Some people can't take it and I've lost long-standing friends for life. My wife said I was a social menace. But I have great insight and I'm a wise old man. The world out there is a jungle."

"Yes indeed," concurred Dambudzo. "I myself am the doppelgänger whom, until I appeared, African literature had not yet met. My phantom still haunts the township where sanity is measured by how much torture one can endure and survive. I have an old uncle who fought in Burma. He thinks that makes him a hero, but he's just another old black man squatting in his mud hut and complaining that the young don't care about the virtues and adventures and pathos of war. But think of Vietnam, Korea, Sharpeville, Dresden, Hiroshima. War is no longer a fact of life but life itself. We don't need some old man's stories of his heroic past. A tongue-in-cheek attitude is the only sane one when confronting the subject of aggression."

I held my breath. Uncle Bernie was capable of exploding on less provocation than this. But Dambudzo's words appeared to suggest a different direction for their disconnected dialogue. "War," he said, "is a joke played by a madman on the sane. In Germany in 1936 they were all doing Hitler salutes. I wore a rubber band round my nose to make me look like a Jew."

"We Rhodesians," responded Dambudzo, "Are the Jews of Africa. I saw a film where Nazis were frying eggs and eating them while with their bayonets they prodded an endless line of naked children into a huge sulphuric acid tank. But look up "nigger" and "Jew" in the *Oxford Dictionary* and tell me if the Nazis were the only ones doing their thing."

"Quite so," agreed Uncle Bernie. "You're too young to remember Stalin. And then that chap that imported communism to the Caribbean. Emily's lover died of an asthma attack beside her in bed one night and she went to Haiti and met this man who was meant to be a voodoo priest or something. I went to visit her and stayed in a very basic hotel and this bloke Raimonde, a teacher earning $10 a month, rice and beans for every meal, he showed me about and I paid him $15 a day. He took me to his house and boy, was it humble. Two metal rocking chairs on the porch and incredibly primitive inside, squalid bathroom with tiles falling off. But in India even the most educated people just had a bucket. Since I had my prostate done I pee in a bucket myself so as not to get up at night."

"In the township," declaimed Dambudzo, "clouds of flies perform Handel's Hallelujah chorus over the turds in the public pit latrines. It is an almost perfect photograph of the human condition."

"On the plane," continued Uncle Bernie, "there were two blacks with dread-locks going to Jamaica for sex. I was frightened of them but the hostess put me in first class because of my limp and I sat next to a man who owned a villa in Barbados where the Queen had stayed."

Dambudzo seemed to swell with something that might have been pride. "Her Majesty," he said in an affected upper class accent, "has twenty-seven toilets from which to choose. *P* lumbing is the key to the British Empire. You perform your duty and politely shake hands and all your filth is swept away in a *g* ush of water."

"The British," agreed Uncle Bernie with enthusiasm, "are they crazy or what? Beagle Hunting. Cornish Floral Dancing. Tombstones. Giant Rhubarb Leaves. Counterpanes. And now, Junk Food, Junk Drink, Coca-Cola Rules the World…"

"Ambi Skin-Lightening Cream," chorused Dambudzo, "Castle and Lion Lagers, Benson and Hedges, Pure Wool Suits and Fanta Orange Tastes So Good…." They clinked their Pimms glasses and I went to refill the jug.

Dambudzo was thrown out of New College the following March. He hung on for a year or so and then I heard he'd gone to Cardiff to live with a woman. I heard he'd gone to jail for cannabis and being illegal, that he'd moved to a squat in London. I was still in Oxford, doing a PhD in Medieval Poetry and tutoring to eke out my postgraduate grant. Susannah, who was working in London, kept me in touch with mutual friends and told me when Dambudzo won an award for his first book. She said the award ceremony was a repeat of the poetry reading in Oxford, only this time it was the chandelier that was smashed. When the Rhodesian war ended and Zimbabwe was born, I celebrated along with the other Oxford Africans, toasting Mugabe and the future of the new country. But I couldn't put out of my mind Dambudzo's words one grey day as we drank at the Mitre. He was unusually depressed, even for him. He had just split up with another of his girlfriends, and his suffering was caused by his own capacity for cruelty.

"Is all this going on because of sex?" he asked. "Or was I piling up humiliations on her as a white woman in revenge for all the years I spent under Ian Smith's boot? Am I a sadist? Or am I in some mad pursuit of vain and complete possession?"

I remained silent, often the only response I could find to Dambudzo's outpourings. This was easy as he didn't really require an answer so much as a sounding board. He went on, "What I'm afraid of is that I'm experiencing personally what will happen to Rhodesia once we gain our Independence. Once we've grasped a chunk of country from the colonizer will we squabble over it and each try to possess it? Will everything disintegrate into a c arnival of c orruption, p ower struggles and administrative d ecay?"

By the time I completed my PhD and moved to London, Dambudzo had gone home. There were reports of him in the park in Harare with his typewriter, homeless as he had been in London. He said things the government considered unpatriotic and they locked him up for his pains. Then one day, I opened a newspaper and saw that he had died. I took my copy of *The House of Hunger* down from the shelf and leafed through it, looking for words to fill the void. At last I found them:

> Bergfrith the beggar
> Whose person was home to a thousand fleas
> And to sundry crimes of buggery and blasphemy
> [...] on whom time hastily hastily scribbled its signature,
> Leaving him toothless, arthritic, bald, rheumatic,
> Fantastic and the bankrupt owner of a repertoire of fantoccini.
> But at last, penniless, homeless, powerless, friendless,
> He crept on hands and knees up the creepy Tower
> Of derelict St David
> And there on bats and spiders lived
> Till he looked and saw the hook where once a Bell hung
> And with a cry recognized it as the fatal scythe.

I closed the book, I closed my eyes. I saw the Radcliffe Camera at dusk, and the cobbled street leading to the Mitre gleaming in the rain. I saw a pile of books on the bar next to an empty pint glass, froth still clinging to the brim. I saw a burning sparrow fly towards me.

Kariba's Last Stand

Robert Fraser

The Poetry Editor was at his usual perch, eating his usual meal. The meal was Italian meatballs and rice: all he could afford. The perch was a corner table in the window nook of the Napoli Snack Bar in Flower Street, conveniently placed for two purposes. The first was fast transit towards the rear of the Panafrica Centre, where the Poetry Editor sometimes performed his verse, and more often drank in the evenings with his friends and fellow authors, Kariba and Omoni. The second was for surreptitious observation of smart young women as they came and went, attired in lyotards or less, through the revolving doors of the Sanctum Dance Centre further down the street. The dressed or undressed young women were the recurrent stuff of the Editor's fantasies, but his glances were habitually unre- turned. He watched one of these unobtainable creatures through heavily lidded eyes, then he turned to the book open on the stained tablecloth before him, and read on:

> He lodged as much by Accident as he dined and passed the Night, some-
> times in mean Houses, which are set open at Night to any casual Wander-
> ers, sometimes in Cellars among the Riot and Filth of the meanest and
> most profligate of the Rabble; and sometimes, when he had no Money to
> support even the Expenses of these Receptacles, walked about the streets
> till he was weary, and lay down in summer upon a Bulk, or in winter with
> his Associates in poverty, among the ashes of a Glass-house.

The book was a facsimile of an eighteenth-century biography: Samuel Johnson's *Life of Richard Savage*. The Poetry Editor often took this classic with him to his cafe. He was thinking of writing a play about Johnson and, besides, there was something about the low-life London described in these elegantly phrased paragraphs that reminded him of his own milieu, sometimes even his own pre- dicament. He took another sip and gawped out of the window again. Vaguely his eyes surveyed a willowy looking young person as she struggled to maintain her balance on high heels along the pavement opposite. Behind him, in the oily atmosphere of the cafe, a sweaty face appeared round the corner of the tea urn and inquired "The meatballs are good, yes?" The proprietor's Neapolitan wife was keen to maintain his custom and, besides, he sensed that she somehow felt sorry for him. The Editor spluttered agreement through a mouthful of over-sugared tea. Her face disappeared, and then it appeared again with a related question: "You like to wash the girls, yes?" This time the Editor did not respond, though his mind expressed a mixture of rueful assent and anxiety that his hidden desires were so easy to detect. He took a sip of strong sweet tea, and then he carried on reading:

> In this Manner were passed those Days and those Nights, which Nature had enabled him to have employed in elevated Speculation, useful Studies, or pleasing Conversation. On a Bulk, in a Cellar, or in the Glass-house among Thieves and Beggars, was to be found the author of the *Wanderer,* the man of exalted Sentiments, extensive Views and curious Observations, the man whose remarks upon Life might have assisted Statesmen, whose Ideas of Virtue might have enlightened the Moralist, whose Eloquence might have influenced Senates, and whose Delicacy might have polished Courts.

The Editor paused and looked up, this time not at the girls on the pavement opposite but at the menu board fixed to the wall to his right. Had the meatballs, he wondered, been beyond his means? Might he perhaps push the boat out a litle more and risk his favourite desert: Bread and Butter Pudding with custard? He decided on the whole he had better not.

Idly, as he closed his book, he asked himself how it had come about that someone of his educational advantages and early promise was obliged to make such a decision. A few months ago he had been a Junior Lecturer at the University of Coketown, spending his surplus income on expensive dinners and suits with fashionably flared trousers and generous lapels, ordered off the peg from the local branch of Burtons. His working hours, in his own mind at least, had been employed in "elevated Speculation, useful Studies, and pleasing Conversation." His live-in girlfriend had catered for these, and for several other needs. She was voluptuous if not exactly beautiful and had taken to luring him away from his left-wing politics of which she disapproved by removing items of her clothing one by one as the clock approached the starting time of the local branch meetings of the Labour Party which she knew he should attend, since he was the Treasurer. As the months had gone on, he had attended fewer and fewer meetings until one night in desperation he had taken her along fully clothed, and she had ruined his chances forever by publicly denouncing Kier Hardie and all his works. Then disaster had struck. The university had not renewed his contract, and his rightwing girlfriend had deserted him for the married Professor of Systematic Theology before running away to the circus where she had become a part-time knife thrower's assistant and full-time organist. Masochism was deep down there in her makeup somehow. He had come down to London, and he had been here ever since, making a precarious living from hack freelance literary work and living in a bedsit in Peckham.

The Poetry Editor rose to his feet, retrieved his duffel bag from under the seat and fumbled in the threadbare pockets of his leather jacket. There were two pounds in there, just sufficient to meet his bill. Tucking the Johnson facsimile under one arm, he walked over to the till, spooned a miscellaneous heap of coins into the proprietor's wife's upturned palm, and made his way into the street. On the whole, he had been wise to pass over the pudding. He had peered into his bank balance that morning, and the condition of it had not been healthy. Clearly it was time for another visit to his friend Charles Goulash, commissioning editor of the Tropical Writers Series of Heineken Academic Books, publishers to parts of the world other publishers would not touch. Goulash was a tolerant soul, and he seemed to trust the Poetry Editor's judgement. Every two weeks or so he would hand over to him a pile of poorly typed manuscripts in brown paper envelopes, each labelled with the name of an author from a country fairly new to the map. There were epic poets from Somalia, writers of limerick from Ethiopia, novelists from the Sudan, tragedians from Malawi. The general standard was uneven but once in a while he came across a pearl in this diverse dungheap. More importantly he was paid £30 a go.

The Poetry Editor made his way through the newly fashionable backstreets of Covent Garden, considering as he went this new mode of life. He was walking through one of the most historic districts of London, once a vegetable market. Dr Johnson would have known it well in his earlier years in London when, having quitted rural Lichfield, he was slowly and painfully attempting to make a name and a position in the capital. Johnson had been an unprepossessing person in those days, and like Kariba, he had left Oxford without taking a degree. He had fallen in with a scapegrace and failed author called Richard Savage, who claimed to be the illegitimate son of a prominent countess who, however, failed to acknowledge him. Excluded by polite society, they had made common cause and walked the streets together, sometimes it would appear trudging all night through. Johnson's *Life of Savage,* written when his own circumstances were beginning to improve, was his tribute to his dead friend, but it was also a meditation on desperation, a disquisition on living on the edge of things, and an essay upon guilt. Perhaps it had also been a vehicle for Johnson's sense of remorse. He had survived, and Savage had not.

Was that, he wondered, how he would eventually come to think of Kariba? Thirty years hence, would he be writing stories about him, as Johnson had once composed a book about Savage? Who could tell? In thirty years time it would be 2009, an inconceivable date. In 2009 he would be sixty-two and looking like his dad. He arrested this train of thought fairly sharply. 1979 was enough to cope

with, what with everything around him apparently breaking down. The winter he
had just passed through was one of the worst he could remember in his relatively
short life. And the politics were dire. There was one advantage or disadvantage
about being a freelance writer and editor: there no point in going on strike. Everybody seemed to had been on strike recently: first it had been the miners, then
the print workers. Fleet Street was in turmoil, and *The Chimes Literary Supplement*, for which he sometimes reviewed books, had ceased publication for several
past months, depriving him of one meagre source of remuneration. The Editor
vaguely supported the strikers, but he could have done with that precious trickle
of cheques. Savage would have understood all this, he consoled himself by thinking, firm in the fraternity of need.

And now of all things the Tories were back in charge. The Editor had been
cohabiting with a Glaswegian communist during the election period. The following morning, when the result was announced she had turned over in bed, switched
the radio on and sneered in her weary Gorbals accent, "Och, it's those voices
again!"

The Poetry Editor passed northwards up Neal Street in the direction of St
Giles' Circus and negotiated the crossroads at the top of the street. As he waited
for the lights to change, he thought about Johnson and Savage, and then he thought
about Omoni, Kariba and himself. They lived in different centuries, but it sometimes seemed to him as if all of them inhabited much the same imaginary terrain.
It was called Grub Street, and it was the place where unsuccessful or would-be
writers scavenged a living from the leftovers of publishing and journalism. Grub
Street was a proud place, a passionate place, and it bred a kind of brotherhood of
need. When Omoni, Kariba and he drank the evenings away in the cellar bar in
King Street they could fancy themselves members of that transhistoric, excluded
company. It was meagre compensation, but it was some. After these drinking sessions, he well knew, Kariba would often spend the night on a park bench. There
was nowhere else for him to go.

The Editor passed into Bedford Square, crossed to Number 22 and mounted
the stairs towards Goulash's lair. When he reached the landing, he peered into
the depths of the small office where Goulash himself sat at the far end near the
window, behind a barracade of files.

Goulash was the son of the reputable South African poet Mark Reagan Goulash, whose neatly rhyming, darkly ruminative lyrics were reproduced in *The
Penguin Anthology of Pretorian Verse*. The Editor had a tattered copy of it at
home. He recalled some of its better lines:

Exiled Iguana
by M. R. Goulash:
Forlorn in my foreign cage I stand,
Alone of all my mottled band.
I was was not born to brave this cold.
My crest is looking rather old.

Goulash *fils* had a benign face, intelligent spectacles and slightly tousled hair. In his own small way he was a legend. The story had gone the rounds as to how as a young publisher, during a period of secondment to South Africa, he had once rescued a radical journalist friend of his, Julius Grape, from the clutches of the thought police. He had, it was rumoured, lent Grape his passport, embarked on a transatlantic liner to see him off and then stayed onboard until mid-ocean, where he had intrepidly dived over the side. Swimming the two thousand miles back to Cape Town he had misjudged both distance and direction, and clambered ashore at Port Alfred. Eventually he had reached England, though not this time by swimming. The notoriety of this exploit had stayed with him, and in a minor way it had altered the world. Currently the noun "Goulash" was forbidden in South Africa, and anyone who used it was instantly gaoled. Menus had been torn from restaurant windows, and every Hungarian chef in the country was held on Robben Island. By way of compensation, dishes of steaming Goulash were regularly served at Anti-Apartheid ralleys in London; there was a soup kitchen selling this subversive stew permanently parked outside the South African embassy in Trafalgar Square.

The Poetry Editor sat down and glanced across at his friend with wan affection. He tried to imagine him diving off the side of a transatlantic liner. He tried to imagine him diving off a diving board. He tried to imagine him diving off anything.

Goulash *fils* looked up from his work and smiled. "Well, old chap, what have you got to tell me?"

The Poetry Editor opened up his bag. He dug deep into its recesses and brought out a pile of tatty envelopes. He brandished one aloft: *Assegais of Hope* by Egregious Obunde. "Bit O.T.T., I thought," he remarked sourly.

"Yes, I expected that," remarked Goulash solemnly, removing his glasses and polishing them. "Full of sound and fury old Egregious. Mostly pure rhetoric."

"If only it *was* pure," the Poetry Editor remarked as he retrieved another thinner envelope from his bag. "Exiguous Matabele?" inquired Goulash "What did you think of that?" "Not a lot." "Pity," said Goulash, "I rather thought you reckoned on young Exiguous. You almost praised that epic he handed in last year. 'An appealing economy of style,' you said."

The Poetry Editor looked up: "Well, it was only three words long. Kariba been in?"

There was a ghastly pause. "Oh!" gasped Goulash as his face hit the desk. "Kariba !"

Goulash let out a wail. His head rested on the desk for several seconds. Was he, the Editor pondered, praying? There had been occasions in the recent past, as well he knew, when Goulash's professional relationship with this wayward author had driven him to the edge of despair. He had tried Buddhism, he had tried yoga. He had now reverted to his youthful Anglo-Catholicism, and was toying with the idea of going on a devotional retreat. Indeed his trials were many. Kariba called round several evenings a week, usually as the office was about to close. He kept a wardrobe of outlandish outfits in a filing cabinet in the corner of the room, and changed into a different one as soon as he arrived. There was a Scottish tartan oufit and a uniform of jodhpurs and spurs in which he sometimes attended ethnic African occasions, denouncing independence in a loud Boer accent. One evening a month previously he had donned a twinset and pearls and made off into Bedford Square determined to enter Transport House and deliver a speech in the persona of the Prime Minister. Goulash had attempted to restrain him, and the two men had ended up wrestling in the middle of the pavement. An astonished police office had stood there observing this ungainly pas-de-deux for some minutes until he had recognised the female pugilist as the incumbent premier, and awkwardly doffed his helmet.

Goulash lifted his head and said, "You better go and see Geneviève." The Editor rose to his feet and opened a door to his right. There in the narrow softness of the outer office sat The Goulash Girls, whom he always thought of with some envy as the firm's secretarial harem. There was Geneviève, and there was Petal. Geneviève was petite and small-boned, and her job was to enter the names of manuscripts that had been read and reported on into a ledger. The Editor respected her intelligence, and he desired her person hopelessly. Three months previously he had squandered several weeks' worth of fees to take her to *Pelléas et Mélisande* at the Royal Opera House in Convent Garden. They had sat through two acts of exquisite *psalmodie* until over interval drinks it had dawned on them both that they had almost nothing in common. The rest of the evening had passed in acute mutual embarrassment before they had parted by briskly shaking hands.

Petal, who sat at the other desk, resembled by contrast a stalky English rose. Once the Editor had spotted her drifting round the London Book Fair, and had fallen into step with her, eagerly explaining the design and contents of the books on display as he went. After some minutes she had looked down at him and said, "Excuse me, but do you mind not following me around the room?"

The Editor entered the details of the manuscipts he had read into Geneviève's ledger, and then he clomped down the stairs. He was just crossing the square when he noticed a poorly attired black man speeding towards him. They were about to pass one another when the stranger stuttered a greeting. The Editor looked up. Surely it could not be? This individual had a full set of teeth. Then he realised that Kariba had recently been in prison after an embarrassing episode at the Panafrica Centre when he had smashed a front widow. The authorities there must have provided him with some dentures. The dentures grinned, and continued their stuttering. The Editor said "Hello, Kariba, off to see Goulash?" He just prevented himself saying "Off to plague Goulash?"

As they stared incredulously at one another, the Poetry Editor brought to mind some of Kariba's history. This was the one-time mission school boy who, when a student, had demonstrated ineffectively against U.D.I. This was the Oxford undergraduate whose antics had diverted and appalled the Fellows of Old College. His theatrical delinquency had been the bane of his tutor, the saintly young Victorianist Seamus O'Flaherty, who had been obliged constantly to break off from his variorum edition of *The Water Babies* in order to attend to his wayward charge. Kariba had then attempted to burn down the place, and had been offered the alternatives of psychiatric treatment or permanent rustication. He had opted for the latter, and for the next few months had existed in a tent near Iffley composing the dozen-odd stories of *Shack of Shame*. Accepted by Goulash after a torrent of enthusiastic reports (which had not on this occasion included his own), the slender volume had gone on to be chosen as joint winner of the Custodian Fiction Award the following year. At the presentation ceremony he had resorted to hurling champagne glasses at the guests, who had all fled into the night with the exception of the radical postmodern fiction writer Seraphina Cowper, who had stayed to mother him for the remainder of the evening, cooing solicitious nothings into his ear and oozing leftish concern all over him.

"Wha-wha- what are you doing?" asked Kariba through his new teeth.

The Editor indicated the duffel bag on his back. "Been to see Goulash," he said. He added, "He seemed a little despondent when I left," without going into the reasons.

"Oh I'll g-go- round later and cheer him up. In the m-m-meantime, you might buy me a coffee."

The Editor rummaged through his pockets. There seemed to be a few coins left in there. "Oh, alright" he said.

They settled into a coffee bar in nearby Great Russell Street, and the Editor went to the counter to order. It was a procedure fraught with misunderstanding since in the afternoons the Editor always needed a cuppa tea, which Italian ears nearly always heard as cappuccino. This time, however, there would be no mistake. "Two cups of coffee," he called as clearly as he could, in his best prep school accent. He collected them, paid, and went back to the table balancing the cups.

The Poetry Editor looked across at Kariba, and Kariba looked across at the Poetry Editor. Kariba had a pile of hardbacks under his arm which he now deposited on the table. On top was an American edition of Saul Bellow's *Humboldt's Gift*, a novel they both admired. It was a story, not unlike Johnson's and Savage's, of a promising young man overtaken by circumstances and sinking in the eyes of society and his own, until he had ended up on the scrap heap, pitied but still envied by a former friend who had since flourished. The Editor opened it at random and read "He was a wonderful talker, a hectic nonstop monologuist and improvizer, a champion detractor. To be loused up by Humboldt was a kind of gift." Kariba took a sip at his coffee. "I w-w-wonder whom he is talking about," he asked. The Editor noted with approval the "whom." "Sounds like a few people I could name," he replied.

There was a difficult pause. The two friends knew one another quite slightly. Their real and abiding bond was literature. Both had read vocariously across European and American fiction, and Kariba also had a relish for the South Americans, about whom the Editor was less keen. Neither of them cared much for politics, or for any of the great causes of the day. In this one respect they recognized one another as being of the same tribe. Ideologically the Editor divided his friends into two great camps: the either/ors, and the both/ands. The either/ors who, whether they knew it or not, had been influenced by the teachings of Kierkegaard concerning the necessity of choice, seemed to be in the ascendant these days, and stressed decision and commitment. Either you were right-wing or you were left-wing, black or white, upper class or lower class, religious or not. The both/ands by contrast were people who lived by the old African maxim often quoted by an up-and-coming bishop from Cape Town called Desmond Tutu: "Wherever there stands one thing, there is another thing to stand beside it." The Editor knew which side he was on: secretly he distrusted many of the causes to which he apparently subscribed. Kariba too weaved dexterously and somewhat mischievously between ideological extremes. Opposites abounded, and you slid from one to the other, as the mood took hold. They were both paradoxical people encumbered and hemmed in by the literal minded. For this reason their jokes were often misunderstood. Kariba opened a grubby cigarette packet and held it out: "Cigarette?"

"I don't smoke," said the Editor.

"You do!" said Kariba.

It was not true, but out of politness the Editor lit up: he detested the taste of tobacco.

Kariba said, "Is *The Chimes* coming out again?"

"Not yet. And nor is *The Chimes Literary Supplement*, worst luck."

Kariba leant forward, his eyes widening and conspiratorial. "Look, you know that Scotsman at UCL, Max Fergusson. He's started a rival rag. Fortnightly. It's called *The London Survey of Books*. A bit pseudo-Left Wing. We should get some reviewing work."

"You honestly feel like reviewing?"

"Not a lot. But I need the m-money. You need the money. The office is just along from here. It's in B-bloomsbury Square. Come on." The great gig-lamps of his eyes flashed defiance. They drank up and left.

Five minutes later they were loping side by side past along Great Russell Street towards the Museum, where the Editor often spent his afternoons reading. They passed its wrought iron gates, and made towards Southampton Row. Just before they reached the T junction, Kariba lurched to the right into an institutional-looking doorway. "It's in here," he said.

Still smoking, they mounted the stairs. "You do the talking," said the Editor unwisely. Kariba was ahead as they entered a large airy office. At the far end, at opposite ends of a large table, sat two girls, typing. They looked as if they had just come down from university with low class degress and high class boyfriends. They were both well dressed and almost offensively pretty. They resembled women from the Sanctum Dance Centre. They looked like the Goulash girls. They looked terrifying.

One of then looked up and regarded them as if they were exotic insects. "May we help you?" she asked, as English people occasionally do when they mean "Bugger off!"

The question seemed to be addressed to the Editor, who by prior agreement indicated his friend. Kariba looked alarmed. He looked sheepish, as if he was experiencing second thoughts and already wished to leave the room. He opened up, "W-w—we just wondered..."

"Yes?" said the other girl, looking up from her keys.

"He's Kariba," the Editor said sharply, hoping that this would help. Clearly it had not. The first girl was looking increasingly like Lady Bracknell, the patrician relative from *Charley's Aunt*. Her look had a way of diminishing you. She clearly thought they were both tramps.

Kariba started again, but his stammer was getting worse. "I-I-I-I am from Zimbabwe," he began, not entirely helpfully. The girls both looked as if they would refer to it as Southern Rhodesia. "I am f-fr-from Zimbabwe, and I am a writer, you know. I wrote a book, quite a good book actually. It was r-r—reviewed in the *N-N-New S-S-Stateman*. It w-w-won the C-C-Custodian F-Fiction prize..."

There was an awesome silence in the room. The girls looked across at the two disreputable visitors, and then they looked at one another. Out of the corner of his eye the Editor could see one of them begin to lift the 'phone.

"You m-m-might have h-h-heard of it," Kariba was courageously continuing. "It was c-c-called *Sh-sh-shack of...Sh-sh-shack of....*" Suddenly paralysis, physical and verbal, seemed to have overwhemed him. He had one more go at *Sha-sh-shack of ...*" and then yelled out "SHIT!"

To his astonishment the Editor saw Kariba lay hold of his smouldering cigarette, hurl it onto the richly piled carpet, and start leaping up and down on it, like a demented cat. Kariba had now started convulsively shouting "Burn the place down, burn the place down!!" The second girl was by now seriously 'phoning.

Then everything froze. Kariba looked at the Editor as if for a prompt. The Editor glanced back at Kariba, but he no longer saw a friend and literary ally. He saw a pyrrotechnic terrorist and one-time arsonist who had just inadverently invited him to participate in a crime. Panic seized him by the throat. He saw the headlines racing before his eyes, "Former University Lecturer Implicated In Vandalism," "Literary Career Founders in Shame," "Ten Years in Gaol for One-Time Choirboy."

Kariba had stopped leaping up and down on his cigarette, which had mercifully fizzled out. But the Editor was still holding ineptly onto his, and he did not know what to do with it. It felt increasingly like a weapon in his hands. Kariba had sprung into action again. He shouted, "Run for it!" Simultaneously they made for the door, rushing down the stair well abreast on one another, and out into the open street. When they reached the pavement, Kariba turned left, and the Editor right. They made off into the morning in opposite directions, Kariba towards posterity, and the Editor towards Peckham. They never saw one another again.

When the 'phone went, the Poetry Editor hardly heard it. He was busy packing. His pregnant wife was in the kitchen, and they were moving. "'Phone, sweetheart," she intoned in her warm Welsh voice, and then, louder, "'Phone!"

He picked up the receiver with one clumsy hand. "Yes?"

A familar, voice emerged from the far end, deep chested, like a cross between Boris Godunov and Wole Soyinka: "It's Omoni."

"Oh God," said the Editor, dropping his packing case. "Whatever happened to you?"

"Nothing happened to me. I'm still around. Not everybody is, though.... Kariba."

There was an awkward silence. "Well?"

"Dead. Kariba's dead."

The Editor did not quite know how to react, and so he asked stupidly "Where?"

"In Harare of course. He's been there for years."

The Editor sat down and remarked, "Well isn't that a surprise."

The Three Musketeers they used to call them round the bar, and now they were only two. He swallowed and asked pathetically "What does one do?"

"Nothing," said Omoni sonorously. "Deaths are not supposed to make you do anything. And anything you say sounds pitiful. All the same, Jamie wants an obit. Can you do it?"

The Editor thought hard. He said "I thought maybe that you..."

Omoni repeated himself. He said, a lot more slowly "Can you do it?"

"What do I say?"

"That's up to you. You can 'phone the copy through though. They take dictation nowadays. It won't take long."

"You know," the Poetry Editor added. "The last time I saw him he tried to burn down *The London Survey of Books*."

There was a muffled laugh from the other end. "Pity he didn't. You stopped him, I suppose. Fool!"

"No," said the Poetry Editor, scratching an itching heel in his shoe. "We both ran away: he towards posterity, I towards Peckham."

"Well," said Omoni sagely. "You've got your last sentence then, haven't you? I shall look forward to reading it." He paused and said warmly "Goodbye." Then he rang off.

The Poetry Editor explained the situation to his wife, and then he sat still for a few minutes, looking into the mote-laden air in the middle distance. He was squatting near the 'phone when it sounded again, and he heard the ringing through his thoughts. When he picked up the receiver, there was the same voice, but the tone of it was subtly altered. Had Omoni too, he wondered, been sitting gazing into the distance at the far end?

"Work," said the voice grimly.

"What?" asked the Editor, thinking he had misheard.

"Work," boomed Omoni, "while there is still light."

The Editor did not know how to react. Illogically, through the pious lobes of his brain, he heard the clanking echo of his father's favourite hymn:

Abide with me; fast falls the eventide;

The darkness deepens; Lord with my abide.

When other helpers fail and comforts flee,

Help of the helpless, O abide with me.

He looked out of the window. It was late August, and the days were drawing in. He picked up his biro as if to scribble something. His wife was stirring in the kitchen.

There was another pause, and Omoni said, "Goodnight."

Lake McIlwaine*
A Short Story

Flora Veit-Wild

"Why don't we go and see if we can spot some giraffes?"

"We don't have a car."

"We can walk."

"Walking is dangerous. Think of the rhino."

"Rhinos don't come near the cottages, the warden said. We don't have to go far."

"I don't like the wilderness. I loathe everything outside the city. You KNOW that. And, I can't see anything."

"Didn't you bring your glasses?" Marie was trying to remain patient as her friend grew more disparaging and irritable.

"Ha, my glasses," he sneered. "You know I lost them. And I don't care. Why should I see anything in this world of shit? As long as I can read…"

"But they were my father's…"

"Ya, ya, your father's. Offal from your graciously kept bourgeois life that you have deigned handing down to me—me, your ape, your lover-clown, your… Is there any Whiskey left?"

Why on earth had she come out here with him? She'd carefully planned this three-day outing, making sure everything would work out well for everyone. Peter would take the kids to school in the mornings. In the afternoon they would come home with one of their friends. The maid was there to prepare meals. So Marie had packed enough food for the three days. There was beer, wine and whiskey to keep her companion going, yet not enough to get him completely drunk.

"Yeah, I'll get you some," she said, putting ice in the tumbler. The National Parks Lodges, though not expensive, were well equipped with a fridge, stove, sheets and towels—all that was needed for a few days of pleasure. Having time, the whole night and the whole day, away from the rest of the world, to care for each other. It had worked the night before. They had grilled some meat on the *braai*, which the warden had prepared, drank a couple of beers watching the sun setting over the lake. The low walls surrounding the lawn were filling up with

---

* First published in *Wasafiri* 27.1 (March 2012): 8-10.

rock dassies, weird creatures without tails, scurrying about hastily, their grey fur hardly visible against the stones in the dimming light. It was peaceful, no sounds but the twitter and chirping of the birds and now and then the muffled moos of far-away animals.

It could be perfect, Marie thought, but he was again in one of his sullen moods and ruining everything.

Buddy was staring into the greyness. He hated being here, and he hated this woman who had taken him here. He felt trapped. He wanted to get away but couldn't. Once again he found himself dependent on *her*, who held his life in her hands and manipulated it according to her whims and desires. He hated being at a place where only white people went, taking their family and friends for a wildlife weekend, driving around in their cars, binoculars at hand, their "ahs" and "ohs" when they discovered one of the "big five"—a giraffe anxiously nibbling at one of acacia trees, a lonely elephant raising his big ears, angry about the intrusion of these aliens. Noisy spoilt kids shouting, Daddy, Daddy, can we get closer? He couldn't understand this fascination of white people with wild animals.

Darkness fell within minutes. Buddy shivered and tried to keep his eyes wide open. What was this? Had he heard a noise? Did he see a huge figure walking towards him? How he hated this countryside, full of the witches and evil spirits of his childhood. He had refused to go back to greet his family after his years in exile, to spare himself their bloody rituals, cleansing his spirit from the foreign world across the ocean—what the hell did they know about his life at Oxford...

"Buddy?" There was a voice close to his ear, two arms clasping his neck from behind. Oh yeah, he was here at that goddamned place with *her*...

"What do you want? Leave me alone."

As he brusquely shook off her arms, Marie felt tension rising in her body.

"Oh no, not this again," she pleaded, "let's just enjoy ourselves. It was you who wanted to get away from the city, just the two of us, three entire days for ourselves..."

"Oh yes, me, always me, you seem to know exactly what I want, do you? But let me tell you"—his voice was swelling with anger and scorn—"you don't know anything. You don't know what it feels like to be here, me, the penniless black man, with a posh white lady, being ministered upon by a black servant—this warden blah blah—he comes from the ghetto just as I do, and now he is waiting on me! Ha, what do you know about my life..."

"But usually, when we go out, you mix with white people at places where most blacks won't go, you don't seem to mind, you always seem..."

Marie stopped herself. "The stench of our lives. Gut-rot was what one became. Stains and scars and blood and wounds..." Words from his first novel seeped into her mind. Had she been oblivious again of his deep feelings of shame and self-disgust?

"Get me some of the wine and let me read my book."

Marie opened a bottle of Chateau Burgundy, one of the few creeds of wine a German winemaker had started to cultivate in the unfavorable climate of Zimbabwe. But Buddy liked it: he did not care as long as it was alcohol and could ease some of his tensions. She was also taking out tomatoes, green peppers and onions to prepare a stir-fry, not forgetting the chili pods that her friend adored. He used to munch them pleasurably as if they were peanuts, and, with a smile to her sons who were complaining about onions in their food, say: Hey guys, you should try these, they are really delicious.

No smile for anyone today, she thought, as she came to the verandah where Buddy was sitting with his book under the gas lamp. There were moths fluttering towards the light, big and small ones in all shades of brown and grey—stupid, she thought, can't they see that this is not getting them anywhere, just bumping against the lantern again and again. Out in the dark, a few meters away, swarms of Christmas beetles buzzed and whirled around, floundering up and down as if they were drunk. Finally, with a popping noise and crackling of their black scales, they would drop to the stony ground. Why do they all fall down, her children would ask, when they were sitting outside in their garden on a night like this. Are they dying? Yes, she would answer, it is the end of the season, the rain has made them come out and live for a couple of days, then they die, but next year their babies will be here.

"What are you reading?" she asked cautiously.

"Oh, nothing you would know," he mumbled, "what do YOU know about literature? I can't even talk to you about the books that matter to me. Kurt Vonnegut, if you care to know," spitting the *Kurt* out like a sword to slash her in half.

"Of German origin, by the way, but why should you bother. You could never relate to the hell that he and some of us have gone through, yeah, a slaughterhouse it was here just like in Dresden, when the Rhodesians were bombing the camps of our freedom fighters, killing thousands of civilians at the same time, and erecting Concentration Camps in the rural areas, "keeps" they were called, but in the new novel I am working on I am calling them by their proper name, because the Rhodesians did to us just what you Germans did to the Jews. So why don't you go home to your blond, blue-eyed husband, fascists as you all are, and leave me stranded here as usual."

"Stop it!" Marie shrieked, not able to control her rage any longer, "you are torturing me, blaming me for all the mess in your own life. When Susi comes to fetch us tomorrow, we'll drop you at your flat, and that IS IT…"

Yet a couple of weeks later, she would be knocking at his French window again, peering inside to see whether he was home. So it goes...

Marechera the Performer
Adapting Marechera's Fiction for the Stage

Dobrota Pucherova

Black Sunlight (1980) has always been considered Marechera's notoriously "difficult book" that has never been so well received as the prize-winning *The House of Hunger*, neither in Britain nor Zimbabwe. The book marked the end of Marechera's relationship with Heinemann; it was banned in Zimbabwe for its alleged "obscenity," as its satire was found too impertinent for the idealistic post-indepedence atmosphere, as well as its "imitation of modern writers" (Veit-Wild, Source Book 291). Yet, for some critics *Black Sunlight* remains Marechera's most complex and sophisticated text. In Flora Veit-Wild's reading, the book is a parodistic destabilization of various discourses, including imperialism, Christianity, and Black nationalism, reflecting Marechera's "hybrid consciousness and cross-cultural imagination" (Veit-Wild, "Carnival" 95). According to Annie Gagiano, *Black Sunlight* uses postmodernity as both a political and a philosophical critique of imperialism masking as modernity (as in Conrad's *Heart of Darkness*), and at the same time is "a devastating mockery of, *as well as* the existential angst resulting from, being black in the 'white' twentieth century" (Gagiano 34). The book's reissue in 2010, 30 years after its publication, signals a wide reassessment of Marechera's postmodernist project.

In adapting the novel for the stage, I wanted to bring forth the audacity and deeply sophisticated comedy present in *Black Sunlight*, which, in my reading, contains some of the most comical scenes in African literature, as well as tragic recognitions of the harmful effect of European racism towards Africans. The novel's challenging humour, its intertextuality with European modernist texts such as Conrad, Beckett and Kafka, and cryptic references to Orwell, Bakunin and Sartre, among others, were what made the novel so "difficult"; on the stage, I felt, the novel's meanings could be literally "performed" and come to life, and the Barthesian "play" present in the text could be explicated and made intelligible. In addition, its parodic references to Oxford University made it particularly suitable for an Oxford production.

The finished play ended up being a modernist collage of a number of Marechera's texts, including "The House of Hunger," *Black Insider*, "Black Skin What Mask," "Oxford Black Oxford," and "Amelia" poems. The title, *A Portrait of the Artist in Black and White*, refers to several of Marechera's own titles,[1] and at the same time to the most recurring themes in his work: the alienation of a black person in a white world, the danger of seeing the world in "black and white," the role of the artist in society, the instability of identity. The play is a visual reflection upon the ambiguity of the meanings of "fiction" and "reality." Monochromatic costumes and set, and a racially differentiated cast, were to visualize the key themes.

Written in 16 scenes for 8-10 actors, the play charts the story of Charlie, a Rhodesian undergraduate at Oxford, who falls in love with his fellow student Blanche, one of his many doubles in the play. After being expelled for provocation and substance abuse, Charlie returns to independent Zimbabwe, where he is taken captive by cannibals. Liberated by Blanche, he finds himself in the gay, hallucinatory atmosphere of a Zimbabwean night club, where he meets a childhood friend, the prostitute Susan. Susan convinces Charlie to join an underground anti-government movement, where Charlie meets Chris, a comic guerrilla leader with sadistic tendencies, and his own *doppelgänger*. After the guerrilla base is bombed, the narrative returns to Oxford, where Charlie is having a tutorial with the sinister Professor Warthog. The play ends with Charlie dancing a *danse macabre* with the corpse of Blanche. The narrative is complicated by recurring flash-backs and hallucinations that take the audience constantly back-and-forth between "the present," "memory" and "dream."

The relationship with Blanche is central in the play. Blanche—the white woman who is an important symbol throughout Marechera's texts—represents the contradictions that split apart Charlie's identity and result in his breakdown: she symbolizes the Western civilization, as well as racism; she represents innocent Victorian femininity, as well as its dark foil—imperialism; she is a Virgin Mary and a whore; a sex symbol and a mother figure. As such, she is a compilation of all white female figures in Marechera: Blanche, Patricia, Amelia, Helen, and the homeless white woman in the "Journal" in *Mindblast*, but also Marie, who is never racially defined. Love for the white woman in the play, rather than being a Fanonian desire to be recognized as—and therefore become—white (Fanon, *Black Skins*), is a desire for a world where people are free from imposed identities. As Gerald Gaylard also analyzes in his contribution to this volume, through his love for and identification with the white woman (the raced, gendered Other), the Marechera protagonist redefines traditional African identity (racially exclusive), masculinity (strong, violent, virile, heroic) as well as stereotypical femininity (passive, submissive, beautiful) and transcends race and gender, becoming both white and black, male and female.

---

[1] See e.g. "Portrait of a Black Artist in London," Marechera's unpublished choreodrama, in Veit-Wild's *Source Book*, 250-268, as well as other well-known titles.

This love, however, remains unconsummated, and transcendence through love becomes impossible. Just before Charlie is about to kiss the white woman in his arms, she turns into a corpse. Blanche's body, which before tantalized him with her beauty, is abjected in horror, in a perverse sexual embrace with a corpse. This image, repeated several times in Marechera's writing (end of *Black Insider*, "The Anniversary," "Amelia," "The Visitor") suggests that Marechera is aware of the Levinasian ethical dilemma of epistemological "merging" with another through possessive desire, which threatens to destroy the other's individual identity and autonomous being. In an interview with Flora Veit-Wild about poetry, he says:

> I know that Amelia will never be mine, wholly mine, my own. To love somebody is to want them all the time, to want to drown their identity in one's own identity, that everything they do or say or decide or think is centred on what I am. (Marechera, *Cemetery of Mind* 215-216)

Instead, the deepest connections in the play are created through the acceptance of the separation of interlocutors, in situations where the gap between the characters' epistemologies create new meanings and paradigms. In the play, Patricia, who is blind (and therefore innocent of racism), has a very different perception of the world around her. Through her music, Patricia expresses Charlie's pain and fear that he can't put into words, becoming a projection of his own self, his distressed state of mind that he is unable to express. Misunderstandings between Charlie and Blanche lead to the recognition that love won't abolish the differences of experience between them, and that they can only love each other if they learn to create space for these differences.

The play was rehearsed in spring 2009 in Oxford, with Ery Nzaramba, a Rwandan actor, as Charlie, and Oxford undergraduates as the supporting cast. The production collapsed due to technical difficulties and the challenge it posed to the amateur crew and cast, but a rehearsed reading took place during the Marechera Celebration in Moser Theatre, Wadham College, Oxford, on Saturday May 16, 2009.

A Portrait of the Artist in Black and White
(excerpts)

Scene 1
[Enter **Charlie**, **Blanche**, and the rest of the cast, who stand on the sides looking
at them. They are looking at each other.]
Charlie: Is she what I was, what I would be, what I have never been?
Is she the ghost of my youth's bitter longings, the almost
Crazed visions of life's beauty which then I sought in excursion and
         friendly rhyme?
The crust of the unattainable on my tongue [he touches her arm]
Unleashed me from home and country – to regions of searching mind
And nerve-racked imagination till like Pygmalion I felt
Her first fragrant breath on my cheek and the hot blood [B. kisses him]
Coursing through her veins – my life's work at last fulfilled!
But before a year was out, from all sides, jeers, sneers upon us stung [on-lookers
jeer]
And she, my human hunger, grew pale, lost appetite, became haggard
Shunned by her own kind. [on-lookers tear them apart]
Outraged storms, as if fired from some
Celestial cannon up there, day after day blew down upon us. Amelia drowned.
[she falls]
I shunned man and his daylight ways. I made the terrible pact
And nightly may visit her in spite of her horns and forked tail![2]
[All exit]

Scene 6
[**Charlie** is typing in his student room. He is stuck. He is visited by two Muses.]
Muse 1: Translate the shocking pain
         Into words brain rains.
         Translate the vein of terror
         Into mainland tribal error.
Muse 2: The clock standing still
         Or the bed dreams kill
         Chimes the cruel hour
         Into painful recesses of power.
Muse 1: The sapphire fish in the Suffolk basket
         Plead fiery attire, pledge Prufrock's musket.
Muse 2: Were Eliot African and mermaids dusky grasses

---

[2] Dambudzo Marechera, "The Visitor," *Cemetery of Mind* 174

Would the verse weaken and our flesh respond to
Irresponsible passes?[3]
[Knock on the door, which he does not hear. Enters **Blanche**.]
Blanche: Hi!
Charlie: Hi!
Blanche: Can I come in?
Charlie: [unsure] Sure. [quickly covering over Apuleius' *Golden Ass*]
Blanche: What are you writing?
Charlie: Nothing.
Blanche: [peers] Wow! Do you write poetry? That's so cool.
Charlie: No. It's just my attitude.
Blanche: What do you mean?
Charlie: Never mind.
Blanche: Can I see what you've written?
Charlie: Noo! [covers page with his hand] Would you like a drink?
Blanche: I'd love one. [sneaks around his book-case, takes out a book]
    Do you like Lawrence?
Charlie: Sure. He was definitely a visionary for his time. To see the
    things his way, you have to be a visionary.
Blanche: [sits on his bed] Who's your favorite writer?
Charlie: I don't have one favorite writer. Do you?
Blanche: I have favorite novels. Like, I don't know, *Jane Eyre* is one
    of my all-time favourites. [**Charlie** looks at her with a mixture of terror
and desire]
Blanche: Have you read it?
Charlie: Have I read Brönte? Sure. And Dickens. Trollope. Kipling.
    Defoe. Tennyson. Wordsworth. [he gives a very bad school-
    boy recitation of Wordsworth's "Daffodils" while pacing the
    room; gesticulates wildly]
    I wandered lonely as a cloud
    That floats on high o'er vales and hills
    When all at once I saw a crowd
    A host, of golden daffodils.
    Beside the lake, beneath the trees
    Fluttering and dancing in the breeze.
Blanche: Do you often talk to yourself?
Charlie: All the time. I need to make sure I haven't forgotten all this
    stuff. You see, English Literature gives one the status of being
    an honorary divine.

---

[3] Dambudzo Marechera, "Hook A-Gallop," *Cemetery of Mind*, 70.

Blanche: [puzzled look]
Charlie: It's like being an organism living off another.
Blanche: What do you mean?
Charlie: Do you know about changelings?
Blanche: Uhm—like in *Midsummer Night's Dream*?
Charlie: It's like being a changeling and not exactly what one appears
  to be. There's so much missing inside as though something
  indefinable was taken out. So whenever I want to mean something, I am
  always just striking an attitude.
Blanche: [looking puzzled]
Charlie: It's like my emotions don't belong to me—they are attitudes that spring
on me like jacks-in-a-box.
Blanche: Even right now?
Charlie: Even right now.
Blanche: Can you ever be yourself?
Charlie: Only sometimes.
Blanche: Like when?
Charlie: Like when I'm writing.
Blanche: Oh. Can I see any of your poetry?
Charlie: Maybe next time. [he is getting impatient]
Blanche: Who's your favorite African writer?
Charlie: I don't know. Aye Kwei Armah.
Blanche: What does he write about?
Charlie: It's not for girls. It's like a baptism of shit.
Blanche: Oh. Do you have any romantic novels in Africa?
Charlie: Like *Jane Eyre*?
Blanche: Yes.
Charlie: No.
Blanche: Oh.
Charlie: And that's precisely what the problem is.
Blanche: [mystified] What is the problem?
Charlie: That the only romantic African story is Tarzan.
Blanche: [Laughs; gesticulates] Me—Jane. You—Tarzan.[They look
  into each others' eyes, almost kissing. She lowers her eyes.]
Blanche: That's interesting. The palms of your hands are pink.
Charlie: So does that redeem my blackness?
Blanche: That's not what I meant!
Charlie: Guess what—the soles of my feet are also pink!
Blanche: What's your point?
Charlie: Do you want to see if I'm pink anywhere else?
Blanche: You're weird.

Charlie: Fuck off! I'm not the subject of your anthropological study!
[Exit **Blanche.** Charlie types frantically. Words appear on the screen.]
    I am the rape
    Marked on the map
    The unpredictable savage
    Set down on the page
    The obsequious labourer
    Who will never be emperor…[4]

Scene 13

[**Charlie** is gagged and tied to the totem pole in centre stage. **A cannibal** keeps a watch over him. The **Great Chief** is examining a photographic camera, and spilling other items from Charlie's rucksack, including a photograph of Blanche. He wears a raffia skirt, a necklace of human finger-bones, and is fat, huge and frightening, suggesting "sudden and barbaric impulses, crude and insatiable appetites"[5]]

Enters Messenger: Greetings, Oh Great Chief! I am carrying strange
    news. I have seen the most astonishing being. It was white from head to
    foot. It was bathing by the Blunt Rock Falls.
Great Chief: What madness has struck you? Was it a spirit?
Messenger: It was human in form, but I tell you it was white, so pale
    you could almost see the red flesh the white bones and the blue veins,
    see them through the white skin.
Great Chief: We will have white meat one of these days. [he has a
    gigantic erection. **Charlie** laughs at the Chief's erection.]
Great Chief: Throw him down the pitlatrine!
Charlie: [struggles with his gag, finally frees his mouth] Not again,
    not again, Oh, great chief!
Great Chief: [sly] You want mercy, ah?
Charlie: Have I not been a good court jester?
Great Chief: Then suck my cock!
Charlie: [flinches] Please, throw me down the pitlatrine this minute!
    [Cannibals stand up. Big Chief gestures them to sit down.]
Great Chief: So. You don't like our chief ornament, eh?
Charlie: One man's ornament is another man's anathema. Besides,
    you could save it for that white woman who is bathing at Blunt
    Rock Falls, as the messenger said. It would give you an even greater or-
    nament than you have now, if you see what I mean. Imagine it, Oh great

---

[4] Dambudzo Marechera, "I Am the Rape," *The Black Insider* 125.
[5] Dambudzo Marechera, *Black Sunlight* 6.

chief, mating with a thing that cannot possibly exist and then eating it in a cicada sauce! You are not a sodomite!

Great Chief: A what?

Charlie: In the Little Oxford Dictionary, a sodomite is one who has
  unnatural sexual intercourse with another of his own sex, especially between males. You can't be a great chief and a buggerer in the same
  breath. You're either one or the other.

Great Chief: And who do you say I am?

Charlie: [draws himself up] Our great chief.

Great Chief: Where do you get all these words you come up with?

Charlie: My years of exile in the wide world, even across the seas to
  the land where these white people live. Their hair is long and shiny even
  between their thighs. Their eyes are green or blue and look like gems
  underneath an x-ray. Some of their women are of great beauty and if you
  have them from behind for the first time the sky will come down. It is a
  sweetness you cannot imagine.

Great Chief: You have experienced it yourself?

Charlie: Well… Yes and no.

Great Chief: Elaborate.

Charlie: I can't.

Great Chief: [to his men] Hang him by his heels in the chickenyard! I
  will deal with him later.

[Cannibals hang Charlie by his heels, then go to sit down at a distance, drumming their drums.]

Charlie: [to the audience] So this is humankind! These are my people.
  I am their people too. Crucified upside down by my heels. My Golgotha
  a chickenyard. Father! Father! Why the fucking shit did you conceive
  me? I've spent my life carrying my smashed peace of mind from one
  bit of earth to another, in search of my true people. But wherever I went
  I did not find people but caricatures of people who insisted on being
  taken seriously as people. Take this for instance. I bring them music
  and laughter and poetry and they hang me in the chickenyard. Perhaps I
  am on the wrong planet. Or in the wrong skin. You know. In the wrong
  skin.
  That lecherous gleam in his glittering eye!
  Blanche! Blanche is the Tarzan to rescue me from my plight! Blanche,
  where are you, my female Odysseus! Penelope awaits you, warding off
  suitors by this stratagem of weaving words. Tales, songs, poems, dra-
  mas, and last but not least they shake out my thoughts by my heels.

[He swings gently, trying to liberate himself while not attracting attention. The Chief takes out his medicine bag and consults the bones. He begins to chant rapid magical gibberish that is underlined by the drumming of the drummers. Charlie swings more and more until he lands on the ground with a thump. Enters **Blanche**, pointing a pistol.]

Blanche: Hands up, everyone! Nobody move!

Cannibals: [look surprised, clearly, they have never seen a fire-arm]

Blanche: Are you alright, darling?

Charlie: [shocked] I'm a bit alright, Blanche, just a little sun stroke…

[Blanche, Charlie and Cannibals start a mad chase in circles, cannibals throwing spears, Charlie dodging spears, and Blanche firing with her gun behind her. At last, exhausted, they all stop.]

Charlie: We are all brothers!

Great Chief: [approaches, looking lustful] Ah! We're gonna have
           white meat these days! Not just white arses, but white cunts!

Blanche: Alright. But you must use these. [she takes a string of
           condoms out of her rucksack]

Charlie: [terrified, grabs her arm]: Blanche!

Filming "The House of Hunger" and Zimbabwe Now*

Chris Austin

Making fiction can get out of control—if it's fiction that surprises you in the creative act, that threatens to disrupt and subvert your intentions as you wrestle with the truth of it. Making a hybrid form that intertwines fact with fiction gets out of control from the start, especially if the "fact" is an unfolding reality propelled by a raging egomaniac shouting dreadful truths that others manage to deny or conceal.

During the shooting of this film, Marechera's last words to me were "Fuck off!" This from the doorway as he walked out on us three days after arriving back in Zimbabwe. I was torn between fear that the idea of the film was falling apart and relief at the thought I might have to make it without him. How had it go to that point so quickly?

Those were the days, my friend... A land of hope and freedom, we thought. I thought I was telling the story of a man who'd had it bad and was now going to have it good. The return from exile to a liberated zone, the leader of the "front-line" states in the war against apartheid, a land that was the hope of Africa. I wanted it to be all *affirmative*, to tell of the return of the prodigal son to a family transformed.

Marechera was having none of it, from the start. "Nothing has changed at all!" Declaimed in a parody of Oxford tones, *and* as we drove *from the airport*! How could he? I wanted to call Cut! and re-write the line. But he was re-writing the whole script, and he was right, as it turns out.

The first news Marechera received on the day of his return was that his country had just banned his second novel. "Sell outs!" he yelled at the other writers –why had they not risen up to defend his work? Because they were all, in one way or another, working for or in hock to the new regime. It was symptomatic of so much. It was the time of reconstruction, not uprising, of compromise, of "unity" and of the artist being "useful." I was guilty of expecting him to accept this, when everything in his work and life screamed, and sang of total artistic freedom, when

---

* This essay accompanies the film included on the DVD.

I had known and been drawn to this "inflamed individualism" that was utterly maverick. I provoked the break between us by attacking him for his "negativity." I was driven to this on two very different levels.

As a filmmaker I wanted the film to look like the script I'd written. We'd already filmed with Marechera in London; raging alienation mixed with "astonishing humour and lucidity." That was what I'd wanted. We'd already shot the scenes from the novel as discontinuous, elliptical frames of the fictionalized bad times of his past. They were going to be woven into the story of his regenerative present as he returned, in reality, to the new Zimbabwe, to reunite with family and friends. So when he arrived and revolted *against the present*, once more becoming the alienated outsider, I saw my preconceived structure heading for the window.

As an exile from South Africa, I felt the political imperative to make an inspiring portrait of the newly liberated Zimbabwe – and here was Marechera calling it no different from Rhodesia! I had to find something positive to counterpoint this. So we turned to the story of Chief Rekai Tangwena, the legend from the liberation war who had played the prophetic Old Man in the fictionalized past, who foretold the exile of Marechera.

We found Tangwena tilling his fields, in his land regained, but where were his cattle? "Ian Smith stole my cattle! I demanded them back and Smith said ask the British. But they didn't take them. Smith did and he must return them. Seven hundred and sixty three cattle!" Smith never gave them back, and you could say that twenty years later, Tangwena's heirs are now taking them by force.

At the time, *Jeune Cinema* described the film in a positive review as "primarily the encounter of a Black Zimbabwean writer, Marechera, and a white South African filmmaker, Chris Austin. [...] Beyond that encounter, there is convergence of two men through the same political struggle. And yet, there is conflict." This wasn't the script, I wasn't meant to be in it, at all. And yet I had to find a form to tell of what happened. Much later, when I held a preview in Harare for a group of writers at the first International Book Fair, I met Marechera for the first time since his departing curse in the doorway. Would he throw something at me? After the screening he got up and hugged me. "You told the truth!"

When I finished the film I felt I had made only the messy record of an attempt at something. I was heartened when Nadine Gordimer wrote to me: "You said you set out to make a film about Zimbabwe, and failed. But you succeeded in doing much more. You do not claim too much, in my opinion, when you say that with the breakdown in the relationship between you as filmmaker and Marechera as subject, the film became both a symptom and an examination of the whole relationship between the Third World artist and European media." (And, I would add: between the white African artist and Third World African material.)

"Your very consciousness of attacking cultural imperialism with being—not *while* being, note—a part of it, has made it possible for you to make an entirely new kind of film, instead of having to abandon the project. You make the discovery, for us, that there is no artistic vocabulary within the distinctions of film as documentary (external reality?) and film as fiction (internal reality?) to deal with a consciousness as culturally blasted as Marechera's.

Not by mistake, but by accepting that a new film language had to be found for what really was there to be expressed, you have made a mode to carry a new consciousness. The film is a positive revelation of what still lies to be understood in the colonial experience, and in its interpretation by all those whose art is bound up with the fact that they were part of that experience."

A year later, at the opening ceremony for the next International Book Fair, he publicly berated the Minister of Information for selling out, for betraying the people and censoring the arts. The police locked him up for the rest of the week. "This society has no place for people like him."

What would he say of Zimbabwe now? That the people were being betrayed again, I think, manipulated by the same elite who sold them out in the beginning and became corrupted by compromise. When the people called them in they cynically resurrected the struggle for land, but despite the historical truth of the claim they've succeeded in dividing the people against themselves as never before.

I don't think he would be surprised—he didn't share our illusions at the time. He would attack the blind greed of the white Rhodesian landowners who wouldn't give an inch until too late, and attack the collusion and self-interest of the new political class who accommodated them for so long. But he had the courage to do it from the moment he returned. Had the country had the courage to listen to him, the course of its history might have been altered. A huge claim for the power of art, but re-connecting after twenty years-five with the power of that moment, I think I'll make that claim.

Litera[ri]ly Laterally
Re-Visioning Marechera for Educational Films*

heeten bhagat

I Am the Rape, the film and facilitation guide, was originally designed as a teaching tool for the A-Level literature syllabus in Zimbabwe and the neighbouring region, to introduce students to the work of Dambudzo Marechera. The project was inspired by the popular belief that the works of Marechera are "un-filmable." Only one attempt has been made, the BBC Channel 4 film *The House of Hunger* by Chris Austin, in the early 1980's.[1] It is a mixture of documentary and dramatisation. For me, the former is more successful, as it features the author and gives the viewer a brilliant insight into the mind behind such traumatic and stellar literature. This film became an important resource for my own project.

After his death, Dambudzo Marechera was canonized as one of the most original African authors who irreversibly changed the landscape of African literature. Yet, this would have proven an anathema to the author who refused to be pigeonholed by his race or the continent of his birth, angrily declaring, "...I would question anyone calling me an African writer. [...] If you are a writer for a specific nation or a specific race, then fuck you" (Veit-Wild, *Source Book* 221). His writing defiantly stood against the African realist, anti-colonial tradition of writing, in favour of a more personal and experimental articulation. His style was, for its time, radical and tumultuous, challenging the realist narrative structure and simplistic binary definitions. This would, no doubt, appeal to countless generations of teenagers and adolescents, constantly in the throes of protest against the older generations.

Marechera is not taught in Zimbabwean schools. I feel strongly that he should be. He presents an alternative hero, one who was not afraid to express how he felt. Also key to his genius was, and is, his incredible knowledge and understanding of the medium of his expression, that being English. This is such a valuable accolade, especially for us Africans, who still live in a world that has been defined for us, and one by which we must live if we are to "succeed." He wrote in English as a way of "expressing the creative turmoil within my head" (Veit-Wild & Schade 7). His self-conscious bastardisation of the literary structures expected

---

* This essay accompanies the film included on the DVD.
[1] This film is included on the DVD.

from "African writers" make his work sublime. However, access to his books is still difficult in the country of his birth. There have been brief moments in the last decade when a ruling party directive issued orders to "celebrate" this "son of the soil," but in most cases this action is disappointingly superficial, as are the collections of youth who momentarily immerse their troubled beings in his controversial fame. Most often it is his anarchic exploits that they seek to mimic and not what, for me, reflects his true genius—his extraordinary contribution to world literature. The challenge then stands: How does one make a film of a text that in a sense defies any previous classification? I think it was exactly this that made the dramatised part of Chris Austin's film unsuccessful. There is a rawness and innate brutalism in "The House of Hunger" and Marechera's other works that we filmmakers in Zimbabwe have only now begun to explore, understand, and develop a visual language for. The language of Zimbabwean filmmakers is, thankfully, nascent and as such provides room for this new growth, for perhaps extreme experimentation. Armed with this and the plethora of analysis of Marechera, the adaptation/interpretation of "I Am the Rape"[2] was made.

Channelling Marechera

Although written in 1979 in London as a reaction to the racist pre-election posters of the British National Party, which metonymically embodied "crime" in the image of a black male face, Marechera's poem "I Am the Rape" bears an uncomfortable resonance to the political and social turmoil facing Zimbabweans today. His experiences and troubles with the oppressive authority of the colonial government in Rhodesia (that is reflected in the racist prejudice of the National Party posters) hold an uncanny relevance to the present regime in power in Zimbabwe. It seems clear that there are multiple readings and analyses of Marechera's work, some of which I think he would find questionable. The primary question for me, as a creative professional, was the following: how do I pay homage to his words and not lose myself in the process? How do I not fall into the trap of "translating" but try to take this process further, creatively, and still find ways to make the final product informative and original?

What follows is my initial explication of "I Am the Rape":

> I am the rape
> Marked on the map
> The unpredictable savage
> Set down on the page
> The obsequious labourer
> Who will never be emperor

---

[2] The poem is included in *Cemetery of Mind* 30 and in *Black Insider* 125.

In this introductory stanza Marechera, with contempt and anger, as if through gritted teeth, speaks of the stereotype of the African man as a "savage." What seems like a self-denigrating rhetoric continues as if to fulfil the prophecy of the opening line: *I am the rape* [Or rapist?], [whom you have for all intents and purposes] *Marked on the map*. [You think I am] *The unpredictable savage* [that you will] *Set down on the page*. [You also think I am] *The obsequious labourer/ Who* [you] *will never* [allow to] *be emperor*. The sad realisation by the end of the stanza almost begs for a question mark, in defence of an even more disappointing truth. Yes, *I* will never be *emperor* in your eyes.

> My hips have rhythm
> My lips an anthem
> My arm a reckoning
> My feet flight
> My eyes black sunlight
> My hair dreadlocks

This second stanza comes through more rhythmically, with an almost sprightly energy. In stark contrast to the preceding one, it exposes the elegance and rhythm of Rap music. This style and beauty carries through to the last two verses, naturally building up speed, to end in a powerful thud. The last line, *My hair dreadlocks*, stops the rhyme abruptly, dead.

> Sit on this truth out at sea
> Hit the shit when you go out to tea
> Don't want to hear what ears hear
> Don't want to see what eyes see
> Your white body writhing underneath
> All the centuries of my wayward fear

This stanza shouts its words, imploring the reader to examine a global responsibility for violence and oppression. *Sit on this truth out at sea/ Hit the shit when you go out to tea*; the world sits and watches what is happening in other countries, safe in the belief that their responsibility is reduced by their distance from the unfolding conflict. News programmes favour entertainment over information, spectacularizing tragedy, building up hype and drama to boost ratings. This in turn leads to desensitization towards violence, as confirmed by the next two verses, *Don't want to hear what ears hear/Don't want to see what eyes see*. In the last two lines concerning the "writhing white body" under a "wayward fear," the anger expressed is vitriolic and loud. As Jennifer Armstrong has written, "His fear is wayward because he is not a calm, docile native. He is inclined to react to what is done to him, thus indicating that something *is* actually being done to him (and to the people of his colour)—something which produces a passionate and negative effect" (Armstrong).

> Goodness is not ground out of a stone
> Evil neither. Men gnaw their chicken bones.Know the electric shocks
> that seized my testicles.
> Which now you eat with the lips of a sunrise
> Your white body writhing underneath
> All the centuries of my wayward fear

This stanza takes on an almost teacherly tone in the beginning. The **stone** is perhaps a reference to Zimbabwe, which means in Shona "the house of stone," the name adopted at Independence after the famed ancient ruins located in the central part of the country. The **goodness** possibly signifies a veiled criticism of the impending independence of this country, followed hastily by a balancing **Evil neither**. **Men gnaw their chicken bones** has drawn multiple interpretations ranging from association to food and the homestead to, quite bizarrely, a reference to female sexuality (see McLoughlin 45-46). Most of these analyses resonate; though the savage intentions embodied in the word **gnaw** speak to a meaning more sinister, perhaps. The next two lines speak of freedom, of independence, **lips of a sunrise**, juxtaposed tragically with what it has cost, **electric shocks**. There is the feeling of an inevitable resignation to what has happened as a result of this centuries-old injustice. The last two lines are a refrain from the previous stanza; this time around, they come as a cold, hard statement, written with what seems like the exhaustion and helplessness that this struggles imposes.

There is an undeniable urgency located within this short poem, one that needed to be consumed with a passion, speed and anger. It was, however, important to remember that this film was to be used as an educational tool. The challenge was to avoid the didacticism and patronising tone typical of educational films and make a product that spoke clearly to the aforementioned attributes. Video games became a key source of inspiration, as well as music videos. It is extraordinary how visually and aurally saturated and sophisticated today's young people are. They exist in a hyper-stimulated environment, and the films needed to work on that same if not higher level. Multi-layered imaging and messaging were necessary.

Ekphrasis, or *Ecphrasis*, can be defined very simply as the making of art from/ of art, for art's sake. This concept, Greek in origin, acknowledges the exploration of one artistic discipline by another, to realise its full potential. The creation of a film from a poem is an example of this. Incorporated in this idea is the investigation of *phantasms*, those random, yet intensely visual images that our mind creates (see Covino 33). This happens quite naturally when reading Marechera, since the writing is very vivid. Documenting the images that were generated on subsequent readings yielded a bizarre collection of notes and images. The information collected worked in tandem with the idea that poetic writing has a wealth far in excess of the words laid down on the page. Each word, line, and how they are placed in relation to each other require a deeper reading. Through the concept of *Ekphrasis*, the words become laden with a rich imagery sourced from a growing knowledge of the writer and his world.

Marechera's work has a unique sense of the carnivalesque. According to Flora Veit-Wild, "He was an expert at masking and unmasking, at disguising and stripping; a master of parodic travesty" (Veit-Wild, "Carnival" 93). Marechera often confessed that his use of the English language was based in his contempt for it: "For a black writer the [English] language is very racist; you have harrowing fights and hair-raising panga duels with the language before you can make it do all that you want it to do" (Veit-Wild, *Source Book* 4). The images that these facts throw up become fascinating and allow for an exploration of contemporary artists working with the macabre. Images created by contemporary visual artists such as Cindy Sherman, Joel Peter-Witken, William Kentridge and Jenny Saville, among others, resonate with the messages of the poem. Marechera's knowledge of world literature was extraordinary; his references to writers ranging from Apuleius through Yeats to Fanon imbue his work with an original and compelling imaginative wealth in comparison with his peers at the time. It so follows that a film made to teach a new generation about his work should be equally wealthy in its knowledge and references. Further, Marechera's writing reflects influences by surrealism, dadaism and cubism. All this variety helps to generate a rich source of imagery confirming the "Ekphrastic" character of this film.

Another key aim became contextualising the film for the contemporary world to make it more relevant. Marechera was clearly disillusioned by Zimbabwe's new government; this pessimism stretched to include the continent of Africa. He writes: "We have done such a good advertising and public relations stunt with our African image that all horrors committed under its lips merely reinforce our admiration for the new clothes we acquired with independence. [...] All this for the sake of the African image which is no longer worth the snot it quotes" (Marechera, *Black Insider* 84). This disillusionment about anti-colonial nationalism and Marechera's subsequent attempts in the mid-1980's to leave Zimbabwe become important in the film that is to educate the new generation about Zimbabwe's history. The situation in Zimbabwe today bears a painful and disappointing relation to the oppression that Marechera experienced in the newly-independent Zimbabwe. The fact that political oppression and intimidation have gotten worse speaks of the relevance of Marechera for the next generation.

This inquiry then led to the making of two short films, "The Control" and

"The Experiment." Based on the principle of a chemistry experiment, the former is situated in the didactic genre, albeit with a fair degree of creative licence. This film, four minutes long, explicates and investigates the full poem through multi-layered images and an intricately-built soundtrack. Each of the images and sounds has relevance to both the writer and his works beyond the poem. The second film, "The Experiment," two minutes long, aims to be an anarchic abstraction of "The Control," deconstructing it in favour of the extreme creative impulse that is present throughout Marechera's work.

A Facilitation Guide accompanies the films. It consists of the documentation of the research and conceptual process in a clear and concise manner, as well as notes collected during the visualisation and editing processes. This information aims to draw attention to the wide range of references contained in this short film. The images and sounds explore a deeper narrative within Marechera's work, encompassing the situation in Zimbabwe presently. The guide is there to assist educators to explore the multiplicity of influences gathered and noted in the making of these films. It is not prescriptive; rather, it aims to be provocative.

Enough said—now I think you should watch the films.

The Twilight Zone of Literature*

Nana Oforiatta-Ayim

> Will this moon scrap itself off my poems!
> This twilight zone stretching between English school
> And my cockroach voice?

So begins Dambudzo Marechera's poem "A Shred of Identity."[1] As a writer, Dambudzo Marechera has long been one of my literary patron saints, although a saint is far from what he was and the circumstances of his becoming a writer were as different to mine as they could be. In 1903, W.E.B. DuBois wrote in *The Souls of Black Folk*, "It is a peculiar sensation, this double-consciousness, this sense of always looking at one's self through the eyes of others, of measuring one's soul by the tape of a world that looks on in amused contempt and pity" (DuBois 8). Despite emancipation and independence, our histories still burn under our skins and a future of undoing them shackled us. I grew up a Ghanaian girl in Germany and England, loving Russian literature as much or even more than the stories born of my continent. I wanted to lose myself in the words of my choosing, but could only do so in the shadows. Instead, I was to don the clothes of respectability and become a lawyer, and I felt the heavy obligation to right the wrongs of our colonial past.

Marechera was the first writer that freed me of my burden. He quoted Novalis, Ionesco, Beckett, Tsvetaeva and Goethe in his writing, alongside Okigbo, Ngugi and Soyinka. He drew on the modernist aesthetics of the beat poets, rather than the mythic narratives or social realism that told of our pre-colonial splendour and our colonial horrors. He described the uncompromising underbelly of what it was like to live in a racially oppressive Rhodesia, then in a morally corrupt Zimbabwe. He tightened his bow and let the arrow fall indiscriminately against both black and white. He went further than the slogan, "Black is Beautiful," by adding, "No, I don't hate being black. I'm just tired of saying it's beautiful" (Marechera, *Hunger* 45). Like Zora Neale Hurston, another writer of my personal constella-

---

* This essay accompanies the film included on the DVD.
[1] The poem is included in *Cemetery of Mind* 99.

tion, he refused to be anything other than himself. She was condemned by her peers for refusing to be defined by past pains. "I do not belong to the sobbing school of Negrohood who hold that nature somehow has given them a lowdown dirty deal and whose feelings are all hurt about it," she wrote in her essay "How it Feels to Be Colored Me" (1928), which is pointedly not about how it felt to be black in the United States, but how it felt to be her (Hurston 153). In their reflections, I saw my own expressive freedom mirrored. And when Marechera, with a self-assurance that refused to be reined in by any form of social constraints, declared that, "I am the doppelgänger whom, until I appeared, African literature had not yet met" (Veit-Wild, *Source Book* 221), I found he was my *doppelgänger* too. Not least because of the twilight zone between the "English school" and his "cockroach voice" that he described in the opening lines of the poem.

In many African countries, the majority of the population is at least bi-lingual, learning old colonial languages alongside multiple local ones. Those who have travelled abroad have had to take on foreign languages often to substitute their mother tongue. For Marechera, the linguistic split manifested itself in a deep cultural schizophrenia, with Shona, his African language, embodied in the *cockroach*—the township poverty he came from—and the European language, English, symbolized by *school*—Western education and opportunity. He wrote: "When I talked it was in the form of an interminable argument, one side of which was always expressed in English and the other side always in Shona" (Marechera, *Hunger* 30). My own linguistic background was not so divisive; my African past presented another type of education and opportunity, sometimes richer than my European one, but nonetheless I grew up speaking three languages, wholly unable to find my voice in any of them. I felt like Marechera when he wrote that, "I was being severed from my own voice. [...] At the same time I would be aware of myself as something indistinct but separate from both cultures" (Marechera, *Hunger* 30).

This multiplicity of languages, of being, was something I began to find reflected in the polyrhythmic structures of musical forms, of design, of social structures in Ghana and many other parts of Africa. Rather than it being a disorder or a state in which you only saw yourself as others saw you, it was an added lens through which to see the world. As the Nigerian-born, England-raised, France-based singer Keziah Jones sang in 1993: "What you believe you see in my colour, is nothing but a curious kind of subconscious." It was this sense of multiplicity that led me to making films out of poetry and in particular a film version of the poem "A Shred of Identity" by Dambudzo Marechera.

> To the ant perched on a grain of sand
> My giant's Artistic dilemma is scarcely visible
> Only clearly seen when I raise my foot.

The bee on his sweet sticky errand, seeing me,
Shoots off at a tangent humming his scorn.
The early swallow from his searing flight
Scarcely casts instantaneous glance at my pains.

These next lines in Marechera's poem reminded me of a position that I have always thought of as more male than female. Although the cultural categories of male and female are constructions, their socialisation gives them ontological value. I have often seen and heard my male artist friends complain of and handle their *giant's Artistic dilemma.* They do it with a vociferousness and entitlement that I, as a woman, educated still today to see her primary role as a nurturer, both envy and despise. Of course I am being reductionist; these same traits crop up in women, but in my experience less so, and when they do they are described as "manly."

In the film I wanted to add another layer to Marechera's treatment of the writer, the "female" gaze of acknowledging the suffering and dilemmas of others alongside that of the male artist and thus relieve him, Marechera, to some extent of his existential loneliness.

The dustman shrugs, hurls his concrete burden
Into factory hand adjusts the zip on his overalls
And without a care awaits his Call—factory's siren.
The milkman cycles his round; the soldier
Kisses his girl hurries to carry out orders.

All these actors on the stage of life were in my film given their own sufferings or "cares"; the actor as writer only sees them when he is joined by his muse. Even though I spoke above of the singlemindedness of artistic self-regard, it is clear from Marechera's writing that he was very capable of seeing through his own suffering into the suffering of others, even though perhaps he found no communion in it.

In the main roles of the film, I cast the twins Chuka and Dubem Okonkwo, also known as Chet and Joe, or The Islington Twins, to play the double aspects of the writer. I first met them at an art opening many years ago. They wore matching threadbare dark coats, scarves and fluorescent bags of the type used for newspaper rounds. They finished each other's sentences. They made notes of what I said in their coloured notebooks. And when I met them again a year or so later, they excavated these from their bags to remind me when we had met and what I had said. When I got to know them better, I found that they moved from place to place, house-sitting for a variety of friends and benefactors, that they were the most well-read people I had ever come across as well as the most kind-hearted, and that their accents full of roomy vowels and clipped consonants were of their own creation and masked a painfully dislocated past. In many ways they reminded me of Marechera, his wandering, his erudition, his penchant for myths and masking. Stories abound of him receiving his Guardian First Book Award in a cowboy hat and a poncho, and of turning up to celebrate the independence of Zimbabwe in full British fox hunting regalia. The twins Chuka and Dubem Okonkwo, though less controversial in their dress, are no less dramatic. They seem to exist as two halves of the same whole and yet, once on a closer footing, one becomes acutely aware of their discrete individualities. Their philosophy of "Twinism'" is based on on different wisdoms, including the book *The Conference of Birds* by Farid ud-Din Attar, in which thirty birds go in search of the mythical Simorgh and at the end come to a lake in which they see only their own reflections and those of each other. Farid ud-Din Attar's lines, "Come you lost Atoms to your Centre draw/And be the Eternal Mirror that you saw," reminded me of the *doppelgänger* of African literature.

> They all seem to know their own selves
> While I like a madman continue to decipher
> The print on a shred of blank paper
> The print that is to become the poem behind this poem.

Marechera tried to find a home in many different places, in his homeland of Zimbabwe, in the institutional realms of education at the Universities of Rhodesia and Oxford, in the anarchic squats and the post-independence melting pot of the Africa Centre in London, but he was at odds with them all. In his essay, "African Writer's Experience of European Literature," he writes: "I have been an outsider in my own biography, in my country's history, in the world's terrifying possibilities" (Veit-Wild, *Source Book* 364). Many artists find themselves as outsiders to some extent, and it is precisely this feeling of estrangement that leads them to creation. I myself have wandered from place to place, searching, in my country of origin, amongst the children of independence like me or those who have grown up in-between cultures. I have found a movable home of sorts, one with people, kindred spirits like the cast and crew, who created the possibilities for the film. But most of all in the solitude of writing, that place with no borders or nations or imperatives, the twilight zone, in which the spirits of Zora Neale Hurston and Dambudzo Marechera dwell, and where language shatters the illusion of our separateness.

Why I Want to Tell Dambudzo's Story*

Ery Nzaramba

I was living in Oxford when I met Dobrota Pucherova, who was doing a PhD in African Literature at Oxford University. We met by accident, really, and when she learned that I was an actor based in Oxford, she asked me if I could play the lead part in the play she'd written about a Zimbabwean writer. When she asked whether I knew of Dambudzo Marechera, I had to admit I didn't. She mentioned other notable African writers: Ayi Kwei Armah, Wole Soyinka, etc. And I had to shamefully shake my head "No... never heard of them." She looked at me, puzzled by my ignorance, and to tell the truth, so was I. How could an African, claiming to be working in the arts, not have heard of those illustrious African writers? And Dobrota proceeded with lending me a few books: I had some catching up to do; particularly, in this case, with Marechera's work. She'd warned me Dambudzo would be hard to read but he wasn't. I instantly recognized Dambudzo's voice. He was describing those feelings that I as a Black man of African origin living in Europe and as a Black actor of African origin working in Britain instantly identified with. And he was doing it powerfully and eloquently. He was expressing that duality of feeling at home everywhere but not fitting anywhere. And he was expressing it in a way I was incapable of. In his essay "The African Writer's Experience of European Literature," he writes: "I have been an outsider in my own biography, in my country's history, in the world's terrifying possibilities" (Veit-Wild, *Source Book* 364).

The first thing that attracted me to Marechera's work and personality was that trait of feeling an outsider within the European community AND within the African community. Be it in Zimbabwe or in Britain, Dambudzo was always searching for his individual self, never feeling he belonged to any one community. I can totally relate to that. That constant search for who I am. I was born in Belgium, moved to Rwanda at the age of seven, came back to Belgium at the age of seventeen and moved to Britain ten years later. My cultural sensibility is as much European as it is African. Am I African? My parents were Rwandan, so I must be. Am I European? I was born in Europe and have spent more than two-

---

* This essay accompanies the film included on the DVD.

thirds of my life in Europe, so I must be. Am I Afro-European? Euro-African? More European than African? More African than European? Does it matter? In the grand scheme of things, it doesn't matter; the consensus is that I'm an African who lives in Europe and I should just get on with it. But I'm an actor; and actors are constantly confronted with how others see them, and have to explore their sense of who they are when portraying a character. So I haven't been able to just get on with it. Whether I like it or not, I'm pigeon-holed as an African actor or a Black actor. Here in Britain, most of the times I'm hired to play an African or at least a Black character. When all I want is play A character. And in Dambudzo I discovered someone who was able to express this predicament in no way that I could. He expressed it in his work, he expressed it in his daily life. To me, Marechera's body of work AND his whole life have been about searching for and expressing who he is.

> [...] to insist upon [...] your right to refuse to be labeled and to insist on your right to behave like anything other than anyone expects. Your right to simply say no for the pleasure of it. [...] Insist upon your right to insist on the importance, the great importance, of whim. (Marechera, *Hunger* 122)

> I am what I am not because I am an African or whatever but because it is the basic nature of a maker of descriptions, a writer. (Marechera, *Mindblast* 123)

> If you are a writer for a specific nation, or a specific race, then fuck you. (Veit-Wild, *Source Book* 221)

You could say that Dambudzo's life was a perfect film plot. A tragedy, in his case. The rise of the underdog, against all odds. From a Harare township to Oxford University, to the Guardian Fiction Award and a triumphant return to Zimbabwe for a film about him and his novella "The House of Hunger." Then his decline: the fall from grace in Zimbabwe, becoming a vagrant in Harare, and dying at a young age.

During my research I interviewed Stanley Nyamfukudza, who was a contemporary and good friend of Dambudzo's. I realized he'd had a very similar route—he too had come to Oxford University at about the same time as Dambudzo (though differently from him, he graduated), he too became a published writer and also returned to Zimbabwe. But he would fare differently than Dambudzo. As I listened to Stanley I suddenly realized I could have been listening to my father: he's of the same generation and also got a scholarship to study in Europe (in his case, Belgium), in the same year: 1974. So, at the same time that Dambudzo and Stanley were traveling from Rhodesia to Britain, 1090 miles (1755 km) away, my father was traveling from Rwanda to Belgium. His story would however be different. In fact, any African who spends his or her formative years in Europe before returning to the home country has his or her own story: Dambudzo had his, Stanley had his, my father had his and I have mine (though I haven't returned yet). Or rather, it is the same story experienced differently each time. And this is what I want to explore with the film. It is still going to be about Dambudzo, but with the larger theme of the modern African Diaspora. In Europe we face the battle between being (and behaving as) who WE are, and being (and behaving as) who THEY expect us to be. I haven't returned to Rwanda yet, but from reading about Dambudzo, and having had a taster whenever I've found myself in a Rwandan community, I am convinced that the same battle carries on once you've returned "home." Only, THEY is no longer the "Europeans" but the "Africans." It's the story of the modern African Diaspora, then and now, away and home.

The House of Hunger (1984), dir. Chris Austin © Chris Austin

"1987", *I Am the Rape* (2006) © heeten bhagat and Linette Frewin

"The real emperor", *I Am the Rape* (2006) © heeten bhagat and Linette Frewin

"The emperor", *I Am the Rape* (2006) © heeten bhagat and Linette Frewin

The principal, *I Am the Rape* (2006) © heeten bhagat and Linette Frewin

"Tableau vivant", *I Am the Rape* (2006) © heeten bhagat and Linette Frewin

"The obsequious labourer", *I Am the Rape* (2006) © heeten bhagat and Linette Frewin

Nana Oforiatta Ayim with Chuka and Dubem Okonkwo © Nana Oforiatta Ayim

Production team of *A Shred of Identity* (2009) © Nana Oforiatta Ayim

86

Ery Nzaramba as Marechera receiving *Guardian* fiction award in short film *Dambudzo*
© Ery Nzaramba 2010

Ery Nzaramba as Marechera receiving *Guardian* fiction award in short film *Dambudzo*
© Ery Nzaramba 2010

PART 2

MEMORY AND REFLECTION

A Letter to Departed Buddy*

Nhamo Anthony Mhiripiri

It's funny
So sourly sardonic Buddy!
How times have lured people
Into an abrupt attitude change
Towards you, your books!
Isn't everything a stinking façade?
Like the new toilet at corner Stanley-Second?[1]
Pshaw!
I remember quite clearly Buddy,
(It's all throbbing back into my mind),
I recall tailored gents, feigning folks,
Disapproving with a Christian vehemence
The acid manner you exposed the infectious diseases
Cupped between everybody's moral thighs, yours included.
Grand Sheraton syphilis soiled some dignitary's underwear;
You filched the dirty linen by the witty hook of your crafty pen
And wrung it before the Public's vacant eyes.
People were stunned for the wrong reasons altogether,
And retched out blind malice against the oracle's opened mouth.
(By the way Buddy, those visions
Of mass despair have amassed.
Visions of "Drought Relief graintrucks vanished into thin air
Between departure point and expectant destination," etc.[2]
Now also include among others,
Incriminated *chefs*[3] cases farted out of public hearing
Into an august High Court chamber.

---

* Written on 2 August 1988 for the University of Zimbabwe students' commemoration of the first anniversary of Marechera's death. An excerpt of the poem is published in Veit-Wild, *Source Book*, 389-390.

[1] Harare's Stanley Avenue is now called Jason Moyo Avenue and Second Street is now Sam Nujoma Street.

[2] Dambudzo Marechera, "Oracle of the Povo," *Cemetery of Mind*, 67.

[3] One's social superior, especially from the ruling political party.

It all stinks of arm-twisting and bribery
Somewhere between uncovered scandal and verdict point.)
For such audacity, Buddy, of painting
A heavily patched, mouse-nimbled soiled rag
As the country's national dress,
You got unwarranted detention,
Some fat knuckled pummelling fists,
Plus slamming boots, as your frail body's massage.
Or they simply lashed out adjectives and nouns,
Cheekily questioning your loyalty to leader and nation
And crudely criss-crossing your sanity
Like a mad morphine stoned Parirenyatwa[4] doctor
Grasping a licensed to lacerate lancet.
I recollect the mercilessly abused toilet in *Mindblast*:
This nationwide lavatory.
And your nearsighted inspection,
Your lucid description of reeking circumstances,
Never got anything like the current acclaim mouthed
By both the hottest-headed of varsity students
And the most cowardly fair weather journalists.
Who's fooling whom then!
Pshaw!
I remember all this Buddy!
Funny enough the official opening of the
Corner Stanley-Second toilet was national news:
The media broadcast the opening of the shit-place
By a dignitary. If he demonstrated its use,
The sparkling new chamber flashed, licked and swallowed
All his linen-dirt secrets in a hullabaloo rush.
But Buddy sometimes I can't help feeling the new loo
Is a special tribute to you?
Man, real things are happening
Since your silent departure into the rigid unknown.
Tribute!
Sure Buddy, for it is in your favourite park.
Were you around I'd gratefully owe you
A decent stipend sponsored sloshing spree
At Norfolk; it's such an achievement.
Yours truly! Our world is beginning to accept more real things.
The toilet is so near to Kingston's—remember

---

[4] Parirenyatwa is a state hospital in Harare.

That's where *The House of Hunger* and *Mindblast* are also sold.
I don't recall much about *Black Sunlight*,
Beside its invitation back from the doom of Christian censorship
And its subsequent conspicuous absence from bookshops.
Now, this one is supposed to be a secret Buddy,
You may not have been told about it.
They published a memorial booklet, far from a biography,
(With the way they're rummaging through your scrap papers
Like hungry scavenging squatter dogs,
Chances are more will come out of you.),
And your dreadlocked portraits too on t-shirts.
Selling like hot buns at that Greek's café!
Selling like Mutoko dope[5] in arid ghettoes!
Haunt them Buddy, they should send fat royalties
To that morbid hushed unknown realm.
Don't you still quest for some bittersweet booze
To wash down the dust, the dried cement on your throat?
The new toilet is right in the Park
Where you used to sit and type away
Amidst Hararean jeers and scorn, such sad beautiful lines like,
"I sing no more roses
But wander through Hararean mazes."[6]
The Park is no longer Cecil Square Buddy,
It's now called Africa Unity Square
And the lavatory consolidates the transformation.
Had you been around you too could have empted
Your starved bowels and overloaded bladders in there,
Obviously confessing your own gut-rot—but no need
For a Catholic penance Buddy, no need!
Ahoy! Would the toilet have been a fitting tribute
With you frail, live and around plodding on a type-
Writer's keys seated on a lone park bench?
City tramps stink the whole place with morsels
Of survival devoured from garbage bins.
Students lurch after quaffing liquor in the Ambassador:
They spew acrid bar-room politics even right there
Onto the new toilet's floor.
Last week I vomited my laden soul in there—calmly

---

[5] Mutoko is a rural province in eastern Zimbabwe and marijuana from the area is rumoured to be potent.
[6] Dambudzo Marechera, *Mindblast*

Retching the crude graffiti scrawled on
The remote blackboard of my reeling mind.
An elderly *chibuku*[7] guzzler drawled his calypso,
Crouching and feet on the chamber seat:
"This is a bankrupt highflying Air Zim Boeing 767
The squat toilet at my Mbare[8] home
Is a battered overloaded commuter taxi
The fuck taxi is my pregnant wife trudging uphill
To overcrowded Harare Maternity Hospital
Oh yeah-yeah-yeah-yeah…………!"
His waiting pal cursed about unemployment, lurching,
And the law for letting *chefs* play soccer out of it.
A whore slinked with a client into the Gents quarters.
It's a long story Buddy… This your tribute…
The gentleman clad in a Perrie Cardin winced
Before the gaping molten urinal
His limp member burnt from sugar-daddying,
Carpet interviews, and believe it or not, an incestuous wrath.
It's a long story Buddy… so long…unending …
Had the new toilet been a pit-latrine,
The Blair toilet of rural progress
In stuffing to the brim dignified silo-bellies,
Shitworms would have slithered very fat
In the mad pomp of shitwealth.
The daily façade of cleansing by the tired workman
Hardly kills the breathing stench beneath.
He ponders on how to feed his brood at home
On a wage a fraction of Honourable Minister's son's
Pocket money at a stately kindergarten.
Hungry students on a demo against graft
Chant and choke on tear-gas in the homely park
And they rampage shops in alliance with vagrants
Taking opportune vengeance on stagnant industry and commerce.
The story is so long… but the Toilet was once, or is it still,
A national issue at least!
Dread R.I.P—this place reeks
Nevertheless you and I speak no tosh
"Oh Bumbo Klaat" "The shitstem we got to rearrange."[9] One love!

---

[7] Commercialized traditional beer.
[8] A poor township of Harare.
[9] Peter Tosh statements: *the best of peter tosh 1978-1987*, EMI Records Ltd (2003).

Marechera in Oxford

Norman Vance

Dambudzo Marechera was called Charles when he arrived in Oxford in the Autumn of 1974. He also had neat short hair. Already a romantic figure because he had been expelled from the University of Rhodesia during a period of student unrest, he had come to New College to study English on a special scholarship scheme and I was one of his tutors. I was a recent arrival at the College myself, but I had moved round the corner from Wadham, where I had been a research student, and he had come from a different continent. In addition to research and some teaching, one of my pleasant duties at New College was to live in College and help to sustain its corporate life by being kind and taking an interest in the welfare of the undergraduates, at that time still forming an exclusively male community. So from the outset I had both academic and pastoral reasons for getting to know the romantic newcomer.

The academic side of things should have been straightforward. I was supposed to teach a course on Victorian Literature, and even though I had never previously taught the course I thought I knew all about it. After all, my research was in this area. Marechera quite quickly made me see not only that I did not know all about it but that I had a lot to learn about teaching. I did my best, and I hope I did little harm, but my best was hardly good enough. To begin with he said little in tutorials and I said too much, which made things worse. When he did talk it was not obviously immediately relevant to the author or topic we were officially discussing. Was he doing the reading? But I was not unduly worried. Things were bound to get better in subsequent tutorials, and his essays would help me to see how he was responding to the course. Unfortunately he soon started missing tutorials, and there was no sign of any written work.

I felt I should look into this. Perhaps he was ill? He had a small room in College quite close to mine so I went to see him. Having established that he was not seriously ill I rather hastily made my excuses and left: the atmosphere was quite literally steamy, and stiflingly hot. He had washed his clothes in his room and hung them right across the room to dry over the electric fire. There was a much easier way of washing and drying clothes, with College washing machines and tumbler driers, but no-one had thought to tell him about this, or he had not thought to ask, or he had not understood.

Hindsight has turned this into an early symptom of more general alienation and social awkwardness: it soon became clear that he was not happy or at home in the College, and the College became increasingly unhappy with him. The awkwardness was not just a matter of cultural difference, although that was part of it. Marechera was funded by the special scholarship scheme to which the students themselves had subscribed. While the scheme was wholly benign in intention it could create awkwardness and resentment in practice. Marechera was at times made to feel a beggar, sponsored by the fellow-students he saw every day who might expect him to be grateful rather than difficult.

The normal social tensions of undergraduate life were made worse when personality clashes provoked crass allegations of ingratitude and counter-allegations of patronising colonialist attitudes. Tempers flared. Some undergraduates, trying only to be friendly, were admirably sensitive, diplomatic and long-suffering, but not all of them. Marechera suffered, but not in silence. The College bar was supposed to be a place for a social drink or two but in Marechera's case drinking soon took precedence over sociability. I offered to buy him a drink on one occasion and discovered his preferred tipple was whisky and lemonade. I tried it myself, out of curiosity, but did not repeat the experiment. Conversation with him could be difficult, but I remember him talking with some animation about the mysterious ruins of Great Zimbabwe. Cultural nationalism, or indeed any kind of nationalism, was rather scorned in his later career, but at this early stage there were at least traces of old-fashioned pride in his own place.

After a time the drinking and the anger erupted into my own life. He returned my visit. It was after midnight one night and I was already in bed when he burst in in a very excited state. "You're all Kiplingesque imperialists!" he shouted defiantly, and it was not just the drink talking. Foolishly, and pedantically, I tried to reason with him, suggesting that he was generalising rather rashly and that Kipling himself had a rather more complicated attitude to empire and the colonial subject than he was implying. It did little good: I can only say in extenuation that I was very young in those days. After a time he calmed down a little and left.

I did not succeed in teaching him much about Kipling, or indeed about anything else. After a long interval I did eventually squeeze an essay out of him, on Emily Brontë's *Wuthering Heights*. To my surprise it was beautifully written, in both senses: the hand was neat (this was long before word-processing) and the language was lucid and effective. It was a bizarre and splendid piece of work. It had very little to do with the kinds of things we had been talking about in tutorials—style, narrative technique, social context—but it had a great deal to do with Heathcliff, the strange, malevolent outsider-figure in the novel. Heathcliff was presented very sympathetically as the great romantic rebel, linked with Albert

Camus' figure of the Outsider in *L'Étranger*, and linked also by implication with the alienated figure of Charles Marechera. I had not thought of the novel that way before, but I have since, many times. This was more than twenty years before Terry Eagleton's reinvention of Heathcliff as covertly Irish representative of the colonial Other. In some ways you could say that Marechera was there first.

After that first term I saw less of Marechera. He was now working with much wiser and more experienced tutors such as Anne Barton, fully-fledged Tutorial Fellow in English and subsequently Professor of English at Cambridge. For all their efforts these tutors seem to have had little more success than I had had in getting him to attend tutorials and produce regular essays. But he was spending a lot of his time buying and reading books, even if they were not the recommended books. He ran up a large Blackwell's bill which he could not or would not pay, and this eventually led to County Court proceedings.

Sensing his disaffection and loneliness, which were particularly severe during the vacations, various people in the College tried hard to help him. One of these was Garry Bennett, Chaplain and Fellow in History, himself a gifted but lonely figure who years later, in 1987, took his own life in tragic circumstances (Carpenter). Despite a rather sharp, dry manner, Garry was a compassionate and caring man who took his pastoral responsibilities very seriously, and he was deeply concerned about Marechera. He put him in touch with Colin Winter, the controversial Anglican Bishop of Damaraland in Namibia who had been expelled from the country for alleged communism and hostility to the *apartheid* régime. Garry did his best to help Marechera to make contact with the community of African students Winter gathered around himself, but this came to nothing.

The Warden of the College, Sir William Hayter, was also very concerned. He had been Britain's ambassador in Moscow, and both in Moscow and in the Warden's Lodgings he was ably and generously supported by his wife, Lady Iris. She had the rare gift, invaluable in diplomacy and in College life, of remembering names and faces and being able to talk to anyone about anything and make them feel welcome. She was immensely kind to my sister when she visited me in Oxford, insisting that she stay as a guest in the Warden's Lodgings. The same warmth was extended to Marechera. The kindly but distinctly patrician couple in the Warden's Lodgings and the difficult black student from Rhodesia had almost nothing in common, but Lady Iris was able to get through to him as almost no-one else could and he remembered her with affection in later years.

But despite everyone's best efforts things went from bad to worse. Marechera's behaviour became more and more extreme and he seemed to be doing no work. The College's official patience was gradually exhausted. A self-mythologiser from early days, Marechera alludes to his last days in College in the short story "Black Skin What Mask," included with his best-known work *The House of Hunger* (1978). According to that the Warden gave him the choice of being sent down

or going to the Warneford, the Oxford mental hospital. While this somehow suggests the Soviet habit of containing dissidents by shutting them up in mental
facilities, and the deadpan narrator may have intended his readers to make the
connection, the intention would have been benign rather than repressive. Was
Marechera not just difficult but mentally ill? Should he be receiving some kind
of treatment? Oxford had plenty of experience of overseas students at graduate
and undergraduate level, and of varying degrees of alienation and unhappiness
among them, but few were as violent or as wretched as Marechera.

Alienation was difficult to treat, but for a writer, and Marechera was already
a writer, it could make good copy. The rebellious Shelley had been profoundly
alienated by the fusty Anglicanism of the Oxford of his day and his angry pam-
phlet *The Necessity of Atheism* (1811) had caused him to be sent down. It would
suit the script for Marechera to be sent down for some similarly spectacular act
of defiance. It was widely rumoured at the time and subsequently that eventually,
in his second year, Marechera tried to set fire to the College, founded in 1379,
and was duly sent down. The reality was perhaps a little less dramatic. Vandalism
could certainly be included in the growing catalogue of offences but Marechera's
self-mythologising seems to have improved the story. There was never any doubt
of his ability, but academically he was getting nowhere because that was not
where his interests lay, and it had become painfully obvious that he and the College were not right for each other.

Years passed and I heard nothing more about Marechera until I was contacted
by Flora Veit-Wild, who was collecting biographical materials. I was happy to
talk to her about my memories of Marechera but I could not help her beyond
that. New College had decided that documents such as tutorial reports should
remain confidential. I felt rather ashamed not to have known about Marechera's
subsequent literary fame or the *Guardian* fiction prize for *The House of Hunger*.
I had continued with my Victorian studies and had moved into other areas of my
discipline, but not the emerging field of postcolonial studies which commended
Marechera to the academy. But as a literary historian of sorts I am pleased and
honoured to have a small footnote in the history of one of my first and most difficult students.

Reflecting on the Marechera Cult?
"More Like Hearing a Scream"

James Currey

To what extent is the Marechera cult due to his exceptional writing? Or is it due to an admiration of the way Marechera stood up to the "chefs" who created the Zimbabwe we know today? Or to his early death because of AIDS?

I emailed Henry Chakava in Nairobi: "It's the Marechera celebrations at Trinity College, Oxford this week-end. Marechera would have been very proud, would have thought them his right, and tried to smash them up." Henry Chakava replied the next day: "Marechera has become so great in death. Those who never saw him will hold him out as a role model, worthy of emulation. I am sure that the celebrations will be a lot more successful without him, but not as memorable!" Henry Chakava, the founder of EAEP as the successor company to Heinemann in East Africa, was vital to me in his support for publishing *The House of Hunger.* In his report on Marechera's manuscript (that we would publish as *The House of Hunger*) in 1977, he wrote, "If this is Marechera's first effort, then he has a great future as a writer." Marechera was one of our greatest successes in the African Writers Series. He was also one of our greatest failures.

The cult of Marechera suggests that at Heinemann perhaps we need not have worried so much about trying to get a well-crafted novel about Zimbabwe from him. My account "Publishing Dambudzo Marechera" in *Africa Writes Back* (Currey 278-95) tells how "short manuscripts emerged but all showed signs of having been written in key-board bashing highs fuelled by alcohol and other stimulants." He brought in at least three aspirant novels. Our loyal advisers responded as fast as they could to his fireworks. But their reports, however quickly they were written, descended into darkness. By the time a report reached Marechera he had lost interest in the original script and was shooting off another. He ignored the reports and just sent up another firework. Tom Engelhardt at Pantheon in New York declined *Black Sunlight*, saying that "We are left with an experience of chaos and fragmentation detached from meaning..." I got Heinemann to accept this short novel in 1979 so I could remove the "psychological block" of turning yet another script down (Currey, *AWB* 292). To my surprise it has been chosen as one of the six titles which Penguin South Africa launched as their contribution to the African Writers Series. *Mindblast,* first published in Zimbabwe, will also appear in the African Writers Series for its first international publication. A few weeks after the Trinity celebration I was in Johannesburg, sinking into the rhythm of a performance by the rap poet Kgafela oa Magegodi; suddenly in the chanted Tswana I understood two words "Dambudzo Marechera." His influence spreads far and wide. Elleke Boehmer found during the conference he is a hero to the Zimbabwean traffic wardens of Oxford.

It was not until six months after publication that Doris Lessing got people to pay due attention to *The House of Hunger*. In late 1978 I sent her a personal copy of the collection of stories and she placed a review with *Books and Bookmen* in June 1979; she memorably described the book as "…More like overhearing a scream…." On the basis of this review I got Dambudzo Marechera an invitation to the Berlin Festival—and managed to get him there and back without any papers or passport. I also sent the review to Bill Webb, literary editor of *The Guardian,* and asked him whether this might not encourage him to get it reviewed, even six months after publication. Angela Carter wrote in her review of "his immense, cruel seriousness..." That autumn Bill Webb rang me up, slightly apologetically, to say that it had been decided to award Marechera jointly *The Guardian* fiction prize. Dambudzo Marechera set out to break up his own prize ceremony by smashing the great mirrors of the Theatre Royal, Drury Lane. His mythology was up and running.

My own contribution to this book arises out of my reflections on the, all too often amusing, accounts given by the impressive group of "elders" whom Dobrota Pucherova assembled for the Saturday morning *indaba*. All of them had stories of how they had coped at those times when Dambudzo Marechera had taken over their lives.

During the three days there was a particular focus on Marechera's own engagement with the freakish establishment of Oxford. This proved more revealing than I had expected. Dobrota Pucherova had set up the conference and the performance of his plays *Servants' Ball* and *Blitzkrieg* because she was shocked that he seemed to be forgotten at Oxford. This conference showed that he was better remembered than most people who pass through its demanding system. Money had been raised by undergraduate common rooms for scholarships for five students thrown out of the University of Rhodesia in 1974. All but Marechera got through demanding courses. Stanley Nyamfukudza at Lincoln College not only secured a degree but managed to contribute *The Non-Believer's Journey* to the African Writers Series.

I only came to know Marechera after he had been thrown out of Oxford. He knew how well the names Oxford and New College resonated with the English tribe. The "Edwardian accent," which Robert Fraser identified, was one of his responses to Oxford. Dobrota Pucherova's idea that she should take members of the conference round New College was inspired, even if she got into trouble for invading the Dining Hall where a Sunday morning brunch of staggering proportions was being provided for the undergraduates. To what extent did Wykehamist exclusiveness and effortless superiority gall Marechera? New College would have been a remote place for any freshman who came up from one of the great northern grammar schools, let alone for an African who came from the squalid background evoked in *The House of Hunger*. Porters, scouts and other college servants were like the non-commissioned officers in the British army. They would have referred with deference to Dambudzo Marechera as "the young gentleman" (it was one of the later colleges to take women). The young gentleman was always right until he stepped out of line. But how when you arrive at an Oxford college do you know what is acceptable, what you can do and what you cannot do? Authority is disguised. Getting it wrong leads to ritual humiliation. The mixture was explosive. Burn the place down!

People in New College could see that he was out of his depth and went out of their way to help him. One of his tutors, Norman Vance, had a particular responsibility for the psychological and social welfare of undergraduates. He told a sad story of how he had a feeling that he ought to visit Marechera's room. Damp tropical air swept out as Marechera opened "his oak," that is his door; his laundry was draped round the room because he had not been told about the washing machines which were provided for students.

Dobrota and I were pleased to find in the holy cloisters a stone plaque elegantly engraved in Latin to the memory of Lady Hayter, just below the stone to Sir William Hayter who was the Warden and who had been British ambassador in Moscow. Lady Hayter saw from the first day, when she took Marechera to Marks and Spencers to buy clothes on his arrival, that he was in danger of being out of place. She applied all her lifetime's skills, as wife of a diplomat, to calm the staff when assaulted by this impossible undergraduate.

Marechera joins Shelley and a select group of well-known writers who were thrown out of Oxford. Like Shelley he died young. During the conference some us talked our way past the porter at University College by explaining that Gerald Gaylard was teaching Shelley in Johannesburg. In the very centre of Oxford there is the mausoleum covering the young marble body of Shelley, which is draped a little too beautifully for a person who has drowned.

In so many ways New College has a proud record; the Rhodes Scholars Bram Fischer and Leo Marquard, who went to New College in the thirties, were both to play outstanding roles in the South African struggle. Good for the New College undergraduates who raised the money to fund Marechera's scholarship. But they made clear their resentment of how they felt they had been let down by his behaviour and his failure to do what work his tutor in English set him. The dons of New College had sent down undergraduates for lesser offences. To what extent would another Oxford college also have found itself equally incapable of dealing with the disconnect in Marechera's mind between his worship of Oxford and his wanting to burn the place down? (His story of arson did sound better than just being sent down for not working.)

The absurd interface between New College and Marechera was replaced with the bizarre interface between Heinemann and Marechera. I got my colleagues to agree to all sorts of unprecedented advances, which he quickly came to resent. My aim was to keep Marechera's typewriter out of the pawnshop and to keep him writing. I told him that he must also find reviewing work for journals, must get broadcasting, must find every way of getting some sort of income together to add to the minimal royalties from sales and translation rights. Robert Fraser showed, whether in the time of Dr Johnson or in the strike-bound seventies, just what organised determination was needed to put together a life from literary earnings in London's "Grub Street." Marechera preferred sponging, begging, living in squats and staying with people until they pushed him out. I was infuriated by his inability to put together a manuscript of his verse which Heinemann would have willingly published, and from which some anthology fees would have come. David Caute, then Literary Editor of *The New Statesman*, told Marechera that he would publish a story. Any professional writer would have jumped at such a prestigious invitation. Marechera did nothing about it. After I had left Heinemann in 1984 to set up my own imprint, David Caute heroically went through the manuscripts of my despair and tried to get Tom Engelhardt at Pantheon to consider them.

Alastair Niven, Director of the Africa Centre in Covent Garden in London during the seventies, used to exchange intelligence with me on Marechera's movements. Marechera knew all too well how to exploit our liberal consciences. Alastair Niven's account of the calmness under fire of John Johnson, former High Commissioner in Nairobi, as Marechera wrecked the Africa Centre Restaurant round him made me proud of our diplomats. He deserves a stone plaque like Lady Hayter. Marechera was relentless in his determination about never fitting in. Yet the next day he was probably boasting of having met the High Commissioner to Kenya.

I went most years to the Zimbabwe Book Fair during the eighties. My sympathy was with my Zimbabwean publishing colleagues who had to deal, as I had, with Marechera's impossible behaviour. David Caute's *Marechera and the Colonel* (Revised and expanded edition 2009) has revealed to me how much I undervalued the importance of Marechera's role after his return to Zimbabwe. David Caute says of his book, "Marechera's writing blisters every totem pole. He took delight in satirizing the "chefs" of the post-liberation years. One of them, the incensed Colonel of the title, beat him up in a hotel lavatory. The political arm of the police, the CIO, locked him up without charge."

David Caute, having reported what was happening in Mashonaland before the time of the 1985 election, could see the way ZANU-PF was going. Those, like myself who were so relieved to have the new Zimbabwe, turned a blind eye. At the writers' conference at the 1982 Book Fair, Marechera attacked the minister Eddison Zvogbo who had published poetry, protesting that the returned soldiers of the *chimurenga* had not got jobs. As Nadine Gordimer said in *The Herald* on 15 August 1978, "…among all us of us he was the one who took up a burning social issue…" On the cover of David Caute's book Mugabe is offering Marechera his condolences after his sister, married to a South African ANC man, had been blown up in 1978. Mugabe, surrounded by "chefs," could well be thinking "I wish it had been Marechera!" AIDS did the job a few months later.

I had every sympathy with Flora Veit-Wild's husband being reduced to manhandling Marechera out of their house. That echoed my experiences as I had too been reduced to wrestling with him in front of the Heinemann Bedford Square office in London with staff hanging out of the windows.

The genesis of my own book *Africa Writes Back: The African Writers Series* and the launch of *African Literature* (2008) can be traced to the second interview on Marechera which Flora Veit-Wild had with me on 19 May 1989, three years after I left Heinemann. Were my memories fading? Was I getting the details wrong? I suggested that she look in the Heinemann archives, which are now at the University of Reading. Her magnificent *Source Book* gave me the idea that I should look at those archives as well. They have provided a response to people like Brian Wafereroa of New African Books in Cape Town who strode forward at a publishers' meeting in Zanzibar "Ah, James Currey! the publisher of Marechera!" I wrote *Africa Writes Back* to prove that I had also published many other outstanding writers. Not one of them demanded such inordinate attention as Marechera.

Hippo and Hyena
My Oxford Celebration Diary

Flora Veit-Wild

When I arrived in Oxford yesterday, it was chilly and wet. I drew my hood close to my head thinking, "Oxford Black Oxford." Marechera's Oxford. As soon as I had entered his realm, I found myself in a Marecheran state: penniless and paperless. After using coins at the coach station to phone my host, my wallet vanished, with money, cards and documents. I had to report my loss to the Oxford police station, the very place where the infamous "Rhodesian" had been one of the regulars some thirty years ago. The guided Marechera tour had obviously begun. Jennifer Armstong, who presented today, must be right—he possesses shamanistic qualities. Dambudzo, child of sorrow, trouble-maker, was certainly having fun looking at us "celebrating him"—wherever he is.

I am having fun listening to the Marechera scholars reading clever things into phenomena that, for me, have very banal reasons. Drew Shaw is intrigued by the jacket with the flowery pattern Dambudzo is wearing on some of the photographs; he reads it as a sign of cross-dressing. Sure he can—because why would Dambudzo have chosen to take and keep this jacket from my wardrobe, if he did not feel comfortable in a woman's garment? But mine it was, just as the white coat he is wearing on other photos—though not as conspicuously feminine. As we all know, Dambudzo "borrowed" what he needed, be it books, booze or boots. Or spectacles as a matter of fact. He was delighted to find a pair of my late father's and to discover that the thick lenses of some eight dioptres made him see things clear again, after he had been walking for I don't know how long with what must have been quite a fuzzy view.

On the second day I find myself on a panel with four grey-haired elderly English gentlemen. In the chronological order of when they—and I—first knew our celebrity, it is Norman Vance, James Currey, Alastair Niven, Robert Fraser, and, last in the row, me. Elderly as well but feeling just as young as twenty-five years ago when I crossed paths with the ominous mindblaster. What can I add to all that I have already said and written about him?

Coincidence was on my side some weeks ago. When I was pondering about what to say at the Celebration, my son Max was with me in Berlin, clearing boxes of old books and various items dating back to his childhood in Harare.

With a smile, he handed me a thin folder. "Surprise, surprise, Mum." The folder contained two postcards by Dambudzo addressed to Max and Franz, my other son. They did not carry stamps, so he must have given them to the boys after we had come back from a sea-side holiday in Kenya; my mother, Max (6), Franz (3) and myself. That was around Easter 1984; not long before, Dambudzo had been staying at our house. The folder also contained sheets from Max's notebook, into which he had written work done with Dambudzo in a creative writing workshop for children. As Dambudzo could relate well to children and had written children's stories illustrated by Max, we had planned a series of sessions with a few children. The first one went well; in the second, Dambudzo got drunk and obnoxious and the children, all still quite small, frightened and discouraged. I suppose Max got the most out of it, as his notes with Dambudzo's marks show. "Always think of your imagination," is also what the child Max remembers, when Fiona Lloyd interviewed him for her Radio 1 obituary in August 1987. As an adult, Max had this to say about his writer friend:

> We got on very well. I think he liked me, and children in general. He could relate to our inhibitions and the way life was so uncomplicated and easy to us. He was always very kind and caring towards me. I could tell when he was in a weird mood or might act "unpredictable" and would leave him alone. (Mushakavanhu)

So when it was my turn at the panel, I showed scans of the postcards and Max's notes to the audience in Oxford and added: "With regard to children I can also confirm that they were much better Marechera critics than I was." And I read a passage from a speech I gave at the commemoration of the first anniversary of Dambudzo's death, which the students of the University of Zimbabwe had organised on 6th August 1988. It was headed by Tendai Biti, now Morgan Tsvangirai's right hand and minister of finance in the "Unity Government," and took place at the memorable Cecil Rhodes Square, later renamed Africa Unity Square. We should call on Biti to name it after Marechera, who used to sit there and type his "parkbench diary."[1]

Here is what I said on 6th August 1988:

> For his writing, he needed approval. That is why he got so furious or depressed and desperate, when publishers sat for ages on his manuscripts before they got them out, or worse, rejected them. And he also could not stand any kind of criticism on something he was writing. Though I was

---

[1] Excerpts from Biti's speech, then still going under the name of Laxton Biti, are contained in the *Source Book* (385); on the photo of the commemoration (Veit-Wild, *Source Book* 380) Biti is standing next to me, quite slender compared to the image we have of the man in power today.

aware of this, I once, and this was only a few weeks before he died, made the mistake to usher a very hesitant suggestion on how he could improve a story he was just writing and had asked me to read (he very seldom did that). It was the story "Fuzzy Goo's Guide to the Earth," dedicated to the 1987 International Book Fair in Harare, which had "Children" as theme. I said I liked it but suggested he should give it a bit more of a real plot, children would prefer that. Dambudzo did not look at the story again. It stayed incomplete. My son Max, 10 years old, read the story a few days ago and said, what a shame that Dambudzo had not carried on with it. I confessed to him that it had probably been my fault. So Max got very cross with me: "So you have messed up three things now, Mummy: You have messed up the nice rubber cooking spoon (which I had let get too hot in a pot); you have messed up the sitting room table (I had placed a very hot pot on the glass); and you have messed up Dambudzo's story."

For Franz (who was three when Dambudzo was staying with us), he had lots of sympathy because he identified with him. He used to say: "Franz is just like me, or rather I am like Franz." Meaning: he screams like hell, when we wants something; and he screams like hell when he does not want something. He takes the posture of refusing to do what is expected from him, nevertheless expecting from the world to look after him and his needs.

Speaking at our Celebration today, I hope Max's remarks on "Fuzzy Goo" and my role in its non-completion has helped to dismantle the myth of me as "The Marechera Authority" and ever so well-doing and resourceful writer's friend and literary executor. Let me elaborate on this a bit more. When I came to Harare and met Marechera in 1983, I was 36 years old. I was far off being a professor—would never have dreamt of once becoming one—nor was I yet a literary scholar. Though I had studied German and Romance literature at university, I did not have a thorough knowledge of literature, let alone of literary theory. In my university days in the late 1960's and early 1970's West Berlin we spent much more time reading Marx, Engels, Lenin and Mao than getting engaged in our various disciplines. So when I met Marechera, who was starving for books and for talking books, I was quite a poor counterpart. He was much better informed about literary developments in the world than I was. He made sure that anyone coming from overseas would bring him what was new on the literary market. I remember that he was reading Rushdie's *Midnight's Children* long before everyone else was talking about it—*I* definitely had never heard of it and read it years later. What I did read at the time was Christa Wolf, and other women writers from what still was the GDR. So I got Dambudzo English translations of Wolf's *Kein Ort. Nirgends (No Place On Earth,* 1977) and *Kassandra (Cassandra,* 1983), which he found very inspirational.

At the end of the conference, I had to make a detour to the German Embassy in London to procure myself a travel permit—mine being whisked away by our shamanistic spirit. When finally I sat on the plane back to Berlin, I was pondering the questions I had been asked, during the Celebration and at other times, about my personal relationship with Marechera. Robert Fraser has repeatedly asked why I did not write his definitive biography. Others have wanted to know, in view of Marechera's penchant for white women, whether this included me. For the time being, I had to leave these questions unanswered.[2] The narrative of my life, which has been an undercurrent to the writer's life and to his afterlife, has still to be written. It will contain answers to such questions. For now it suffices me to say that Marechera in all his idiosyncratic anti-authorityness has been a major teacher, mentor, an authority for me. Knowing him has contributed substantially to shaping my outlook on Africa and its literature. Moreover, I am immensely grateful for the chance that came my way to contribute to the preservation of his work and legacy. When in 1994 I was appointed Professor of African Literatures and Cultures at Humboldt University in Berlin, I dedicated my inaugural lecture to Dambudzo Marechera, who "taught me that nothing is whole or holy, least of all African literature" (Veit-Wild, *Karneval* 5).

---

[2] Following the Celebration, Flora Veit-Wild wrote the personal essay "Me and Dambudzo," which we include as the afterword to this book. It contains the answers to some of questions raised here.

Spirits and Projections
A "White Zimbabwean's" Reading of Marechera

Jennifer F Armstrong

Essential to Marechera's writing is his refusal to accept an identity that has to be externally bestowed. That has been my position for over twenty years, ever since migrating to Australia from Zimbabwe. I grew up in tune with "nature," not understanding that a war was taking place at all, except in the most abstract sense. Part of the reason is that we had effectively time-locked ourselves into a mindset that had been more salient in Europe a few centuries before. This was due to media censorship, which kept us unaware of how much the world was changing. Another reason for my innocence was that this is how white girls in Rhodesian society were brought up. We were told very little about politics, or indeed about reality, because our minds were deemed too fragile to come to terms with these issues. These factors put me into a very vulnerable position. In Australia, at the age of 16, I was spoken to as if I were all sorts of very peculiar things, none of which I could emotionally identify with. The Australians seemed to give me two choices: be penitent for your "sins," or be unbowed and be ostracised. I tried the first way, and then the second way for a while, but ultimately opted for a more difficult "third way."

I refer, in terms of a "third way," to the violent psychological struggle that Marechera engaged in throughout his lifetime, in refusing to accept an identity that would make him fit neatly within the logic of larger political systems. One sees his refusal to be in a limited sense "black" or "African" writ large in his early fiction. His short story "Burning in the Rain" (Marechera, *Hunger* 83-87) is a beautiful example of how the author, represented as a youth in a difficult relationship with a woman, refuses to grow up under the terms dictated by the Rhodesian political system. The protagonist will accept being neither an "ape" (86) (a denigrated black man) nor a whitewashed English "lord" (86), but would rather retreat into an exploration of the dynamics of the unconscious. He will work out his true identity in relation to his "anima" (84) (that is, in Jungian terms, the feminine part of a male's unconscious).

Marechera fought the kind of battle that I was to have to fight with all my energies much later: It is based on the principle of ethics that one is not responsible for the nature of the ideological shifts that occurred before one was born.

One has to have shamanistic eyes to see the dangers here. There are loose "spirits"—free-flying archetypes looking for physical bodies to make themselves at home in, to "possess." These archetypes are (in Western parlance) "projections." In African parlance, they are "spirits" that have been set loose into the world by various ideological manipulators; politicians who have an axe to grind, who are seeking to consolidate their power in the world at large. One of the most powerful evil spirits that Western power-mongers have sent out into the world (and I am speaking from the point of view of a white African) is the idea that whites who originate from Africa are inevitably evil, racist oppressors. This free-floating projection is an evil spirit that lies in wait for those who come to Western shores. If they are already vulnerable, due to being traumatised by the transition from one culture to another, this malicious spirit (a product of Western denial of its own racially oppressive history) enters the body of the vulnerable one, and becomes part of their soul. Initially, Western culture treated me with such hostility that I developed an enduring tightness around my throat, and was unable to speak on my own behalf. This sensation of being strangled lasted for a number of years, throughout my twenties.

Only after more severe bullying at work when I was twenty-six—which was orchestrated on the basis that I was a white who was also Zimbabwean (but working at a nominally "leftwing" organisation)—did I finally come to learn the name of the Westerners' most intense fear, their demon which they had projected into me, as if it were not theirs but had originated from me alone. This demon that they wanted to disown so much now had a name. It was "racial superiority." It had nothing to do with anything I had known before, since I had enjoyed horses, the African bush, and lived in a state of relative poverty compared to most Westerners. The culture I came from had been genuinely gentle, that is if you were white, I suppose—"between ourselves."

But then I reasoned that Westerners were frightened of it—so much so that they had projected their own (European) history and generalised misinformation about "all colonial whites" into me, in order to relieve themselves of such identification. Their own projections were of Boers and Nazis (certainly nothing from my original homeland, Zimbabwe, but all the same frightening apparitions––frightening "archetypes"). What to do when one is given a "gift" in the form of a demon, a gift that one didn't want? If it is better than the demon of fear, one might embrace it anyway. So it was that for a time I embraced a Western cultural archetype—the one they had wanted to disown by projecting it onto me. I became "evil" along the precise lines of Western psychological, historical and cultural specifications. Such "evil" was not based upon my own psychological, historical and cultural reference points, but those that I had learned to be the Westerner's own, the manifestation of his own exaggerated fears about me.

After the workplace bullying at the leftwing organisation, I found it logical to wear the exaggerated caricature of a Nazi disguise for some time. I embraced the negative side of the Western metaphysical dichotomy. It didn't resonate that deeply with me, but by this point in time—when I had tried, and failed, to integrate myself into conventional Australian society—it didn't seem any more false than any other aspects of this new society. I figured that since my enemies were so unpleasantly moralistic and condemnatory of those whom they didn't even take the trouble to find out about, evil might after all be interesting. I made this turn towards evil after having failed to redeem myself by behaving like a penitent. But this solution was not much more intrinsically satisfying than the previous side of the Western metaphysical dichotomy.

In taking the third option concerning identity, I also had to take the hardest measures against myself: Rather than face the world reactively, I had to actually let the old identity pass away and start again. Marechera's *The Black Insider* suggests to me that when you face ego death (from encountering tremendous threats to your existence), you also come into contact with "all the versions of yourself that did not come out of the womb with you" (Marechera, *Black Insider* 107). This is what it means to be "shamanised"—to operate with the realm of psychologically projective forces, forces which in African parlance are termed "spirit." Embracing this multiplicity of being (especially in the concrete form of my new Shona and Ndebele friends on Facebook), I no longer feel lonely. By studying Marechera's work and reading between his lines, I have now escaped the net of Western political machinations: the false choices originally given me: to be either sorrowfully penitent, or to wear the Westerner's identifying mark of evil upon one's brow.

Marechera-Mania
among Young Zimbabwean Writers and Readers

Memory Chirere

Marechera-mania among students

Over my last ten years at the University of Zimbabwe's Department of English, I have taught a Level One survey called "Introduction to Zimbabwean literature." Many of these undergraduates, straight from high school, maintain their cool when you take them through texts such as *The Grass is Singing* by Doris Lessing and *Waiting for the Rain* by Charles Mungoshi. But midway, when the students get to read "The House of Hunger" by Marechera, they become visibly overexcited. They pick a cue from somewhere that "The House of Hunger" is the text that will change their lives. When you give them background to Marechera and the novella, there is a deafening silence. There is always a feeling that you are not telling them a new story and that the audience is following through, walking a separate private path, comparing your information with their own from the Marechera folklore in Zimbabwe. This includes the ever-present but unconfirmed notions that Marechera was mad.

When you proceed to read aloud selected passages from the novella and make the "mistake" of choosing the public rape scene, the students will cry out and whistle in amazement. Some of them stand up to dance and clap their hands. In one year there were several nuns amongst the students and I thought they would walk out. They didn't. They stayed alongside the rest, listening to a reading of the "notorious" passage:

> The older generation too was learning. It still believed that if one did not beat up one's wife it meant that one did not love her at all. [...] The most lively of them ended with the husband actually fucking—raping his wife right there in the thick of the excited crowd. He was cursing all women to hell as he did so. And he seemed to screw her forever—he went on and on and on and on until she looked like death. (49)

Clearly, the above passage is more about violence than sex and one is always taken aback by the excitement and cheery response of the students. Coming from an African background where issues of sexuality are not dealt with in a mixed audience, the students cannot believe that Marechera dared to describe such sexu-ally explicit scenes and got published and even won a prize. Their loud reaction to that passage is a spontaneous reaction to what they think is Marechera's exagger-ated tragicomedy. For the whole of Marechera series, students rarely miss classes or come late, and one is assured of a full house. Reading "The House of Hunger" is a rite of passage of sorts.

This excitement with Marechera is more pronounced in young men than wom-en. Female students tend to find Marechera outrageous and frightening, too, be-cause of his scenes of violence against women. They feel that he is "too macho" and that he did not pay much respect to "women's sensibilities." On pointing out that Marechera is in fact actually protesting against the dehumanization of espe-cially women, one of my students felt that "Marechera protests, right, but he still writes about violence against women the way most men do."

After their first experience with "The House of Hunger", at least a third of the male students immediately begin to be overtly outspoken. They begin to grow their own dreadlocks, smoke and drink, scribble their own poetry and prose, and you are waylaid by young men and women who plead with you to look at what they are writing. You sense that they want you to confirm that they are now part of the club. Their poetry is angry and melodramatic, without being very clear about the causes and targets of the anger. You realize that the anger is targeted toward their parents, their siblings, the University of Zimbabwe, elders, and even themselves. In their notebooks you find lines such as, "Nature the yowls of yore in a pun of roguery," which is almost as senseless as "The systematic erosion of my being is the cauldron / of sad dreams. / Skin me alive and sell the carcass for a dollar."

Most of these students are for the first time exposed to freedom of mind and experimentation, in sudden contrast to the relatively conservative high school en-vironment. Marechera's rebelliousness offers a matchstick to the already growing desire of the students to be free from imposed ideas. Unfortunately, this influence is not always positive. In fact, Marechera can be a bad influence because some of these students begin to deliberately miss their lectures and fail to hand in their assignments or meet deadlines in line with what they regard as the Marechera tra-dition. Some of them eventually drop out and one never sees or hears about them again. The more gifted of them, who manage to stay on, tend to become brusque and antisocial, or dreamy and reserved, sitting in your class without taking down any notes.

Marechera-mania outside academia
Outside the academic environment, you find high school drop-outs, job seekers, young farmers, budding guitarists, sculptors, and people herding cattle and goats and house servants who prefer Marechera's *Mindblast* to *The House of Hunger*.

This is probably because of its more contemporary themes that attack the corruption of the newly independent Zimbabwean society. On the bus to rural Mt Darwin, Guruve or Murehwa, one often finds these readers, usually dreadlocked, with *Mindblast* in hand, smiling at Marechera's wit. They want to keep it and refer to it lavishly and out of context, too. You realize that other than understanding a few selected passages, part of their joy is in knowing that they are reading "something by Marechera." They simply enjoy being part of the Marechera legend. These people redefine reading. For them to read is not necessarily to comprehend, to get to the essence of the text, but to know that what you are looking at are the narratives of one of your own, considered (even by foreigners) as extraordinary. It is not rare to find at rural outposts such as Mt Darwin and Guruve people calling a fellow who does not read much or write, "Marechera"!

Marechera-mania among writers: the Marechera apostles

There is a long-standing tendency amongst some serious emerging writers to employ Marechera style and vision as a temporary launch-pad for their own writing careers. One of these "Marechera apostles" is Robert Muponde. On hearing about Marechera's death in August 1987, Muponde reveals that Marechera had actually read some of his pieces and ordered him "to keep on writing" (Veit-Wild, *Source Book* 389-90). In the same eulogy, Muponde describes the passing away of Marechera as "The loud fall of a great mind—burying itself in the shadow of its shadow—never to be found again. [...] My tear is my blood from my bleeding heart. My blood is my ink and I shall spill dams and lakes of this ink unflinchingly..."

Robert Muponde's short stories carry close and vigorous stylistic and thematic echoes of Marechera. His story "The Storm" is a tumultuous story about a literature student at the University of Zimbabwe whose world is collapsing all around him. The university has been closed down after a violent demonstration; in addition, his girlfriend is pestering him endlessly; and in the midst of all this, his landlord violently kicks him (and his girlfriend) out of the suburban lodgings for outstanding rentals. The story begins as follows:

> It was dark in my mind. Dawn had hurtled itself into my consciousness, splashing its reds and yellows on my flyblown window. A cool hesitant breeze had soughed through the old, grey fence that sagged under the burden of a dead climbing plant. I looked out of the window through weary eyes. [...] My whole body ached and itched. [...] I was a ball of fire. Self-devouring. [...] The senseless ball of white fire rolled quietly in the blue sky. Senseless sun. [...] There was a morbid feeling: I was a man who stood besides his own bowels watching them screaming weakly and I was trying to walk away from them [...]. Then I was talking to Langston Hughes. (194)

And compare this with Marechera's:

> Sunlight harsh, stridently bright. Dark but convincing clouds now and then
> challenged the time white brutal heat. Here and there in the milling crowds,
> the First Street glitter fashions [...] Cecil Square fountains, the flush of toi-
> lets, the horrible oogle of the sink. Of rain, not a smell. [...] I did not know
> where I was going. (Marechera, *Mindblast* 119)

Both passages reveal the tendency to take off from a point of sudden inexplica-
ble agony and anger and to describe the external world as a direct mirror of the
internal turmoil of the narrator. Evident too, is the unmistakable "sweet sadness"
of characters who are in circumstances that supposedly trap them. This reflects
the realization that Independence has not really brought prosperity and freedom.
Both Marechera and Muponde use a language laden with abstract imagery to create a mood of regret mixed with anger towards the self and beyond. Muponde's
characters, like Marechera's, feel disappointed by the situation in independent
Zimbabwe and their narration is coarse and nihilistic; there is also the typically
Marecheran naturalist explicitness.

While following closely behind Marechera, Muponde is conscious that
Marechera sometimes damages some of his blind "followers." In Muponde's story called "Touched," Elijah, a Marechera fan and admirer, drops out of university
(in the Marechera fashion) and ends up a rogue temporary teacher. What begins
as an imitation of Marechera, a series of quoting and misquoting passages from
"The House of Hunger," ends in a personal tragedy. Elijah says about imitating
Marechera:

> All this time I was trying to fight him [Marechera] to death. They make a
> myth out of him, and he guards the portals to our creativity. The bastard...
> Somehow the younger generation passes through him first before they can
> write their own poems. [...] He's something haunting their language, some
> beast. How to outpace him, how to tear away from his grip... (206)

Both Muponde and Marechera are protesting against a violent society that leaves
one very little space to live and create, whether one is writing about the 1970's,
1980's, or the 1990's. However, whereas Marechera was defeatist, Muponde is
hopeful and regenerative. Whereas Marechera's humour has a fatalistic streak,
Muponde's is light-hearted. Muponde's characters, as in the story "At the Window", find ways out of entrapment and angst. Muponde is aware that the reason-
able thing to do is to work with the Marechera mode only as far as it is a kind of
apprenticeship. His recent unpublished poetry is a painful reflection on the irony
of knowing that you no longer belong to the lost dream of one's country and

childhood. In these poems you sense the Marecheran God-forsake-us attitude, but the wit and the sting belongs to Muponde:

> Madness
> Wooed my coy senses
> Into a strip-tease of myself
> Am I a character in an organisation carnivalesque?
> I heave after the cartwheeling
> In the headless riproar at independence
> And learn how to tease and escape from my own very shadow
>
> I'm skeleton without spirit
> Weighed low with flappy flesh
> I'm flesh without spirit
> Stale mouldering dough
> I'm without bone without muscle without spirit
> Limp hamstrung
> ("The Fury of Futility")

Ruzvidzo Mupfudza, who died on May 3rd 2010 (and tragically in his thirties, like Marechera), admits that he had "once walked in the shadow of Marechera" before finally finding his own voice (Mupfudza, "Who is Afraid"). When he found it, he said: "Now, I am grown, I have not stopped questing for and exploring new horizons […] the roads and the journeys I take are mine and not Marechera's. Whereas he would balk at the thought of being levelled 'an African writer', I have become a fierce Pan-Africanist" (ibid.). In a 1993 story called "A Picture of Madness," Mupfudza re-dramatizes the stories of broken-down families from "The House of Hunger." He draws his images of madness, death and suicide directly from Marechera's writings and interviews on his troubled childhood. His later short stories, such as "The Eyes of a Walk" and "Mermaid out of the Rain," show that he had evolved from Marechera's intense individualism to search for and sometimes struggle with matters spiritual. From Marechera, he adopted a hypnotic and intense writing style and borrowed Bohemian characters such as the tramp writer in *Mindblast*. In "Mermaid out of the Rain," a teacher shocks the whole community by taking into his home a woman tramp. As a result, he loses friends and fiancé. In such texts, Mupfudza fuses Marechera's nihilism with African folk, myth and wisdom to achieve an effect similar to the magical realism of Allende and Marquez: at the end of "Mermaid out of the Rain," the tramp from the rain just vanishes into thin air. In Harare, you came across Mupfudza sporting the Marechera dreadlocks, but also brandishing a traditional Shona walking stick.

Probably the most daunting association with Marechera today is the Shona poet and novelist Ignatius Mabasa. This is because Marechera regarded his native Shona as part of the "ghetto demon" which he was trying to run away from (Veit Wild, *Source Book* 3-4). Mabasa's Shona novel, *Mapenzi* (Fools) (1999), which has been compared to *The House of Hunger*, is a ground-breaking novel through its sheer innovativeness of form. As I have previously argued, *Mapenzi* strays across genres, including prose, poetry, song, dream, the epistolary form and others, and redefines the novel in Zimbabwe (Chirere).

Mapenzi is a story about one Hamundigone—a veteran of the liberation war. He says he has just been expelled from the teaching field because the authorities allege that he is not mentally stable. Hamundigone reminisces loudly and aggressively about his experiences. His presence and story touches nearly everyone in the novel. The creation and use of a central character of Hamundigone's temperament is a serious innovation on its own in Shona literature. Hamundigone is a wanderer, going from place to place, censoring careless speakers, rebuking pretenders and social hypocrites, chiding mean and selfish relatives, criticizing the status-quo, singing the latest tunes... He is a man of no fixed abode but you sense that he has a private destination—to tell the truth! His voice is reminiscent of the voice of the tramp writer in *Mindblast*.

Recently, leading Zimbabwean poets and critics Kizito Muchemwa and Musaemura Zimunya referred to Mabasa as "the Marechera of Shona poetry and fiction" because "in Mabasa, like in Marechera, there is the riot of sensibility, the controlled exuberance, the parodic style, the acerbic and the tenderness." He is set, so they say to "revolutionarise Shona fiction and poetry." Within the university of Zimbabwe I have often heard it mentioned with a remarkable sense of authority that Ignatius Mabasa is a madman and that he writes the way he does because he is a distant relative of Marechera. There was even a debate on whether Mabasa's novel *Mapenzi* was a novel or just a "heap of broken images." Having known Mabasa myself since boyhood, I think I can safely say that he is not mad and he is not related to Marechera.

More recently, Brian Chikwava, the winner of the 2004 Caine Prize for African Writing for his short story "Seventh Street Alchemy" has been compared to Marechera. The aggressive mood and staccato flow of this episodic story that delves into the lives of the downtrodden of Harare reflect Marechera's influence, especially of *Mindblast* and *Scrapiron Blues*. But more evidence of Marechera's approaches is in the story "The Jazz Goblin and His Rhythm" (2006). The story takes off, Marechera-style, with specific date, place and mood: "Independence Day, Wednesday, 18 April 2001. I still remember the morning clearly enough" (17). Like in "The House of Hunger," the young male protagonist, carrying all his belongings, is bitter about his family and country and is uncaringly wandering into an uncertain future. His artistic spirit is high and that is going to be his mainstay. He is a man put up against a world that is not prepared to tolerate the individual as it continues with its mundane routines. For this character, like for the protagonist of "The House of Hunger," the important things now are the tools of his trade, "the suitcase and sax" and "the cigarette" (132). He is on the road to a Bohemian life in what Marechera often refers to as "good old Harare."

Conclusion

Marechera was not an entirely new thing in the experience of the Zimbabwean people. The restlessness of men and women of art is not a new thing in Zimbabwe. We grew up in a society where the guitar player, for example, was an aloof character, walking and playing the guitar for over twenty kilometres to himself and those who cared to follow and hear. There are also stories about mbira players who went from party to party playing, "forgetting" to marry and settle down, but all the time criticizing the ills of society. However, this level of excitement with Marechera among young writers, readers and critics would not have worried Marechera himself who once declared that he did not find "influences pernicious" and that when he began to write, he was influenced by the likes of D. H. Lawrence, James Joyce, Kurt Vonnegut, and others (Marechera, "African Writer's Experience").[1]

---

[1] This lecture is included on the DVD.

Cult Figure and Pub Legend
Dialoguing on The Legacy of St Dambudzo

Anna-Leena Toivanen and Tinashe Mushakavanhu

Dambudzo Marechera is often referred to as a Zimbabwean cult icon, his repu-
tation oscillating between the genius of his fiction and the controversy of his
personality. In order to scrutinize his evasive legacy Anna-Leena Toivanen and
Tinashe Mushakavanhu set out to dialogue on the issue. While Toivanen positions herself in the field of cult studies, which serves as the framework informing
her questions, Mushakavanhu responds to these questions as a Marechera scholar
and, above all, as a writer and reader inspired by Marechera's legacy.

ALT: Considering that this book is about the legacy of Dambudzo Marechera, it
would be interesting to discuss how you cherish Marechera's legacy in your own
writing. To start with, there undeniably is a cult phenomenon around Marechera.
Although cult phenomena are marked by their objects, the coming into being of
a cult always requires an audience willing to invest in the object in terms of emotion, time and even finance. Hence, no cultural text is *inherently* "cultic." Further,
cults are situated in specific contexts; this has bearing on the attractiveness of
certain cultural texts. Hence, cults should be understood as phenomena that go
beyond their mere object: the followers invest in the object and get something "in
exchange." As to your own writerly identity, what has Marechera given to you?

TM: What I admire in Marechera is the sheer intensity of language, the use of
intense imagery, the fearlessness and openness in his writings and the desire to
be independent from the self and society. In fact Marechera is an attitude—a way
of relating with the world.
   Marechera has been a big source of literary encouragement in my creative
and critical development. I know very well the fanaticism around him, but to me
Marechera just showed the way. He gave me the gift of probing things, of ask-
ing questions, of not believing anything at face value, of using my imagination
against a world that is often militating against the individual. If curiosity killed
the cat, then Dambudzo Marechera is the curiosity that happened in my youth.
In other words, my relationship with Marechera was as a reader of his writings.
He became an unlikely mentor. His works became a literary "sat-nav" that con-

tinues to tour-guide my intellectual journey. The allusions to history, philosophy, politics, cultures, literatures of the world in his works has given me a yearning to discover, for example, why I am a product of contradictions.

And having said that, Marechera is the closest approximation there is to what could be described as "the Zimbabwean writer's writer." His work stands out clearly in its own right, as a precept, a value, which exercises tremendous, if not heterodox fascination for other writers. This dimension of the impact of Marechera's writings certainly reveals the significance of how and whom his works have impressed.

ALT: You mentioned the word "fanaticism." This is interesting, for the etymological origins of the word "fan" stem from the term "fanaticism," which has often led to the characterization of fans as pathological fanatics in the eyes of the *outsiders*. What is at stake in cult phenomena are questions of identity and distinction: the cult object comes to represent a means of identification for the admirers, and, of course, identity is as much a means of belonging as it is a means of differentiation. When you are talking about fanaticism around Marechera and distancing yourself from this aspect of the phenomenon—while not being an outsider either—would you say that Marechera fans can be divided into different categories? There seems to be some sort of a distinction between those who admire Marechera as an extra-literary attitude, and those who are more familiar with his writings.

TM: Most people often ask me: What kind of Marechera lover are you? What kind of writer are you who doesn't drink or smoke? They say you can only be a writer if you are intoxicated, you can only read and understand Marechera if you are intoxicated. But, what am I supposed to do when I was born intoxicated, when I lead an intoxicated life?

The tragedy of the Marechera phenomenon in Zimbabwe is that it has created "literary zombies." They speak and write without thinking, they read without understanding, they see without seeing. I have always wanted to see myself as a *reader* of Marechera, not a *fan,* because there is danger in seeing Marechera as a rough centerfold figure on the pages of Zimbabwean literature and glorifying his bad deeds over his creative genius. He is the poster boy of bad behavior, of recklessness, of womanizing, of laziness. He is the big excuse given by ultimate failures; see we have not made it because society rejected us just like it did Marechera. Marechera is a winner. We all can't stop talking about him. If he had not existed we would have invented him. The misunderstanding is largely because most of these people try to do what Marechera did (and most likely never did).

Marechera is a signpost of our changing history. He represents a certain postcolonial mindset that only "creative artists" can embrace. He represents freedom of expression, fearless criticism, uninhibited imagination, a certain moral conscience of art. He presented us with alternative ways of seeing, of living, of being, of feeling, of emotion. He naturally experimented with form, and challenged the line between fact and fiction. Everything is dynamic, open to new interpretations. The rest of our society deny(ied) him. The politicians wish he had never existed. He has since been condemned into that annex of the mad and yet it seems madness (perceived or real) is an alternative form of expressing truth.

ALT: Your answer embodies the idea that the objects of cult are open to divergent readings and appropriations. It is important that one can define one's own position in relation to the cult object without being labelled. You just defined yourself as a *reader*, not as a *fan*. It seems to me that you prefer to keep a certain distance to Marechera while valuing his legacy, and to make a distinction between his literary production and his public image. Is your position in relation to Marechera strictly that of a reader? Would you say that through your own writing, you are dialoguing with Marechera's writings; that is, (re)writing him somehow? Do you think that in your relation to Marechera's literary output there is also this critical edge?

TM: I don't mean to eulogise Marechera. He is everything and nothing to everyone—depending on who they are and what their circumstances are. In Zimbabwe there are those who got to meet Marechera (or so they claim) and the rest of us who encountered him through reading his works and through embellished pub legends. In fact, those who were old enough when Marechera was alive tend to be possessive of the man and the legend, even his writings—there is an arrogance in them that says "because you never got to know him in his lifetime therefore you are not qualified to talk about him." I have experienced this as a young Marechera scholar and felt it even more before and after my participation at the historic Oxford symposium. In those very moments, I become very suspicious, but also embrace them as a buffer, a necessary critical distancing, that allows me to engage with him from a totally different angle.

I like writers who keep it real. Marechera did. *The House of Hunger* was a revelation. I saw it in the streets in which my mother and father grew up, the streets in which I was growing up—the hunger, the squalor, the poverty, the prostitution. I saw Mai Nhingi, our neighbour, turn to prostitution to feed her nine kids after her husband died. We followed the older girls who had sex in the bushes at the edge of the "location." I remember sisi Immaculate who had a child whose father was unknown. Literature became a motion picture of my existence. I like writers who consistently ask me to stitch together those things that we normally keep apart, and while doing so, taking the most perversely original instance to instantiate the problem. Marechera was and continues to be all those writers to me. Along the way I have had to read the works of James Joyce, D. H. Lawrence, Bukowsky, Shelley, Günter Grass, Shakespeare, Soyinka as footnotes of his writings.

Yes, I connive with Marechera primarily as a reader and writer. Sometimes we agree to disagree. Sometimes I update his writings by (re)writing and locating him and myself in the new dispensation. My desire is to interfere with and interrupt the flows of his thoughts, to engage with and fight with his ideologues in response to my own.

ALT: You mentioned the possessive attitude. This is a question of authority and power over who is entitled claim the ownership of the "truth" about the *real* Marechera. This kind of jealousy is often characteristic of cult phenomena where identities are defined in terms of who is in and who is out. Those who are in are trying to "protect" the cult object from the appropriation of the "outsiders." It is interesting that in Marechera's case this exclusionary practice is so closely connected to the authority of "having known" Marechera, and not to whether, for instance, one is conversant with his production. This is illustrative of how much this is a personality cult. There is this deadly serious edge in this approach; no room for playfulness, not to speak of distancing. Could it be that the fact that you cannot claim the authority of "having known" Marechera gives you more freedom to negotiate with him?

You have mentioned the word "truth" a couple of times, linking it closely to Marechera's work. Is there not a discrepancy between such a concept and Marechera's deconstructive vision?

TM: I first encountered Dambudzo Marechera one August morning at a school assembly when our headmaster was talking about this writer I had never heard of. It was on the tenth anniversary of his death in 1997 and I was 14 years old. Our headmaster must have been a big fan because our school library had a full collection of all his books. *The House of Hunger* was the first book I read, and it made me feel so much cooler than anyone in high school. Marechera seemed to be coming at me with everything. His life seemed at stake in his words, and while I was reading, so did mine.

I vividly remember moments I would sit under library tables or hide behind colossal bookshelves and read a Marechera book. Reading Marechera was like an initiation into a secret society. There was something wonderfully subversive about his writing; he said things that were too dangerous to say, things I had to decode. Marechera didn't want to be too easily understood. As he explains, through his alter-ego Nick in *Black Sunlight*, "I am astonished at the audience's ignorance. I did not expect such a low cultural level among you. Those who do not understand my work are simply illiterate. One must learn" (110). In this way, Marechera prompted me to pursue him. We became comrades.

I love this relationship with Marechera—he has always been like that forbidden friend in childhood who was way older than you and your parents told you to keep away from him because they thought he was a bad influence and corrupting your sensibilities. And yet, you still sneaked out to see him because he had all the time in the world for you, you told him about your troubles and fantasies and he listened and gave you advice, he told you grown-up stuff and you listened and asked too many questions which never seemed to bother him, and he knew everyone else misunderstood him except you. While I have no claim to have met Marechera, his books were my older mates I looked up to, to be streetwise. Are they honest friends? Do they always tell the truth? I have always learnt to read between the lines and take out what I want from the relationship. Truth is always what you want to believe.

124

Matriculation portrait, New College, 1974 © The Warden and Scholars of New College, Oxford

Passport photograph, 1974 © The Warden and Scholars of New College, Oxford

---

STATEMENT

My recent expulsion from the University of Rhodesia has disrupted my studies,especially so since I was a second-year B.A.English Honours studen -t who because the sylabus here dictates so had not as yet written an impor- tant examination.The study of English Literature has always been my sole ambition;as for a career I have always vacillated between an academic and a journalistic post.However,as I well realised,I am a black man and in this country the academic and journalistic fields are virtually closed to African -s.But I was determined that I would first of all obtain a degree here before anything else,since a foreigner in your country will fare better if he has something more than just words.My expulsion on August the seventh has itself become an important element in my decision to study at Oxford.

And what undergraduate in Africa has not heard of your University's long and unending tradition.It is a naive reverence,I admit,but nonethless this vague awe is not unimportant.

A more important reason then the one above is that for the first time in my life I will be studying among a people whose tradition is now firmy founded upon human dignity and equality;I will be among students whose main preoccupation will not be the colour of my skin,among lecturers who do not hold that a black student can never be half as good as a white student;among friends who have actually set up a body (W.U.S.)to help x needy students.Abov -e all,as a student with literary pretensions -I write poems and short storie -s,have written a bad play,and am writing a novel- I believe that the rigorou -s standards of your University will cure me of my artistic illusions or hop- efully will reinforce my rather inflated belief in my imaginative and creativ -e powers.

CWMarechera

(NB:You will find a hand-written version of this statement attached to this sheet.)

Marechera's application essay to Oxford © The Warden and Scholars of New College, Oxford

Stories from Marechera's Children's Writing Workshop, Harare 1984 © Flora Veit-Wild

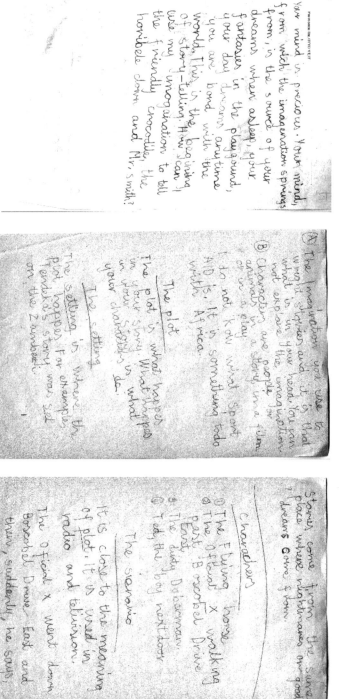

Your mind is precious. Your mind, from which the imagination springs, is the source of your dreams when asleep, your fantasies in the playground, your day dreams anytime you are bored with the world. This is the beginning of story-telling. How can I use my imagination to tell the friendly crocodile, the horrible clown and Mr. Smith?

(A) The imagination you use to what is fiction and it is that what is in your head. You can not explain the imagination.

(B) Characters are people or animals in a story in a film or in a play.
I do not know what sport AIDS is. It is something todo with Africa.

The plot

The plot is what happened in your story. What happened in your story is what your characters do.

The setting

The setting is where the plot happens. For example Tendai's story was set on the Zambezi.

Stories come from the same place where nightmares or good dreams come from.

Characters

① The Flying horse
② The Official X working past
③ Basotfed Drive
④ The dirty Doberman
⑤ Tell the boy next door

The scenario

It is close to the meaning of plot. It is used in radio and television.

The Official X went down Borrobel Drive East and then suddenly he saw…

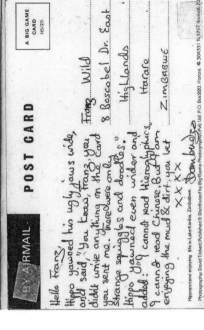

POST CARD

A BIG GAME CARD H5/20

Hello Franz,

Hippo yawned his ugly jaws wide and said, "You know, Franz, you didn't write anything on the card you sent me. There were only strange squiggles and doodles."

Hippo yawned even wider and added: "I cannot read Hieroglyphics. I cannot read Chinese. But I am enjoying the mud & dirt, you bet

x x x x

Dambudzo

Franz Wild
8 Roscobel Dr. East
Highlands
Harare
Zimbabwe

Hippopotami enjoying life in Lake Kariba, Zimbabwe.
Photography: David Trickett Published & Distributed by BigGame Photography (Pvt) Ltd. P.O. Box 200, Horace. ☎ 304331 Tx:3757 Scobell, ZU

Marechera's postcard to Franz Wild, 1984 © Flora Veit-Wild

POST CARD

A BIG GAME CARD J1/5

Listen to this, Max:

"Weaver birds?" said the hyena.

Jackal nodded and said,

"Yes, lots of them. I saw them. My friend Max saw them. The whole of Kenya saw them!"

Hyena was very jealous. He said, "I suppose you'll be parachuting next.."

x x x

Dambudzo

Max Wild
8 Roscobel Dr. East
Highlands
Harare
Zimbabwe

Sidestriped Jackal, Zimbabwe.
PHOTOGRAPHY BY DAVID TRICKETT. PUBLISHED BY BIG GAME PHOTOGRAPHY PVT(O) LTD. P.O. BOX 200, SALISBURY.

Marechera's postcard to Max Wild, 1984 © Flora Veit-Wild

128

Top: Marechera with Max and Franz Wild, October 1983 • Bottom: Commemoration of the first anniversary of Marechera's death, Harare 1988 © Flora Veit-Wild

Marechera in the yard of his flat, Sloane Court, Harare, February 1986 © Ernst Schade

PART 3

SCHOLARSHIP

A "Postmodern" at the Margin Innovations in Dambudzo Marechera's Texts

Carolyn Hart

Introduction

Dambudzo Marechera is remembered for being a writer of great imagination whose numerous texts are remarkable for their subject matter and experimentation. He is remembered perhaps as much for his theatrical and sometimes shocking behavior as he is for his writing, including everything from speaking with an upper-class English accent to his drinking and way of dress. He is also remembered for his shocking statements, many of which are highly quotable. One of his best-known statements concerns his identity as an international writer:

> I think I am the *doppelgänger* whom, until I appeared, African literature had not yet met. And in this sense I would question anyone calling me an African writer. Either you are a writer or you are not. If you are a writer for a specific nation or a specific race, then fuck you. In other words, the direct international experience of every single living entity is, for me, the inspiration to write. (Veit-Wild, *Source Book* 221)

Although Marechera considered himself to be a writer of international scope and experience, at the same time he believed himself to be a writer for readers who shared his experiences, as expressed in the following, albeit semi-serious, statement: "I write for the reader who is exactly like myself and has experienced what I have experienced and has got the same feelings as I have..." (Veit-Wild, *Source Book* 311).[1] Similarly, in regard to writing *Mindblast,* Marechera stated: "For instance, the last section of *Mindblast* from the journal—that is simply a factual record of what was happening to me each day whilst I was homeless. In it I recorded even anything that walked by as I was typing, how I had slept the night before etc." (Marechera, *Mindblast* 37).

This article suggests that the aesthetic innovations of Marechera's texts, and in particular the innovations in language and use of non-linear narratives that lack closure, cross borders as they share commonalities with texts by writers of Africa

---

[1] This interview with Fiona Lloyd is included on the DVD.

and the Diaspora that are experimental or "postmodern." At the same time, these innovations in his texts reflect his experience as a Zimbabwean, and more specifically his urban experiences growing up in Vengere Township, such that his texts were groundbreaking and stand out even in relation to other experimental texts produced at the time.

It is my intent to place Marechera's writing within an international context of contemporary, experimental or "postmodern" writers and writing. The article explores links between the aesthetics of Marechera's texts and the texts of writers of Africa and its U.S. Diaspora that incorporate innovations in language as well as non-linear narratives that lack closure and reflect musical structures, in particular jazz. Although scholarly debate has so far included comparison of Marechera's texts to other postcolonial literatures (Veit-Wild and Chennells; Gaylard), links between his texts and contemporary texts of the African Diaspora have been little explored, especially in relation to these aesthetics.

I suggest links between the language and aesthetics of Marechera's texts and the texts of other "postmodern" or experimental writers not through textual analysis, but rather through discussion regarding the reception of the texts and their production, including the writers' own descriptions of the creative process. It is not my intent to define or categorize Marechera's texts as "postmodern," but to acknowledge the experimental nature of his texts: James Currey, editor of Heinemann African Writers Series (AWS) at the time, stated that Marechera's writing was highly exceptional, that his writing "yelled from the page," and that it was a financial risk to publish his texts—so much so that if he had received them several years later (when the AWS had less money) he might not have been able to publish him at all (Veit-Wild, *Source Book* 223). This assessment of Marechera's writing by his publisher as "high risk," and as highly exceptional, corroborates the critical reception of Marechera's texts following their publication (Veit-Wild and Chennells).

Language innovations in Marechera's texts

"That's it, man. Swear it out of your system. It does a man good to swear" (Marechera, *Hunger* 13). Marechera seems to have believed in this statement, for his own writing incorporates a good deal of swearing. His texts have in common with the texts of other "postmodern" or experimental writers their use of so-called "shocking" language and graphic scenes describing the body and sexuality. Such writers include the Ghanaian Ayi Kwei Armah whose experimental texts are exceptional among those published with the AWS. Richard Priebe notes "how very different" Armah's *The Beautyful Ones Are Not Yet Born*, published in 1968, and Kofi Awoonor's *This Earth, My Brother*, published in 1971, are from earlier Ghanaian novels. These "experimental narrative styles," he writes, are "more in line with post-modernist fiction in Europe than developments in Ghana." The earlier novels follow "an objective and realistic mode of representation with a strictly linear chronological structure" while these are "impressionistic," with "a very fragmented chronological structure" (Priebe 15). Like Marechera's fiction, *The Beautyful Ones Are Not Yet Born* is characterized by the use of graphic language. Currey discusses the repetition and emphasis on "shit" in Armah's novel noting that his colleagues "reluctantly" accepted that it be published with the AWS, expecting that the novel would not sell to schools in Africa—an assumption that turned out to be incorrect (Currey 73).

The "developments" in "post-modernist fiction" of the West that Priebe mentions apply to well-known American writers of experimental texts, such as Kathy Acker, who was born in 1949, and Fiction Collective members Ray Federman, Ron Sukenick, Steve Katz, Clarence Major and Cris Mazza, among others. Founded in 1974, the Collective was a group of writers living in New York City, as well as in California and Colorado, who successfully established a non-profit co-operative that published experimental texts, including among many others Ronald Sukenick's *98.6*, Russell Banks' *Searching for Survivors*, Marianne Hauser's *The Talking Room*, Raymond Federman's *Take It or Leave It*, Steve Katz's *Stolen Stories*, Clarence Major's *My Amputations*, Fanny Howe's *Holy Smoke*, and Mark Leyner's *I Smell Esther Williams*. The Collective received regular support from the New York State Council for the Arts and the NEA, as well as grants from other institutions, and many of the authors have won prestigious awards. The Collective has since evolved to become the Fiction Collective 2 (FC2) (DeShell et al.). As I will discuss further in relation to non-linear narratives and Marechera's texts, writers of the Fiction Collective have provided critique of Western realist, linear narratives; in the words of its member Ray Federman, new fiction should be "'deliberately illogical, irrational, unrealistic, non sequitur, and incoherent'" (Balogun 252). Although graphic or obscene language is common among writers whose texts are considered to be "postmodern" or experimental, the use of such language has been received with controversy even beyond the literary establishment.

Marechera's texts share similarities in their language and aesthetics, and also their reception, with the experimental texts by the Fiction Collective writers. The Zimbabwean Censorship Board considered Marechera's *Black Sunlight* to use language deliberately shocking and intended to offend (Bryce, "Inside/Out" 222). In terms of language, the texts of the Fiction Collective were considered obscene, therefore not fit for funding from the National Endowment for the Arts (NEA). During the 1990's, Representative Peter Hoekstra, head of the congressional Subcommittee on Oversight and Investigation, raised an inquiry regarding the support of the NEA for FC2 (DeShell et al.). Here, I wish to point out that among other qualities of Marechera's texts that contributed to Currey's assessment of Marechera's texts as "high risk" in terms of their publication and reception in the literary establishment were the language and "obscene" nature of the texts. Thus Marechera's texts were made note of by the Zimbabwean Censorship Board for breaking with the acceptable conventions and boundaries of the national literature; the experimental texts of the Fiction Collective were similarly noted by the U.S. government as they broke the boundaries of the "national literature" of the U.S.

In addition to using graphic language, Marechera's themes about the urban experience in Zimbabwe and living as an "outsider" in Oxford and London set his texts apart from other "postmodern" writers including Armah whose texts explore issues particular to Ghana, as well as writers whose experimental texts explore very different issues, including most of the writers of the Fiction Collective, Kathy Acker, et al. Jane Bryce and Flora Veit-Wild have discussed the carnival nature of Marechera's texts and their exploration of urban themes, noting that the subject matter and language of the texts reflect Marechera's own life, not the life or language of the British or Zimbabwe elite (Bryce, "Inside/Out"; Veit-Wild, "Carnival"). The following passage from "The House of Hunger" is poetic in its repetition but it also uses so-called "shocking" language with the effect of creating a picture of a harsh reality—the type of daily reality that Marechera experienced:

> There is nothing to make one particularly glad one is a human being and not a horse, or a lion, or jackal, or come to think of it a snake. Snakes. There's just dirt and shit and urine and blood and smashed brains. There's dust and fleas and bloody whites and roaches and dogs trained to bite black people in the arse. There's venereal disease and beer and lunacy and just causes. There's technology to drop on your head wherever you stop to take a leak. There's white shit in our leaders and white shit in our dreams and white shit in our history and white shit on our hands in anything we build or pray for. (59)

The language emphasizes shit and urine, but the fact that Marechera relates this language to racism makes his writing exceptional even among experimental texts; and the themes reflect Marechera's experience as a Zimbabwean. Writers such as Armah, and African-American writers such as Ishmael Reed and Clarence Major, are among the few whose texts are noted for their experimentation with language and aesthetics, while at the same time they use this type of scatological language to explore issues of racism. African American writer Ntozake Shange is exceptional among contemporary writers as she, like Marechera, cites issues regarding racism (among other reasons) for her experimenting with the English language.

Shange was born in 1948 in New Jersey, and lived in Los Angeles to complete her education before moving in 1975 to New York City. She began publishing in the 1970s and is known for her experimental texts blending fiction, poetry and drama; she is perhaps best known for her controversial and experimental choreopoem *for colored girls who have considered suicide / when the rainbow is enuf,* first produced in 1975. Shange is a prolific writer and has written numerous plays, poems, novels and essays, including *Sassafrass, Cyprus and Indigo, See No Evil* and others. Nancy Gray's study *Language Unbound: On Experimental Writing by Women* discusses Shange's writing alongside that of Virginia Woolf, Gertrude Stein, Monique Wittig and others.

The experimental nature of Shange's writing in terms of language and aesthetics is reflected in the following response she gives to critics "'[who] had accused me of being too self-conscious of being a writer [...] / [so] that my writing approached verbal gymnastics like unto a reverse minstrel sho': 'I cant count the number of times I have viscerally wanted to attack deform n maim the language that I waz taught to hate myself in / the language that perpetuates the notions that cause pain to every black child as he / she learns to speak of the world & the 'self'"" (Shange, *See No Evil* 21). Similarly, regarding his use of language, Marechera stated, "Shona was part of the ghetto daemon I was trying to escape [...] This perhaps is in the undergrowth of my experimental use of English, standing it on its head [...]. For the black writers the language is very racist [...]. It is so for the feminists" (Veit-Wild, *Source Book* 4). Although Marechera (as he himself stated) did not write to promote Zimbabwe as a nation or to promote his own race, he did explore issues regarding racism and like Shange, his use of language could be said to confront racism, as in the passage above quoted from "The House of Hunger." Marechera's innovations in language therefore cross borders, as the language of his texts shares similarities with innovations in language of experimental texts produced at the same time in the U.S. But the nature of experimentation in language regarding racism in Marechera's texts is exceptional, as is the language Shange uses in her texts. The fact that Marechera combines this use of language with the exploration of urban themes in Zimbabwe further distinguishes his texts so that they stand out even among contemporary writers of Africa and the Diaspora who, like Armah and Shange, are known for experimentation.

Aesthetics of Marechera's texts:
non-linear narratives and "jazz writing"

Both the subject matter and aesthetics of Marechera's texts—such as open and non-linear narratives found in *The House of Hunger, Black Sunlight, The Black Insider* and other texts—challenge the standards of realist, linear writing that, as Drew Shaw explains, was not indigenous to Africa but imported as part of the colonial project (Shaw 11-12). In terms of post-colonial and anti-colonial literature, Abiola Irele sums up the response from the Empire: "The pattern involves notably the refusal of privilege to the language, literature, and thought systems of the colonizer [...]. What is implied here is a determined inversion of the order of precedence decreed by the colonizer" (Irele 73). In Marechera's case, "standing a language on its head" can be interpreted as such an inversion of order, as can the non-closure of his texts. For Marechera the realist, linear narrative limited creative expression: "Thoughts that think in straight lines cannot see round corners; the missionaries and teachers saw to that. [...] Logic is an attitude. It freezes us forever in the icy tumult of all the cursed attitudes they stuffed into us" (Marechera, *Black Insider* 37).

African-American writer Gayl Jones is known for her texts that incorporate non-linear narratives and lack of closure; she also explores "taboo" topics concerning women. Jones was born in Kentucky in 1949, and began publishing in 1975 after completing her Master's degree at Brown University in Rhode Island. Her novels include *Corrigedora*, *Eva's Man*, and *The Healing*, among others; she has also published several collections of poetry and has received critical attention from scholars such as Claudia Tate. Jones stated in an interview with Charles Rowell that took place in 1982, "[M]any Euro-American writers—whether it's admitted or not (*and particularly the most innovative ones*)—have been influenced by Afro-American 'oral arts and traditions' (*this includes the music*) as well as their own" [my emphasis] (Rowell 34). A prominent avant-garde writer, African American Ishmael Reed was born in 1938 and has published many experimental novels beginning in the 1960's, including *Yellow Back Radio Broke-Down, Mumbo Jumbo,* and *The Last Days of Louisiana Red.* He believes that "Afro-Americans [...] are very suspicious of what has been called the avant-garde. Now, what I'm doing is not avant-garde, but a classical Afro-American form. And that's been beaten out of them" (Martin 1).

The repetition of sound and words used in oral arts including poetry, and the non-linearity and non-closure that is characteristic of jazz—an Afro-American form of music that Jones discusses in relation to her texts—are present in the texts of some of the most innovative writers, as Jones suggests, including Marechera's texts. In my article "In Search of African Literary Aesthetics: Production and Reception of the Texts of Amos Tutuola and Yvonne Vera" (Hart), I explore the aesthetic resource-base for Tutuola's and Vera's texts (which incorporate repetition and non-linear narratives that lack closure) in relation to oral arts, including music and in particular drumming, indigenous to Africa. Reed's statement that his writing "is not avant-garde, but a classical Afro-American form" and Jones' comment on the contributions of "oral arts and traditions" to innovative texts serve to corroborate the influences of oral arts on the creation of their texts. The ideas they express in regard to the creation of their texts are similar to Marechera's statements about his writing in relation to linearity, i.e. colonial imports, and "thoughts that think in straight lines."

In regard to Jones' idea that Afro-American music has influenced innovative writers, numerous fiction writers in America have been influenced by jazz, such as Maya Angelou, Toni Morrison, Langston Hughes, Thomas Pynchon, Donald Barthelme, and others (Albert 1996). Fiction Collective members have acknowledged the influence of jazz in their work; Steve Katz, for example, acknowledges his early exposure to jazz musicians in New York City as an influence on the writing of his experimental texts. He has dedicated pieces in his latest collection *Kisssss, a Miscelany* to Cecil Taylor, Ornette Coleman, and Steve Lacy, three jazz greats (Pelton). Jones makes it clear in her novel *The Healing* that she is taking liberties with the traditional chronological narrative. Early in the text, there is this interruption of the story:

> Not now. Before. I'm telling you about them old days… You know, like them flashback scenes. You got to always explain them flashback scenes. They just understand that chronological order. Seem like to me anybody seen a modern movie, even them old-time modern movies would understand a flashback scene. Or if you listen to jazz, seem like you'd understand them flashback scenes (68).

In a later passage, the narrator makes similar comments, this time referring to the movie and book about Billie Holiday, *Lady Sings the Blues*: "The book moves back and forth in time, more than the movie. You think you're in one time and the next chapter you're in another. Joan says it's kinda like jazz" (126-27).

Observations such as those of Jones and Reed corroborate Marechera's insistence that he was an "international" writer as the aesthetics of his texts cross borders and share characteristics with African American art forms and other experimental texts; as Jones describes, these are aesthetics that are also present in jazz. Such observations suggest the idea of resistance among these writers against what Marechera considered to be the imposed aesthetics of rationality and linearity that were imports of the colonizers; aesthetics that limit creative expression for "postmodern" writers as expressed by Ray Federman. Marechera's writing breaks the standards of "Western" realist, linear narrative texts and is considered to be "experimental" even while, as he himself noted, linearity and closure were not indigenous to African storytelling but were imposed as part of the Enlightenment project (Shaw 11).

Conclusion

Shaw states that *all* Zimbabwean writing is "a syncretic mix of African and European themes" (Shaw 9). But as Shaw discusses, and as Marechera himself stated, Marechera consciously resisted the ideology of the Enlightenment and therefore also realist master narratives (Shaw 11). Marechera explored issues particular to his experience as a black African living in Zimbabwe and in British exile, and at the same time he shares commonalities with numerous "postmodern" or experimental writers of various nationalities, races, ethnicities and gender in that his texts experiment with language and they are non-linear, lacking closure. Marechera's language combined with his exploration of urban themes set in Zimbabwe, as well as his refusal to follow other black Zimbabwean writers who would as he put it "write works which would re-inforce the bone marrow and thinking of Ian Smith's skull" (Veit-Wild 223)—that is, his refusal to write texts that reflected the views of either the British or Zimbabwe elite – make his texts unique among contemporary writers of Africa. Marechera's texts at once have themes and aesthetics that cross borders, but they also are particular to his own experience. It is the unique combination of experimental elements in language and aesthetics that makes Marechera's contribution exceptional and groundbreaking at the international level, even among contemporary, experimental and "postmodern" writers.

"House of Fools"
Madness and the State of the Nation in Marechera's "The House of Hunger" (1978) and Ignatius Mabasa's *Mapenzi* (1999)

Katja Kellerer

> *"In 'The House of Hunger' I do not preach about politics, I do not preach about anything at all. I merely state exactly what 'The House of Hunger,' Zimbabwe, is like."*
>
> Dambudzo Marechera[1]

> *"That's what I want to do. I would be glad to find a place to slip far away from Harare. Far away indeed from this madness. This madness which sees lunacy in others while refusing to acknowledge its own lunacy."*
>
> Ignatius Mabasa[2]

During the past half-century, Zimbabwean writers have produced a rich and versatile body of literature. While some well-known Zimbabwean writers, including Dambudzo Marechera, Tsitsi Dangaremba, and Yvonne Vera, have chosen to write exclusively in English, there is a significant body of literature in Shona and Ndebele that is little known outside the country (Veit-Wild, "De-Silencing" 195).[3] These two strands of Zimbabwean literature—in English on the one hand and in Shona and Ndebele literature on the other—developed separately for a long time (Veit-Wild, "Zimbolicious" 695). In this essay, I want to contribute to the emerging dialogue between these two bodies of literature by comparing one English novella, Dambudzo Marechera's "The House of Hunger" (1978), to one Shona novel, Ignatius Mabasa's *Mapenzi* (1999). These two works are suited for a comparison since the publication of *Mapenzi* triggered a wave of commo-

---

[1] Sweetman

[2] Ini ndizvo zvandinoda kuita. Ndingafare kana ndikawana kwekuvererekera kuri kure neHarare. Kure chaizvo nehupenzi huno. Hupenzi hunosanganisira kuona hupenzi hwevamwe ivo vasingaoni hwavo. (Mabasa, *Mapenzi* 30). All English translations from *Mapenzi*, unless otherwise indicated, by Joyce Mutiti.

[3] In her 1992 *Survey of Zimbabwean Writers*, Veit-Wild has found that more than half of Zimbabwean writers are strictly unilingual, more than three quarters write mainly in the vernacular, either Shona or Ndebele, while only ten percent write exclusively in English (116).

tion throughout the Zimbabwean literary scene, prompting rumours concerning a close relationship between the two authors. As Memory Chirere has observed,

> [a]t the University of Zimbabwe, where I teach, I have often heard it mentioned, with remarkable authority, that "Mabasa is a madman." He has even been considered "a distant relative to Dambudzo Marechera," the late prizewinning Zimbabwean author who wrote almost entirely in the English language. There was even debate on whether *Mapenzi* is in fact a novel or just a "heap of broken images." (221)

A brief glance at the autobiographies of these two men, however, reveals that Mabasa is neither a madman nor related to Marechera. In fact, in contrast to Marechera, whose excessive drinking bouts and eccentric public appearances left many of his contemporaries questioning his mental stability, Mabasa appears to lead an ordered life—he works as the Deputy Director of the British Council in Harare.

Yet, on a literary level, the works of the two authors are clearly interconnected. *Mapenzi* contains direct references to Marechera; within the text the author is mentioned by name. In addition, the novel's unique and innovative style and language are evocative of the late author's work. Thus, a striking aspect of *Mapenzi* is that "it can be read as a sort of Marecheran text in (mostly) Shona" (Veit-Wild, "Zimbolicious" 695). Moreover, despite the fact that *Mapenzi* was published twenty years after "The House of Hunger" and is set in a different historical setting—independent Zimbabwe under Mugabe's ZANU(PF) regime in contrast to the Rhodesian settler state that constitutes the historical backdrop of Marechera's novella—both works share one compelling theme, reverberating throughout both texts: madness.

With regard to the meaning of madness within the two works, the theoretical approaches of Michel Foucault and R. D. Laing are particularly pertinent. By tracing the different meanings madness has been imbued with in Europe, from the Renaissance to modern times, Foucault illustrates in his seminal work *Madness and Civilization: A History of Insanity in the Age of Reason* that it is an inherently constructed concept—its meaning hinging upon the dominant ideology of the time. By emphasizing the essential role power plays in the process of defining madness, Foucault questions why someone is labelled mad and by whom. Foucault's ideas were picked up by the anti-psychiatric movement that criticized the prevailing practices in psychiatry in the 1950's and early 1960's. With regards to madness, Marechera aligned himself with one of the movement's founders, R. D. Laing (Veit-Wild, *Writing* 60). In stark contrast to the tenor of the time, the psychiatrist believed that psychopathological behaviour was not a biological or psychological fault of the person but was rather triggered as a response to a distressful social environment, particularly the family. According to Laing, for instance, "the experience and behaviour that gets labelled schizophrenic is a special strategy that a person invents in order to live in an unliveable situation" (115).

Taking these two theories as a point of departure for my analysis, I argue that in both works under discussion madness functions as a device to critique the state of the nation. By exploring the blurred lines between sanity and insanity, Marechera reflects on and strikes back to colonial oppression under Ian Smith's white minority rule, while simultaneously counteracting African nationalism. Mabasa, writing in post-independent Zimbabwe, unravels the madness of the Mugabe regime and critiques its ruthless promotion of "patriotic history"[4], which is mainly expressed in parodying Zimbabwe's liberation war of 1966-1979, the second *Chimurenga*.

Madman or mad genius?

Marechera's life and his work are closely intertwined. Yet, "The House of Hunger," despite being interlaced with autobiographical elements, cannot be read as an autobiographical work. The author constantly reinvented and recreated his identity and explored competing identities. Consequently he developed different versions of his life-story. For instance, in an interview with Alle Lansu, he explained that his father was mysteriously killed by the army (Veit-Wild, *Source Book* 12). According to Veit-Wild, however, "[t]his version of his father's death has not been confirmed by anybody else. The general version is that he was run over by a car when he walked home on the road at night" (ibid.). Thus, Marechera blurs the line between fiction and autobiography, narration and reality. He creates characters "that resemble the author himself, or a facet of the author's identity"; yet, by defining identity as an "unstable, fluid, and ever-changing" category, necessitating "constant redefinition," Marechera's writing, as well as the story of his life, are constructed and deconstructed from the author's "particular point of view at a particular point of time" (Levin and Taitz 164). Laurice Taitz and Melissa Levin poignantly convey this constant interplay between reality and fiction that underlines Marechera's work: "While characters represent fragments, they are fictional creations. It is this fictionality that Marechera recognizes in the construction of himself through his characters and it is at this point that the autobiography becomes a fiction" (164).

Correspondingly, to read the mad tendencies of the narrator in "The House of Hunger"—his constant wanderings along the brink of insanity that culminate in an outright nervous breakdown—as autobiographical references, as signs of men-

---

[4] The term "patriotic history" has been coined by Terence Ranger who contrasts it to and differentiates it from the concept of nationalist history.

tal illness afflicting the author himself, is too simplistic. Yet, throughout his brief life, Marechera was repeatedly labelled a madman, and, according to Veit-Wild, "[t]he question whether or not Marechera was mentally ill, in the clinical sense, has preoccupied many who met him" (*Writing* 56). The writer was very aware that others perceived him as insane. Indeed, for him, the public image of him as one "who slept on the benches in the city-square and is going nuts," was a myth that starkly contradicted his self-perceived private image—a "quiet, shy, retiring person who prefers to be with his library than anything else" (Veit-Wild, *Source Book* 37). Moreover, since Marechera had a heightened sense of self-awareness, and since he perceived identity as inherently constructed, he probed, struggled, shaped and played with his public image: "Sometimes I will act insane because that's what they expect me to do" (Veit-Wild, *Source Book* 37).

David Pattison argues that Marechera's writing is a reflection of his deteriorating mental health. "The pattern of increasing incoherence and fragmentation" that Pattison detects in the author's work is, for him, an indication of a schizophrenic mind (194). However, I align myself with Veit-Wild's perspective that the issue whether Marechera was "mad" in the clinical sense is not important for understanding his work; on the contrary, it is misleading (Veit-Wild, *Writing* 60). Instead, I am taking up Marechera's "own concept of a *de-ranged* person as someone who is set apart from society and has extraordinary powers of insight and imagination" (60). By constantly blurring the line between sanity and insanity, the author did not only gain an extraordinary level of imagination, but also an extraordinary insight into the political and social developments around him.

The main character of *Mapenzi*, Hamundigone, a veteran of the war of liberation who lost his job as a teacher because he is allegedly mentally ill, can be read as a Marecheran figure, especially in the way he recalls the persona of the "writer-tramp"—roaming the streets of Harare and silencing his inner demons with booze. Mabasa explicitly illustrates the link between his character and the late author, by letting Hamundigone refer to Marechera within the text:

> Now I truly appreciate Dambudzo Marechera's sufferings as he carried around his idiosyncratic ideas and those who didn't think the same way as him calling him insane. If you saw a lunatic staring you in the face would you know one?[5]

Hamundigone compares himself to Marechera and, like the author, he suffers from the allegation of insanity levelled against him. Indeed, the question whether the protagonist is mentally ill or not is a recurring theme throughout *Mapenzi*.

---

[5] Iko zvino ndave kunyatsonzwisisa nhamo yaionekwa naDambudzo Marechera achifamba zvake akadengezera musoro wake, dengu rizere pfungwa dzisina vazhinji, vaye vasina pfungwa sedzake vachingoti hero benzi. Imi mapenzi mukaaona munoaziva imi? (Mabasa 16)

Hamundigone is introduced to the reader as an elderly man, sitting at a public place, eating maize cobs, drinking beer, wearing a slightly soiled suit, and nodding and smiling to himself while reading *The Sunday Mail*. The reader is told by a third-person narrator that "people would glance at him and walk on by"[6]—an indication that something is unusual and slightly repelling about this character. Indeed, the way in which Hamundigone's behaviour is portrayed bolsters the image of him as a madman. He highlights some words in the newspaper with his pen as if marking a school essay, salutes at the bus stop, talks to strangers, urinates in public, leaves his fly open and does not care that bits and pieces of maize are stuck in his beard. Throughout the novel, the character holds fervent, impromptu public speeches and drinks excessively—a habit that he picked up in order to silence the songs in his head. His presence irritates, annoys, and embarrasses other characters who cross his path. The people who are caught with him in a minibus on the way to Harare, for instance, "looked at him, their faces questioning why they had ever gotten into a kombi with such a nut."[7]

However, despite signs of madness that underline Hamundigone's behaviour, hints of doubts about his mental instability are scattered throughout the story. The fellow passengers in the minibus to Harare, for instance, start to wonder whether he is truly mad: "His fellow commuters laughed with relief, thinking how unlike a usual violent madmen he was, that is if he was even mad; it could be merely drunkenness."[8] Moreover, one of the characters, Bunny, is particularly reluctant to buy into the charges of mental illness against Hamundigone, who he refers to as uncle: "I don't know, maybe it is us who are mad; the one who is really mad is difficult to know just as Reuben's uncle Ticha says" (my own translation).[9]

However, the last part of Bunny's observation is only partly true. Although Hamundigone struggles with the accusations of insanity against him and although his actions and behaviour oftentimes demarcate him as a madman, he incessantly fights against the charges of being a lunatic. He repeatedly proclaims that it is not he who is mad but everyone else around him:

> Nuts! I don't know who can tell this kind of crazy. Me crazy? Now that's real nutty. No-one likes a profound thinker who speaks his mind. That's me, wide awake and always on the ball. I'm a genius but they call me mad!

---

[6] Vanhu vaingodzitarisa vopfuura (Mabasa 6).

[7] [...] vanhu vakamutarisa zviso zvavo zvichiratidza mubvunzo wekuti benzi iri rambokwirirei mumota ino [...]. (Mabasa 10)

[8] Vanhu vakaseka zvavo kungwara kwemudhara iyeye pamwe nekufara aiita kunge benzi rakasiyana nemamwe aye ane hasha, ndokunge ari benzi, nekuti kwaigona kunge kuri kudhakwa. (Mabasa 11)

[9] Hameno, pamwe isu tisu tinopenga; anopenga chaiye anonetsa kuziva semutauriro wasekuru vaReuben, Ticha. (Mabasa 44)

Do they recognize madness when they see it? [...] By God, they are all nuts!"[10]

Throughout the novel, Hamundigone insists that he is speaking nothing but the truth. This self-assessment is also reflected in Chirere's description of the character, as

> a wanderer, going from place to place, censuring careless speakers, rebuking pretenders and social hypocrites, chiding mean and selfish relatives, criticizing the status quo, singing the latest tunes. He is a man of no fixed abode but you sense that he has a private destination—the truth. (221)

Thus it is Hamundigone who offers the most candid and truthful insight into present-day Zimbabwe. Since the allegation of madness stifles his words before they leave his mouth, he casts off social constraints and freely speaks his mind. By wandering along the brink of insanity, he is set apart from society, he moves in a borderline space that allows him an exceptional insight into the social and political developments around him.

Although in "The House of Hunger" Marechera does not speak about madness as such, the protagonist also sets himself apart from society, thus occupying a liminal space, and this allows him exceptional insight into his socio-political surrounding. This is already elucidated in the novella's remarkable opening line: "I got my things and I left." Although the protagonist's journey ends at the township's beer hall, where he sits down with a bottle of beer tucked between his legs and starts to review "all the details of the foul turd which my life had been and was even at the moment," the novella begins with the protagonist setting himself apart from the "house of hunger"—a metaphor that refers as much to his family as to the state of the Rhodesian nation, and to his own mind (Foster 59)—by packing his belongings and attempting to leave. Consequently, the reader is taken on an open-ended journey through the thoughts, reflections, and consciousness of the story's protagonist. By offering an insight into the mad mind of the protagonist, his alienation and fragmentation, Marechera comments on the state of the whole nation, which has descended into madness as a result of colonialism.

---

[10] Kupenga! Ha-a, hameno kuti kupenga kwakadai kuchazoonekwa nani chaizvo kuti kupenga. Ini chaye *kudhunya*? Ndiko kunonzi *kudhunya manje*. Vanhu havadi munhu anofunga zvakadzama achiona zvakadzika-dzika nekutaura asingakakamire. Ndinika wacho inini. [...]. Kupenga vanombukuziva here? Nhai mai, kupenga munokuziva here? Kuye kunoita kuti vanhu vagare vakakusunga necheni dzegejo? Vanhu vanoita zvekutamba nekupenga chokwadi. NaMwari chaiye vanhu vanopenga. (Mabasa 7-8)

Nation of *Mapenzi*

According to Maurice Vambe, "'The House of Hunger' deals with the effects of colonialism's psychological violence on Africans in Rhodesia" (Vambe, "Instabilities" 71). The destructive effect of colonialism on the psyche of the colonized is reflected in every character in the novella. The "House of Hunger" equals a mad house in which the violence of Ian Smith's minority rule spreads down and manifests itself within the African community, in particular the family (71).

Peter, the protagonist's brother, for instance, compensates his feelings of powerlessness in the face of colonialism by acting overtly aggressive. In order to assert his masculinity, he beats his girlfriend Immaculate "into a red stain" (Marechera, *Hunger* 14). Violence toward women is a phenomenon reverberating throughout the community: "The older generation too was learning. It still believed that if one did not beat up one's wife it meant that one did not love her at all" (64). The protagonist's father tries to escape the hardships by excessive drinking that exacerbates his violent behaviour towards his family: "I knew my father only as a character who occasionally screwed my mother and who paid the rent, beat me up, and was cuckolded on the sly by various persons" (95). Neither does the protagonist's mother provide a refuge from the omnipresent violence:

> But mother was more feared than respected. [...] [S]he was good in fights, and verbal sallies, never losing face; and more important for me, she had nothing better to do than to throw her children into the lion's den of things white. (96)

Stretching from the family into the community, township life is portrayed in the novella as a spiral of violence and moral decay—which, combined with the confusions and blocked aspirations stemming from his Western education, pushes the protagonist over the edge of sanity. In accordance with Laing's perspective on psychopathological illnesses, he responds to his social environment by suffering a nervous breakdown "a few weeks before my sixth-form examination—which I then had to write with the assistance of white tranquilizers and pink triangular pills" (41).

In *Mapenzi*, it is implied already in the opening chapter that madness is a sickness that has taken hold of the entire Zimbabwean nation:

> My mind is now numbed by some new infirmity now in Zimbabwe, which is neither AIDS nor any kind of VD. One looks at what you are and realizes it needs changing but finds no time, strength, hope, or even a place to begin.[11]

---

[11] Pfungwa dzave nechiveve. MuZimbabwe muya mave nechirwere, chirwere chisiri njovhera kana

Reminiscent of Marechera's descriptions of township life in Rhodesia, the characters of *Mapenzi* are caught in their struggles to survive, to make ends meet, which translates into a loss of any moral compass or, as Itai Muhwati and David Mutasa state, "it is not possible to uphold morality because survival takes precedence over morality" (Mutasa and Muhwati 7). We learn from Magi, a young university student, that most female students, including herself, prostitute themselves in order to subsidize their meagre student loans:

> Also the money that we are given is too little for us to get what we want, I just did what every girl here is doing. They knowingly have affairs with married men and tell you that they are only looking for money to survive. Many of them deny that they are whores but the truth is that we are all whores.[12]

Magi ends up being raped by her married lover, Mangwiro. Violence and sexual exploitation appear to be ubiquitous: Saba sleeps with prostitutes in front of his wife, May Tanya, and his behaviour is so abusive that he finally kills her; Eddie, the husband of Heaven, is a loafer living at his mother-in-law's house and forces her maid Saru to have sex with him; Heaven sexually abuses Reuben, the son of her sister, Maud, who stays with her for a few days after his mother died of HIV/AIDS.

Thus, Hamundigone's repeated exclamation that, "These people are mad. We are all mad people, mad" (qtd. in Chirere 222), contains some truth. In fact, within the novel, the collapse of morality and the insane and destructive behaviour of the characters are linked to the corruption and mismanagement of the government, whose rule has plunged the country into a devastating economic crisis and has shattered the dream that surrounded Independence.

The slashing of meta-narratives
This link between the nation's descent into madness and the Mugabe regime's (mis-)rule of the country is most clearly established through the protagonist, Hamundigone. It is him who voices the harshest critique of the government and its institutions and repeatedly laments the state of the nation. He openly accuses the government of corruption, saying "these rude people who get their jobs corruptly are such a pain"[13] and openly complains about the inefficiency of the government (Mabasa 16).

---

mukondembera. Munhu unotarisa zvauri woona kuti zvinoda kushandurwa. (Mabasa 5)

[12] *Also* nenyaya yekuti mari yetinopiwa ishoma kuti ikuitirewo zvaunoda, *I just did like what most girls are doing* pano. Vanodanana nevarume vevanhu vachinyatsozviziva, asi *they tell you* kuti vari kuda kungowana mari yekuti vararame. Vazhinji vacho vanoramba kuti havasi mahure, asi chokwadi ndechekuti tese titongori mahure. (Mabasa 48-49)

[13] Vakandiita kuti ndinzwe hasha chaizvo. (Mabasa 16)

His harshest critique, however, is his observation that those who are now in power legitimize their positions by having fought in the war, despite the fact that many of them never did and were not scarred by the Boers' bullets:

> I am not mad but I know those who are mad. We know those who are mad. It is those who claim to have fought in the war when they did not. And those who claim that they saw too much blood and no longer feel well yet they lead the nation.[14]

Thus, Hamundigone turns the allegations of madness around. It is not him who is mad; on the contrary, the people in power who declared him insane are actually the mad ones. Indeed, he explains to Bunny that the accusations of mental instability against him were a strategy by the government to be able to fire him, to silence him, since he told his pupils "the truth about events that happened during the war, things my comrades are lying about today."[15] This recalls Foucault's theory that madness is constructed by the powerful—or powerful social structures within society—in opposition to reason in order to silence the voices of the "mad"—individuals who refuse to fit into or fall out of the hegemonic structures of society. Yet, in *Mapenzi*, Hamundigone repeatedly emphasizes that, if he is mad at all, it is the personal greed and hunger for power by the man in charge, that pushed him close to the edge of insanity: "I fought so that we all could be haves, all eat, and all prosper so that if we starve, we all starve, not for only one man to have access."[16]

It is not only him who suffers from this discrepancy—between having believed in and fought for an ideal that has been slashed by the post-war reality. Instead, the character of Hamundigone can be read as a Marecheran figure mirroring the state of the whole nation. According to Muhwati,

> the whole nation is being pursued and tormented by the very historical processes which sought to liberate its people—the war of liberation. [...] For the majority, the war was a goal-oriented undertaking. The betrayal and the abandonment of such goals triggers various psychological and physical reactions. (Muhwati 16)

---

[14] Ini handipengi, asi vanopenga ndinovaziva. Vanopenga tinovaziva. Ndavaye vanoti vakarwa hondo ivo vasina kurwa hondo. Ndevanoti vakaona ropa rakawanda saka havachanzwi zvakanaka ivo vachishanda kutungamira vanhu. (Mabasa 134)

[15] Ndaivaudza chokwadi chenyaya dzakaitika kuhondo, nyaya dziri kunyepwa nevamwe vangu nhasi uno. (Mabasa 139)

[16] Ndakarwa kuti tese tiwane, tese tidye, tese tigute – kuti kana toziya, toziya tese, kwete kuti munhu mumwe chete ndiye anenge achitambura nekudzvova tsvi. (Mabasa 140)

Hamundigone summarizes his experiences as a former war veteran in post-independent Zimbabwe, his disillusionment and alienation:

> Zimbabwe has mauled me so that even today the wounds remain unhealed and unfaded like the scars that I brought back from Mozambique. It scooped out the very heart of me, like you do with Vaseline and left a gaping hole that can't be closed. I have seen much in life for which I have no words to explain.[17]

The war has left deep scars, not only on his body, but also on his mind. In post-independent Zimbabwe, however, he does not reap any benefits from the deeds he has done for his country. On the contrary, he is declared mentally unstable for speaking his mind, he has lost his job, and he is left to struggle for his daily survival.

In *Mapenzi*, Mabasa offers a counter-narrative to the ZANU-PF version of Zimbabwe's past, which Ranger has termed "patriotic history." The patriotic history glorifies the Second *Chimurenga* and the actions of the men who fought for the independence of their country, masking the internal ethnic and gender-based divisions and the injustices that were committed in the name of these identities. Indeed, ZANU-PF justifies its grip on power on the grounds that it freed Zimbabwe from the shackles of colonialism. Yet, the story of Hamundigone turns this narrative upside down: those who fought in the war are now at the bottom of society.

Such a take on national history reflects Marechera's views and his refusal to contribute to the body of African literature concerned with national reconstruction.[18] In "The House of Hunger," cultural nationalism is satirized by the character of Steven, who "was mean, a bully; a typical African bully at an ordinary African school" and who espouses the negritudist trend of thought of firmly believing that there is "something peculiarly African in anything written by an African" (63). Although Marechera reflects on and condemns colonial oppression, he questions any grand ideology, including African nationalism, on the grounds that it reifies and essentializes black identity, and thus denies "the complexities of class, race, gender and generational conflicts that presently define African realities" (Vambe, "Instabilities" 71). Although Marechera wrote twenty years earlier than Mabasa, he predicted, with almost prophetical insight, that the war would not result in freedom, equality, and national unity, as promised by the proponents of African nationalism.

---

[17] Zimbabwe yakandimara zvekuti mamaranzurwa ayo nanhasi ari kuramba kupora nekufudzika kunge mavanga andakabva nawo kuMozambique. Yakandinombora kunge *vaseline*, ndikasara ndave neburi risingavharike. Ndakaona zvakawanda muupenyu zvisina mashoko ekuzvitaura. (Mabasa 14)

[18] See Shaw as well as Chennells/Veit-Wild.

Mad metaphors, mad writing

"Stitches," "wounds," "stains," "blood," and "stench"—these are some of the key words that repeatedly leap off the pages of "The House of Hunger," sketching a violent, disruptive, and distressing mood. Indeed, Marechera perceived his writing to be a kind of "literary shock treatment" intended to cure his readership from "slow brain death" (Veit-Wild, *Source Book* 41). Yet, in order to be able to express himself and his own experiences in the English language, he had to "have harrowing fights and hair-raising panga duels with the language before you can make it do all that you want it to do" (Veit-Wild, *Source Book* 4). It is this process of appropriating the English language—"standing it on its head, brutalizing it into a more malleable shape for my own purposes" (4)—which enabled Marechera to hammer "the cries of the colonized into the language of the colonizer" (Veit-Wild, "Zimbolicious" 693).

Although Mabasa admires Marechera's ability to tame the English language, he has chosen to write in Shona—he claims that inspiration comes to him almost always in his mother tongue and only a few exceptional individuals, like Marechara, are successful in shaping the English idiom in ways that express their own experiences (Mabasa, *Why I Write*). Nonetheless, his use of language in *Mapenzi* has revolutionized the Shona novel. Instead of sticking to a standard Shona, the author uses a style of language that reflects the socio-linguistic reality of present-day Harare. Thus, *Mabasa* intersperses the text with slang-words and frequently interlaces the narrative text, as well as the dialogues, with code-switches from Shona to the English language.

For instance, the author interweaves English words into Hamundigone's speech: "*ndakafitwa here nekuti hiri-hiri ini*" (Mabasa, *Mapenzi* 7). As the example illustrates, an English root, "fit," is embedded within the Shona verbal structure, creating the expression *ndakafitwa* ("it fits me well") (my own translation). He also sprinkles slang words into his character's speech. An example for this is Hamundigone's exclaimation: "*Ini chaiye kudhunya?*" (7). *Kudhunya* is a Shona slang word for mad; hence, the sentence means "Me really mad?" (my own translation).[19]

Critics such as John Gambanga argue that "making excessive use of English in a Shona novel" is tantamount to "daily assassinating our beautiful language, allowing it to play second fiddle to others. That is wrong and unpatriotic" (quoted in Chirere 223). Yet, as Chirere has rightfully observed, the practice of code-switching is neither arbitrary nor artificial:

> By making his characters code-switch from Shona to English, he portrays their social and academic status, thus adding to their characterization.

---

[19] A glossary of slang words, translated into Shona, are listed in an appendix to the novel.

> The young tend to code-switch but the old, like Maud's mother, stick to a "standard" Shona and its idioms. It would, however, be unrealistic and out of character for an educated person like Magi to speak in traditional Shona with its archaisms. (Chirere 222)

Besides reflecting the social change, status, and difference, code-switching often-times infers social critique. This is exemplified as Hamundigone meets a former comrade of his—they fought side by side during the war of liberation—on a street corner in Harare. However, now, the latter is a *shefu*, a big man in politics, owning a Mercedes-Benz, while the former is an unemployed social "nothing" (Veit-Wild, "Zimbolicious" 696). The *shefu* expresses the social rift between the two men as he switches from Shona to English as he calls out to his driver: "Hey Mr. Driver *itai kuti* security *ibvise munhu uyu pano*" (Hey Driver get security to remove this person from here) (Mabasa, *Mapenzi* 19).

Mabasa's creative use of language is further conveyed in that he invents new words, phrases, and proverbs—most of which are imbued with irony and social critique. For instance, Hamundigone's most scathing critique of the government is summarized in a riddle he poses to bystanders at the bus stop in Bindura: "The pot was burned cooking sadza. But only the plates from their shelf went to the table."[20] As Veit-Wild points out, with this riddle, the author,

> wants to point at the discrepancy between those who were injured and did the actual fighting ("burnt") in the war of liberation and those who stayed behind, "on the shelf" (who were working in offices in foreign countries, were studying abroad or stayed behind in Zimbabwe). These are now the ones in display and in charge (used for serving the food "on the table"). ("Zimbolicious" 696)

Indeed, riddles, allegories, and fables—all of which containing an element of social critique—appear extensively in Hamundigone's speech. The folktale of the owl that he tells his nephew Reuben is yet another example of a fable with an underlying message of social critique: Owl forces the other birds to do whatever he wants by pretending to have horns (Mabasa, *Mapenzi* 132). Yet, the meaning of his words is obscured by his inclination to speak constantly and often incoher-ently—ironically a characteristic he himself ascribes to mad people (Musengezi 2009). Sometimes, he even makes up words, such as *sikarabhonya*, in order to express the images of his jumbled mind (Mabasa, *Mapenzi* 8). Thus, his speech is very much akin to the ramblings of a madman. He even says so himself: "You

---

[20] Poto yakatsva ichibika sadza pamoto, Asi kutebhuru kukaenda ndiro dzaive musherefu? (Mabasa 9)

people are all listening to one man—do you think I am sane? These are but the ramblings of a lunatic—let them be."[21]

This again links *Mapenzi* to "The House of Hunger" which ends with the ramblings of the old man. His stories, which can be read as a meta-narrative to the novella, are "oblique, rambling, and fragmentary" (Marechera, *Hunger* 79). Yet all of them are allegories containing elements of social critique. In one of them, for instance, a man and his wife eat a magic egg that later returns in order to haunt them (Marechera, *Hunger* 81). According to Vambe, the story implies "that the system of colonial violence generated its own contradictions that were to be resolved through African cultural nationalism" (Vambe, "Instabilities" 71). Yet, in the other stories, the old man also exposes the flaws of African nationalism. For instance,

> In one such folk-narrative alluding to cultural nationalism, a hunter of women ends up hunting within himself. There is in the story criticism of the narcissism of cultural nationalism's belief in originary and intact cultural roots. (71)

While both Marechera and Mabasa create characters who utter profound truths about the political developments of the time, their message is hidden behind a fragmentary and figurative speech—one has to scratch the surface to grasp the meanings of the words. Both works allude to and play with the proverb: Fools and madmen speak the truth.

However, in the writing of the two authors, madness appears most strikingly on yet another level, namely on the level of language itself, particularly in their use of metaphors.

> I leaned back against the *msasa* tree and lay still, trying not to think about the House of Hunger where the acids of gut-rot had eaten into the base metal of my brain. The House has now become my mind; and I do not like the way the roof is rattling. (Marechera, *Hunger* 24)

This passage illustrates that the linchpin of Marechera's metaphors is his unique combination of completely different semantic fields. On one side, words such as "acids" and "base metal" are technical terms, predominantly used in the field of chemistry. On the other, "gut" and "brain" belong to the field of the human body. While the ones are hard and biting, the others are soft and fleshy. These semantic clashes which permeate all of Marechera's writing belong to the major source of

---

[21] Saka nemiwo muri kutonditeerera muchiti ndakakwana here? Ndakanzi ndiri benzi saka zvangu siyanai nazvo. (Mabasa 33)

his creativity and of the shocking and provocative quality of his imagery. While the linking of the gut-rot metaphor with the metal quality of the roof offers an incredible insight into the peculiar quality of that House, its "rattling" then tones this down to a mundane level and makes it utterly funny and (self-)ironic. The protagonist's mental state reflecting the madness of his social surroundings jumps at the reader from the page, from the very linguistic level.

Similarly, in the first chapter of *Mapenzi*, entitled "Munhu" (person)[22], unusual metaphors insinuate an abnormal, mad mind—which can be read as an element of foreboding in regard to the disquieted mind of Hamundigone and the distressing state of the nation:

> But the horns of my thoughts are locked. They are fastened together in a knot. They stop me from grappling with raw ideas, [I can only grapple] with ideas that have been chewed until they are soft (transl. by Rettová 217).[23]

Here, again, the strength of the metaphors is rooted in the deliberate clash of semantic fields: terms from the realm of concrete rural and domestic life (horns, knot, raw, chewing) are brought together with abstract concepts (thoughts, ideas). The thoughts are obscure and intangible—since they are entangled into a knot. This leaves the anonymous narrator with a jumbled mind, unable to absorb and understand ("chew") new, unprocessed ("raw") ideas.

Conclusion

The publication of *Mapenzi* signifies a milestone in Zimbabwean literature. The novel has revolutionized Shona literature, particularly in regard to Mabasa's creative use of language. John Gambanga even speculates that Mabasa "could be the Shakespeare that we have been waiting for" (qtd. in Chirere 221). Moreover, the writer has started to interweave the hitherto separate strands of literature in Shona on the one hand, and literature in English on the other. As has been shown, Mabasa establishes an especially strong connection not only through a direct intertextual reference but also and more importantly, through his particular handling of madness as a topic and a literary device. Hence, as I have argued, Ha-

---

[22] This chapter is set apart from the others, by being narrated by an anonymous, unknown voice that addresses "a not so definite audience" and that "asks no questions and expects no answers" (Chirere 222).

[23] Asi, nyanga dzepfungwa dzangu dziri kukochekerana. Dziri kusungana, kuita pfundo. Dziri kundirambidza kurwa nemazano mambishi, kwete mazano akatsengwa akawota. (Mabasa 5). I am quoting Rettová here, since she provides a more accurate translation of this sentence. Also, note here, the usage of the noun class 10, with the prefix *dz-*, is also reserved for animals and inanimate objects and might imply here an unusual, distressed mind.

mundigone can be read as a Marecheran figure mirroring the state of the nation.

Mapenzi was published twenty years after "The House of Hunger" in a different historical era: the Rhodesian Settler regime had been finally defeated in 1980 and, for a bit over a decade, Zimbabwe could proudly count itself amongst the African states that had forcefully unshackled the grip of colonialism. Yet, by investigating the meaning of madness within both works—its form and function—it quickly becomes evident that while the historical setting may have changed, the state of the nation has remained distressing and disruptive. In both works, characters appear who, by hovering on the brink of insanity and moving in a liminal state, illustrate an exceptional insight into the social and political developments surrounding them.

While the narrator-protagonist in "The House of Hunger" delineates how in response to Ian Smith's minority regime, his family, community, and the whole nation have turned into a mad house, Mabasa affirms Marechera's prophecy: the war of liberation, fought under the flag of African nationalism, will not and did not provide the cure. Instead, as his novel illustrates, the corruption and mismanagement of the country under Mugabe's rule have plunged the nation into a state of madness.

"A Melodrama of the Voluptuous"*
Marechera's Love Poetry

Gerald Gaylard

What connects us? What is desire? What makes us desire another? What are the politics of desire and love? These are questions which the subjects of desire and love perennially raise, but which are politically sharpened in a postcolonial context due to the social exigencies (or "rhetoric of urgency" as Bethelehem put it) in operation. The intense pressurising of the personal and cultural by the contextual that takes place in the postcolony is perhaps nowhere more evident than in the extremist writing of Dambudzo Marechera in newly independent 1980's Zimbabwe which argued for the "rights of desire" (Coetzee 89). Whilst there has been interesting recent work on Marechera, for instance Annie Gagiano explores his writing on war and Dick Mafuba undertakes a close reading of his long poem "Throne of Bayonets," his love poetry has received scant critical attention. This is regrettable both because of the rarity of love poetry in the Zimbabwean context (partly due to the sense of social urgency referred to above) and because Marechera deals so insightfully with the intricacies of relations between self and other within a racialised and bordered world. In order to approach Marechera's treatment of love between self and other I shall survey the recent theoretical work on this topic in postcolonialism, partly in order to illuminate what Marechera's writing might add to postcolonial theory within the ambit of desire as resistance, an idea suggested by Achille Mbembe's *On the Postcolony*.

Much postcolonialism has taken a Levinasian turn of late, arguing that the best postcolonial literature ethically confronts the reader with unassimilable alterity. Southern African literary criticism, for instance, has been centred on progress and ethics: work on the Truth and Reconciliation Commission such as Mark Sanders' *Ambiguities of Witnessing*; Derek Attridge's book *J.M. Coetzee and the Ethics of Reading*; Mike Marais's work on Levinasian ethics in Coetzee; Stefan Helgesson's *Writing in Crisis: Ethics and History in Gordimer, Ndebele and Coetzee*, are all examples of this focus. Helgesson articulates the central argument of this recent Levinasian ethical criticism when he insists that

---

* This paper was previously published in a substantially different form as "Love in the Time of Illness: Marechera's Love Poetry." *English Studies in Africa* 50. 2 (2007): 89-100.

the other cannot be *known*. Knowledge and understanding are both imperialistic categories, incommensurable with the ethical dimension of the face-to-face relation. The intentional operations of knowledge appropriate the other, totalise it and deprive it of its alterity. Instead, the other, *qua* other, surpasses understanding, surpasses philosophy with its traditional focus on the ego. The untotalisable other can only be compared to an irreducible infinity. (194)

The refusal to appropriate the other and the attempt to respect the radical incommensurability of that other are most appealing in this argument, and generally characteristic of postcolonialism. Attridge's Levinasian reading of Coetzee runs thus: "we encounter the singular demands of the other. Coetzee's works both stage, and are, irruptions of otherness into our familiar worlds, and they pose the question: what is our responsibility towards the other?" (xii). This ethicalising alterity entails "responsibility": the other interpellates, makes "demands," is an "irruption." In other words, alterity in this Levinasian postcolonialism appears to derive from theology, modernity's individualism and the existentialist emphasis upon responsibility. Indeed, it could even be claimed that this particular version of alterity within postcoloniality is a reflection of white guilt or colonial cringe. Whilst it is true that Levinas writes of love and desire in *Totality and Infinity* pointing out that "Love aims at the Other" (256), and he does write of eros, fecundity and filiality, this is not a central argument or concern in his work.

If we analyse this version of otherness promoted by Southern African postcolonial critics, it becomes apparent that it is indeed just one version of alterity. Whilst it is necessary to keep this absolute otherness of alterity constantly in mind, if it is not unforgettably "in your face" (particularly within violent colonial and postcolonial contexts), the postcolonial Levinasian argument tends to ignore that the other is not always absolute and essential. The Levinas that postcolonial critics foreground understands alterity theologically and tends to make alterity extreme, if not apocalyptic. At a general level, one might counter this argument with the seeming banality that not every other is as "Big" as Lacan or Levinas's infinity-God Other, and that there is usually some common humanity, at least in terms of basic needs for air, water, food, shelter and community, between human others. Incommensurability between self and other is not always a clear gulf, but often a porous and shifting boundary. The aspects of sameness and self that the other echoes may provide an avenue of approach. Moreover, difference itself and the exotic can be the mechanism of the initial engagement between self and other. The postcolonial argument about alterity disregards the fact that whilst the other may be an object of subject-construction, of self-othering, it may also be an object/subject of allure, not only because of what it can mean for the self, but precisely because of its own self, its exotic difference. As Baudrillard points out,

"In order for there to be alterity, there must be some reversibility. Not the opposition of separate terms like me and another person but the fact that the two are in the same boat, with the same fate" (*Radical Alterity* 126).

To advance my argument at its broadest, my heretical sense (a sense I think Marechera shared) is that literature is as much about desire as it is about ethics, improvement or progress. Levinasian postcolonialism tends to ignore desire, *jouissance* and, dare I say it, love, in favour of ethics and responsibility. This ethicalising argument seems to me to have shifted the political overdetermination of postcolonial writing, particularly African, towards an ethical overdetermination, eliding in its good intentions desire and freedom, let alone *jouissance* and wickedness. This tends to limit literature in my view; as Tolkien famously put it, the only people worried about escape are jailers. If we want to take the literature of desire and literature as desire seriously then we might turn away from Levinasian postcolonialism to other theorists who have overtly written of love and desire. The work of Baudrillard, Kristeva and Irigaray is prominent in this area and suggests most strongly the link between postcolonial others and desire.

Identification with the other is what Derrida, Lacan, Kristeva and Irigaray, in different ways, have called *jouissance* or play because it involves desire. The emphasis upon desire has its roots in the Surrealist "pleasure principle" that desire makes the world go around, a principle derived from the omnivorous Menippean tradition of literature. Postmodernism inherited this Surrealist idea; Baudrillard, for instance, summed up *jouissance* as "the haemorrhaging of value, the disintegration of the code, of the repressive logos" ("Beyond the Unconscious" 70-71) and related alterity to seduction and provocation in *Radical Alterity*. Moreover, *jouissance* may be social as well as psychological. This is perhaps most apparent in Bakhtin's carnivalesque which advanced the idea of *jouissance* as a socially liberating transgressive desire: "as opposed to the official feast, one might say that the carnival celebrated temporary liberation from the prevailing truth and established order; it marked the suspension of all hierarchical rank, privileges, norms and prohibitions" (10).

Kristeva similarly describes freedom as *jouissance*, an idea she developed from Barthes and which seems similar to Bakhtin's more sociologically orientated concept of carnival. *Jouissance* for Kristeva is an "experience" of "nonsense" akin to an amniotic lack of boundaries and borders. There would be no *jouissance* if there were not escape from repression: "she experiences *jouissance* in nonsense through repression" (*Desire in Language* 154). *Jouissance* is similar to the abject which is a reminiscence of the infant's unity with the mother in the pre-Oedipal stage; the abject confronts the subject with the spuriousness of the self created by the infant when it rejected the (m)other in entering the symbolic order. How does this *jouissance* occur? According to Kristeva, *jouissance* occurs via "A polyphony – but also to wipe out sense through nonsense and laughter. This is a difficult operation that obliges the reader not so much to combine significations as to shatter his own judging consciousness in order to grant passage through it to this rhythmic drive constituted by repression and, once filtered by language and its meaning, experienced as jouissance" (*Desire in Language* 142).

Taking this idea into the postcolonial, my feeling is that postcolonialism not only involves the ethical demand of incommensurable alterity, but also the *jouis-sance* of desire for the exotic other. Exoticism can bring self and other into a de-familiarising propinquity which disturbs habitual consciousness, allowing a brief respite from the repressions of the self and its home culture, a respite experienced as *jouissance*. This is distinct from imperial otherings which typically keep the other at an abject distance. Irigaray in *The Way of Love* expands on this linkage between desire and the other by showing that desire is a "bilateral approach" which involves "drawing near" to the other: "the approach here must be bilateral: I not only have to draw near to the other, we must succeed in drawing near to one another" (65). For Irigaray,

> To approach implies [...] becoming aware of the diversity of our worlds and creating paths which, with respect for this diversity, allow holding dialogues. Being placed side by side does not suffice for reaching near-ness. This local, cultural, national proximity can even prevent the approach because the forgetting of the fact that going the path towards the other is never achieved, requires an unceasing effort and not a standing in the same. [...] For an incitement to such a task, it is not enough to let oneself be there where we already are. (68-70)

Irigaray, like Levinas, insists that the other remains other, that the space between the self and other not be colonised by projections and a self-satisfied surety, but she emphasises desire far more than Levinas. In Irigaray's view, the other is not necessarily an apocalyptic difference, an absolute separation, from the self, but may be desirable and pursued/accepted. There is a connection, a pathway, between the self and other in this view. In other words, desire may not always involve projection, but can be the desire for difference.

What I am attempting is a catachrestic misuse of Kristeva's *jouissance* and abjection via Irigaray's notions of love to demonstrate that there can be a positive mechanism of interaction between self and other in the postcolonial. Baudrillard and Guillaume, using Victor Segalen, point out that the interaction between self and other can be a form of "radical exoticism" that need not replicate the "fiction of the Other" that characterises Modernity, imperialism and tourism (47-48). The self who embraces the other, often via the exotic initially, strays from their home culture:

strays instead of getting his bearings, desiring, belonging, or refusing. [...]
He is on a journey, during the night, the end of which keeps receding. He
has a sense of the danger, of the loss that the pseudo-object attracting represents for him, but he cannot help taking the risk at the very moment he
sets himself apart. And the more he strays, the more he is saved. [...] For
it is out of such straying on excluded ground that he draws his *jouissance*.
(*Powers of Horror* 8)

So the embrace of difference via the exotic is dangerous and frightening, for it
requires trust not only to embrace the new and unknown, but also to abandon the
self and its culture: "'I' am in the process of becoming an other at the expense of
my own death" (*Powers of Horror* 3). In other words, the exotic exposes the desire and fear at the heart of all culture. We desire to escape, but fear embracing the
new and unknown. Otherness in postcolonialism is both desire for escape from
the entrapping, and the playful and dangerous desire for the new and strange. We
play joyfully to usher in the other, and with trepidation in order to defer a dangerous other.

   Postcolonialism in this view can be seen as the desire to break colonial racial
and sexual borders, to become a citizen of the global by being a citizen of the
other; a desire for something else, the other. But it is also a desire to escape the
self, the local, the repressive, abjection within the home culture. In this fearful
desire for freedom what we have is the creation of a hybrid, and a confrontation
with how difficult hybridity is. As Kristeva has it: "But when I *seek* (myself), *lose*
(myself), or experience *jouissance*—then 'I' is *heterogeneous*" (*Powers of Horror* 10). In other words, postcolonialism creates hybridity through the other and
the desire that the other engenders in the self.

   So far I have emphasised this propinquity between self and other at an interpersonal level, and this is certainly visible in recent work on the politics of
transcultural friendship such as Fabio Durão and Dominic Williams' *Modernist
Group Dynamics: The Politics and Poetics of Friendship*, Elleke Boehmer's *Empire, the National, the Postcolonial, 1890-1920: Resistance in Interaction* which
traced the influence of Tagore on Yeats and Leela Gandhi's *Affective Communities: Anticolonial Thought, Fin-de-Siècle Radicalism, and the Politics of Friendship*. Moreover, interactions also take place at a cultural level, and we might see
the long history of imperial exoticisms as a negative instance of that. However,
the current vogue for transnationalism is also an acknowledgement that positive
interactions between self and other have always been historically and socially
ongoing alongside less positive relations.

   So whilst one might not normally associate French postmodernism with postcolonialism, I hope to show that the postmodern concern with desire in Kristeva
and Irigary helps to explain some of the most radical literary practices of postco-

lonial African writers that connect the personal to the political. In Coetzee's *In the Heart of the Country* and Landsman's *The Devil's Chimney* cross-racial love for the other is not merely a desire to embrace difference, but to extinguish an identity about which the colonial protagonists feel white guilt. This desire when consummated does not result in an equitable, sustained relationship with that other, primarily because there is too much of a power hierarchy involved. This begs the question, can a desire to embrace alterity result in a positive engagement? Outside of oppressive colonial power and identities, some writers suggest that there is a possibility of such a positive engagement.

A postcolonial exotic that desires and trusts alterity in Africa is to be found in the ludic fiction of Marechera and Sello Duiker, amongst others. This fiction, because it gives desire free rein, allows for various forms of embracing the other. Both authors, in their lives as well as their fiction, embraced otherness as a route towards a redefinition of self. What their writing reveals is the Dionysian underbelly of desire and eroticism that seems to be silenced in conventional Southern African society and fiction by a form of macho repression. Sello Duiker's protagonist in *The Quiet Violence of Dreams* utilises homosexuality as a defamiliarising alterity, as a way of reinventing himself. Marechera's promiscuous desire and love for the other also challenges the postcolonial orthodoxy that the other confronts us with existentialist responsibility, suggesting that we need a new postcolonialism beyond that influenced by Levinas. Marechera has two poetic sequences in which he explores his desire for the exotic other: the relatively chaotic *écriture automatique* of 1983's "My Arms Vanished Mountains" (which was actually destroyed in a fit of rage by the poet and reconstituted from the tapes of his reading of the poem in the published version) and the more coherent "Amelia" poems written between 1984 and 1985 (both collected in *Cemetery of Mind*). Some of the poems in "Heaven's Terrible Ecstasy" (1984) also deal with love and desire.

The Amelia poems are a sequence of thirteen poems, perhaps suggesting Marechera's characteristic bad luck (Dambudzo in Shona means "bad luck"), exploring the full gamut from ecstasy to despair of his relationship to "Amelia," a white woman, in post-independence Harare. Flora Veit-Wild's essay in this book, "Me and Dambudzo: A Personal Essay" makes it clear that this white woman was herself (though other women may have also have played a part in the construction of the character and image of Amelia). Veit-Wild portrays their relationship as tempestuous, not least because she was married and a mother at the time. Marechera's desire for Occidental alterity, a European lover, estranges his self, a theme he is able to convey via a defamiliarising free verse poetry that refuses to be bound to any convention. Perhaps unsurprisingly, Flora Veit-Wild recalls in her personal essay in this book that she also "had always had a longing for the wondrous, the fantastic, the outlandish. Dambudzo appealed to the clownish, melancholic, poetic part of me" ("Me and Dambudzo" 192).

In his introduction to the Amelia sequence, Marechera claims that "the self-consciousness of the structure, the form" (168) of these poems is an immortality strategy, suggesting that whilst love and lovers are mortal, the "poetry [...] when it is good, is immortal." Marechera refuses "to be bound by any period of human history" and makes "selective use of myth and legend" in this immortality strategy. This myth and legend is often Eurocentric, ranging from classical references ("Amelia's at Apollo's Shrine" 178) to Trotsky ("Agony Column" 179). Yet along with this metaphorisation of love via classical and modern European culture, there are also repetitive references to primal animals and animality (cockroaches and crocodiles 176); death, loss, phantoms, ghosts and haunting; pain and suffering (concentration camp lampshades 176). As Marechera makes clear in "A Phantom of Delight," the second poem in the sequence, "love's hellish vision" is a phantom of loss, a spectre that defamiliarises our Eurocentric or conventional understandings which beautify and etherealise love, removing it from suffering and the physically grotesque. His project is thus not just to meditate upon love and desire but to show that our habitual modes of doing so, both imagistic and linguistic, are hidebound and inadequate as part of his characteristic iconoclastic quest for liberation. Rather than "returning" to an African authenticity which was the common cultural move at that time, Marechera attempts to defamiliarise love by engaging with, and deconstructing, European culture. Modern Eurocentric individualist romance falls apart in the Zimbabwean context riven by historical and social divisions, a context in which gothic imagery that connects the primal chthonic to social violence is more appropriate.

Marechera's insurrectionary quest for psychosexual freedom involved a number of important literary and socio-cultural interventions. Not only would he deconstruct received cultural tropes and images, but he had to be prepared to both use and abandon any and all traditions, particularly those that associated identity with sexuality and power. He had to be prepared to challenge gender roles, in particular any sense of himself as a conventional phallogocentric male and the idea of femininity as passive. He had to embrace alterity, particularly in the form of European others, which led him into a Kristevan territory of *jouissance* and abjection, what he calls in his introduction to the Amelia sequence "the delight of pure sexual pleasure [...] when thought and calculation are banished out of sight. A melodrama of the voluptuous" (167). And, finally, he had to find a new and appropriate style and register in which to write this new form of love.

That this examination of self in relation to the romantically desired other was central to Marechera is apparent in the self-conscious introduction to his Amelia poems: "Give loneliness a platform and its speech will be poetry. To become one with another is simultaneously to lose and acquire one's identity. When I look in the mirror it is Amelia's face which—in astonishment—gazes back at me"

(167). Poetry was a means to examine the self-othering of desire. What he found
is that this poetic discipline had fallen into decline during the struggle years in
Zimbabwe. "When Love's Perished," the first poem in the sequence and in four-
teen line sonnet form with a conventional octave and sestet, shows that the love
poem between two culturally different people has been "sticky with centuries'
sleep/ And anaemic from lack of iron discipline/ And pallid from years' diet of
political slogans/ And wedged under the door between Europe and Africa" (169).
Marechera's project is to resuscitate this sleeping beauty poem and he does it by
transculturating the romantic sonnet via the violent imagery of interpersonal and
cultural conflict. Just as a title, "When Love's Perished" bodes ill and suggests
that this will be no sentimentally romantic sequence but every bit as excoriating
as Baudelaire's *Le Fleurs du mal*, for instance. It is worth noting I think that ap-
proximately seven other poems in the Amelia sequence are close to sonnet form,
though Marechera does not scruple to play with the form via enjambment, single
word lines, and, most importantly, unlovely imagery. This suggests Marechera's
conflicted relationship with the heritage of European literature, a literature that
he both uses and abuses in his attempt to locate himself within and beyond its
carnivalesque Menippean stream (Marechera, "The African Writer's Experience
of European Literature" 101).[1] The subject of the poem is an individual, presum-
ably Marechera himself, who is in a state of primal fear about commitment: "One
whose slow measured pace to the altar/ Raised more dust than buffalo stamped-
ing—/ The soft sweaty palm in limpid handshake/ Hid a grizzly bear's powerful
claws" (169). Underneath the politesse of his limp handshake are the claws of the
hard-wired neural cortex in a fight or flight conflict to the death. This suggests
not only that Marechera partially rejects the Western heritage of the romantic in
his emphasis upon the psychology of primal drives, but also that this psychology
was uniquely his own.

Flora Veit-Wild in *Dambudzo Marechera: A Source Book on his Life and
Work* claims that "The most significant event in the writer's childhood was his father's death in February 1966" (51), and certainly it was the case that his faith in
masculinity was impaired by the death of his impoverished and disempowered father in a car accident when he was thirteen. However, his conflictual relationship
with the mother who had named him "bad luck" or "trouble maker," passed her
grandmother's witch spirit into him (*Source Book* 53-4) and later turned to drink
and prostitution (*Source Book* 17) surely also sculpted his psyche. Moreover,
he contracted venereal disease from his first, drunken, sexual experience with a
prostitute which left him feeling that "I can never really divorce the feeling that
the very desire, the lust, the passion for a woman, will make me come out of this
more and more diseased" (*Source Book* 14). He also noted in an interview that

---

[1] This lecture is included on the DVD.

his sexual disgust was exacerbated by the general abuse of women in the township: "Poverty can drive one into obscure sexual passions: if economically you cannot assert yourself, you try to assert yourself as a human being sexually. This means, any woman, any girl out there will do. [...] That's why women were the ultimate victims of racism in this country" (*Source Book* 13). Further, he claimed that his first love was a coloured girl called Margaret Miller (*Source Book* 15), perhaps as a result of his persistent desire for difference and escape from the house of hunger. As he noted, the desire to escape from poverty and deprivation in the township "meant ignoring the poverty of others. [...] It's very selfish. I had been reading all these books from the rubbish dump and I knew there was another world out there. And I wanted to break into it" (*Source Book* 17). As a result of these biographical details, Marechera tended to be fearful of women and relationships as well as scornful of masculinity and modernity. This Oedipal psychology permeates the Amelia sequence and partly explains its alienation and violence. When this psychology occurs in a relationship of cultural difference within a very conservative society with a history of racism, not to mention the problems of marriage and disease, it should be no surprise that the relationship breaks down.

Throughout the sequence the difficulty, if not impossibility, of an intercultural relationship between a black man and white woman is emphasised, and this is just as much a result of context as of psychology. "A Phantom of Delight" (170), shows that love involves disillusionment—"Love's hellish vision," "love's false City." The poem is full of the imagery of destruction: destruction of the self and its illusions about romance. The next poem, "Her Hands My Eyes Closes" (171), makes clear that this disillusionment is inevitable for more than psychological reasons: not only is Amelia from another culture, but love is crushed by "Church and Parliament," by the "past and future's glasshouses" of idealisms, by the "clay" and "pottery" of human frailty (the poem suggests via the phrases "bitter detail" and "well-kneaded" that Marechera was jealous of Amelia's marriage), by the "kitchen, bedroom, bathroom" of mundanity and domesticity. Amelia is now a mere memory, turning the poet inwards into his "hideous darkness" of loss. Yet, even in that inner darkness of loss, love's candle burns: "before me her serene eyes/glowing softly."

Likewise, the poet-persona's relationship to the European "Stephanie" (actually Veit-Wild—see "Me and Dambudzo" 194) in "My Arms Vanished Mountains" is one of frustration; dreams of a stable reciprocity between "Der Alte Kanal" of Nuremberg and First Street in Harare via the *metissage* of the lovers turn out to be "illusions" of exoticism because the lovers speak a different language, "Frenetic, verbose, language without a core" (130). Without sufficient contextual support, pragmatism, determination and will to overcome cultural differences, this love was doomed. Cultural differences here are due as much to the desire for control and dominance as to exotic projections: "I am the place she staked out, pegged, registered" (122). So the inability to overcome cultural differences and stay together results from a lack of trust within contextual antinomies: "This graphic display of black and white/ Clenching in barren greeting/ These two elms each diseased by circumstance" (133). Self, other and context are mind-blastingly intertwined.

So Marechera's poetry exposes a number of difficulties in cross-race, cross-culture love relations: the respective psychologies of the lovers, Veit-Wild's marriage, gender stereotypes, the chiaroscuro of exotic projections, mechanisms of cultural exclusion, the inheritance of racism and exploitation. Given his risqué experiments with love and the multiple closures effected by his context (of which more below) it is not surprising that there is some debate about Marechera's sexuality, particularly in terms of his liaisons with white women in newly independent Zimbabwe in the early 1980's. According to David Caute, Marechera was a rapacious chauvinist with a taste for the equally hungry travelling European women who visited Zimbabwe shortly after independence looking for the frisson of the exotic (103-6). His rather judgmental view has been countered by Veit-Wild who argues that:

> The myth of Marechera's wild sex life was another aspect of his public persona. He did have many different partners but his sexual behaviour was much more conventional than many people might have suspected from his books. He made it clear that his sometimes shocking descriptions of sexuality stemmed from extensive reading and not from personal experience. [...] He longed for intimacy and tenderness but found this incompatible with his own physical desires. For him, sexuality was haunted by the vision of women being raped, humiliated by men through the sexual act, and by their burden as child-bearers. (Veit-Wild, *Source Book* 320)

Veit-Wild sympathetically emphasises Marechera's need for intimacy and tenderness rather than his more selfish Dionysian tendencies. Marechera's love poetry invites us to explore this dialectic between desire and vulnerability without finally collapsing into either side of the debate; we do not have to adopt either Caute or Veit-Wild's perspective but can explore the fertile interstices between their perspectives. In particular, it might be germane to consider his relationships as not merely symptomatic of personal complexes and idiosyncrasies as these two readings tend to, but also as reflecting the problems of his context and time, as I do below. What I have to say below shifts the focus from the psychological dynamic between lovers to the psychosocial closures of Zimbabwe.

Both Caute and Veit-Wild's (different) emphases upon Marechera's subjectivity in relation to his love affairs tend to elide Marechera's sexual and gender radicalism. This radicalism exists in four major areas. First, Marechera exposed gender stereotypes, amongst others, in his writing, a risky activity in a conservative society like Zimbabwe:

> Male sexuality is not dependent on mutual understanding but on conquest, that it is the woman who is conquered every time she is with the man. That is the kind of attitude I grew up with in Vengere township. [...] The idea that a man who does not beat up his wife occasionally is said not to love her at all. [...] This is also what silences me sometimes, usually when I feel that I love somebody. I then remember all the things I have been brought up with. [...] Sheer sexual pleasure, without impregnation, where both are enjoying themselves, is something which is considered extraordinary here. The woman is not supposed to enjoy herself, and if she does, that is seen as a sign of her immorality and perversion. (Veit-Wild, *Source Book* 320-1)

Second, it is often love across the colour bar that is at stake, a politically radical act in newly independent Zimbabwe. It is a truism that indigenous patriarchy and black male sexuality were severely damaged by the colonial incursion, a psychosis manifest in the insecurity of the new power elite, and visible in the expedient traditionalism and hysterical homophobia of Robert Mugabe, both cemented during the years of white minority rule. Colonial Zimbabwe's version of apartheid prohibited sexuality across the colour bar and miscegenation. As John Pape notes in his examination of Zimbabwean sexuality during this period:

> "Black peril" incidents of alleged sexual violence by black men against white women, was at times a fully hysterical obsession amongst the white population of colonial Zimbabwe. Fear of "black peril" spawned a wide range of legislation, including the prohibition of sexual relations between white women and black men. In addition, dozens of blacks were executed, both legally and extra-legally, for supposed "black peril" violations. Yet, for the most part, "black peril" was a manufactured phenomenon, with the number of such cases being extremely small. (699)

The central issue in the demonisation of black male sexuality in colonial Zimbabwe was the myth of priapic African men threatening the chastity and fidelity of white female employers. Pape notes that "viewed in the broader context of hysterical legal proceedings, sexual deprivation of black workers [the cities were full of black male workers, black women were not allowed in], and labouring conditions of constant degradation, black males emerge as virtual paragons of sexual restraint. [...] The promotion of 'black peril' fear was an effective tool for white males to protect their women from directing their attention elsewhere" (710). Indeed, white women demonstrated against the hypocrisy of legislation that prohibited sexuality between themselves and black men whilst white men's vast sexual interaction with black women went unlegislated and ignored. Remarkably, in 1921 half the adult white women in Rhodesia signed a petition against this hypocrisy. Perhaps these white women recognised that underneath the demonisation of black male sexuality was fear of omnivorous white female sexuality and the stereotype of the bored colonial housewife? Although no white male was ever executed for sexual abuse of a black woman, over 30 black men were hanged for abusing white women in Rhodesia.

Given that Zimbabwe inherited this demonisation of black male sexuality, Marechera's tender intervention humanised what had been outlawed: love between a black male and white female. This risqué topic had been bravely broached by Doris Lessing in 1950 with *The Grass is Singing* in which the contextual closures brutally ended the affair between a white woman and her black lover. Marechera rehearses this novel in his poetry, suggesting that not much has changed since the 1950's, but debunking the colonial myth of rampant black male sexuality in the process. His love poetry is Romantic in the full sense of intense Dionysian passion. Sensuous and sensual, it foregrounds individual subjectivity and the poet-persona's interiority, involves tragic impossibility, alienation, loss, heightened aesthetics, overturns the colonial heritage, and is political in the widest and deepest sense of the term. His critique of the association of sexuality with power possibly found its fullest expression in *Black Sunlight* where he specifically lampooned the traditional African autocrat as unconsciously identifying with a bullying phallus, and thereby exposed the sexually corrupt father at the heart of nationalism. So Marechera's psychosexual complexes mirrored those of Zimbabwe: a sense of disgust at grotesque physicality from his childhood experiences and colonial missionary education; triply compounded patriarchy and the subordination of women linked to political dictatorship; Dionysian desire despite these associations of love with power; the quest for psychosexual freedom. Marechera was aware, as Boehmer puts it, that "the overcompensatory mechanisms of a defensive African masculinity, and its accompaniment, the celebration of a symbolic but circumscribed motherhood, is more fully understood as an often coercive form of postcolonial nationalism" (146). Marechera's humanisation of sexuality in his love poetry, particularly in the insistence on remaining vulnerable, was radical in its ability to counteract the association of sexuality with power.

Third, Marechera's love poetry was not only sexually and politically radical in post-independence Zimbabwe, but also social in its deconstruction of institutional and cultural mechanisms of control and exclusion. Marechera was of his time in the sense that he sought relationship ideals without the drawbacks of claustrophobic commitment, a fecklessness that Zygmunt Bauman calls "liquid love" in his book of that title which analyses the vagaries of love in our "liquid modernity." However, this contemporary romantic idealism was exacerbated by particular social, cultural, urban and racial dynamics in post-1980 Harare. "Primal Vision" (172), for instance, makes it clear that some sort of betrayal has occurred; the speaker "dreamed Amelia unfaithful in heaven/Exchanging kisses and more with some Angel," and this is accompanied by jealous insecurity in that his verses are now "enough to entice to bed – and no more" for Amelia. The problem seems to be that much of the attraction between the two lovers was ethereal, in another realm. In other words, exotic allure remains just that if it is not able to ground itself, and such grounding in practicality is very difficult to achieve across cultures, not to mention across a marriage. Most cultures or societies require exclusivity of commitment and are unhappy with go-betweens. Just how intolerant cultures are is made clear in "The Visitor" (174):

> ... The crust of the unattainable on my tongue
> Unleashed me from home and country—to regions of searching mind
> And nerve-racked imagination till like Pygmalion I felt
> Her first fragrant breath on my cheek and the hot blood
> Coursing through her veins – my life's work at last fulfilled!
> But before a year was out, from all sides, jeers, sneers upon us stung
> And she, my human hunger, grew pale, lost appetite, became haggard
> Shunned by her own kind.

The heaven of love here becomes a hell of alienation: "Hell is Heaven and Heaven Hell where our love is/ concerned" (172). We have an image of the narrator as a vampire with "dripping fangs" —clearly this affair with a white foreigner has filled him with guilt, and it is also as if he is now an outcast from the "natural" order of things which makes him feel spectral, otherworldly, a living dead. The middle ground between two cultures occasioned by love, if it can be created at all, is a no-man's land, and often a hellish one. There is no underrating of the difficulties of cross-cultural interaction here, although Marechera's sense of humour remains intact in the final line which adds a light, albeit sardonic, touch to this intense Dantesque imagery: "But my Amelia I will avenge on unsuspecting nuns!" (172).

Fourthly, Marechera exposed the shadows of exotic projections between self and other, a psychological project that involved aesthetic and linguistic inventiveness. Marechera's, often Eurocentric, imagery is that of the collective unconscious:

> Every act of love is a recapitulation of the whole history of human emotion. That total innocence which is actually the seed of cynicism and ultimate despair. But when we have gone beyond despair, then we can dream. And it is in dream that we discover our mythical self. The ghosts which hover

> over Great Zimbabwe are the same as those which tormented Troy, those
> which overwhelmed Carthage, those which watched over Aenias. And love
> is basically *recognition*, an eternal déjà vu, and this introduces the sense of
> terror, the desperate fear and longing of the loved one. (167-8)

For Marechera, the other is a mirror in which he recognises himself beyond the
ghosts of psychological projections. The other is an exotic allure that, when
touched, disintegrates, revealing it as a projection and this in turn shows that
a truly different other does stand there. Yet, despite this postcolonial rejection
of projections, Marechera does not abandon desire even though he knows it is
a fantasy; he continues to reach out to the other in himself and to others outside
of himself, creating a space for many others within and outside of himself. He
knows that to denigrate desire would be to abandon that which can attract others
together.

    This explains not only the partly Eurocentric imagery of these poems, but
also their consistently gothic character, for love involves loss, fear and death.
"Th' Anniversary" (173) paints a gruesome picture of love lost; the anniversary of the narrator and Amelia's love declarations fills his head with the "rot-
ting" gothic imagery of death. As with "Primal Vision," the poet-narrator rails
against the injustice of an all-too ethereal, otherworldly love: "my lips scarlet
with curses against traitorous Heaven." For love poetry, this is fairly grim fare;
these titles characterise the "Amelia" sequence: "When Love's Perished," "A
Phantom of Delight," "Her Hand My Eye Closes," "The Visitor," "The Cemetery
in the Mind," "The Future a Mad Poem," "Agony Column," "Dido in Despair,"
"Cassandra's Ball (a fragment)." This gothic imagery is not only due to the difficulties of manifesting love on the practical plane, to cultural intolerances and to
Marechera's Dionysian excesses, but also results from an involvement with the
other causing a death of the self:

> And love is basically *recognition*, an eternal déjà vu, and this introduces
> the sense of terror, the desperate fear and longing of the loved one. To love
> is to die. And, as Sylvia Plath said, dying is an art. Hence the visions of
> Amelia [are] in direct connection with the women of Troy, the women of
> Argos, the tragedy which love/life is. To love is to come into direct con-
> tact with mortality. To realise that the loved one is doomed – it drives me
> insane to think of the loved one in any peril. But there it is. Amelia is not
> immortal. (168)

Moreover, Marechera's emphasis upon the darkness and danger of love also acknowledges that his love, particularly his love for white women, replays psychological aspects of imperial domination. Ania Loomba, utilising Fanon, points out

that the psychology of colonial domination places the black colonial subject in an "Oedipal scene of forbidden desire" (124) because colonialism emasculated and infantilised the black father and mother. The colonial subject was left with the phantasy of the white mother. Because Marechera's poetry expresses desire for the white woman it would appear to remain within this ambit of the colonial subject as transgressive child, yet its transculturation of love poetry into something altogether stronger and more bitter foregrounds this colonial psychology and shows that desire for the inaccessible colonial mother is a phantasy. This is apparent in Marechera's mythologisation of practical, intercultural and psychological difficulties: "Outraged storms, as if fired/ from some/ Celestial cannon up there, day after day blew down upon us" (174). As he says, he wants to point out how "universal" such difficulties are through "selective use of myth and legend" (168), but perhaps he simply cannot accept responsibility for something he feels is beyond his control in postcolonial Zimbabwe. The multiple closures of this context often destroyed his love as well as making it phantasmal. Marechera's poetic persona in the Amelia poems is left walking on air because of the virtuality of his exotic love:

> Black sunlight, granitic water
> Flames encased in sheets of ice,
> My heart can only read in the dark,
> My footsteps are planted firmly on empty air,
> My eyes, seeking answers, peer backwards into my brains.
> ("Dido in Despair" 180)

Alterity has not solved his problems but led him into a cartoon virtuality ("My footsteps are planted firmly on empty air") and left him peering into his self; the other has been a mirror for himself. Hence Marechera's imagery is dark, gothic and experimental, defamiliarising our expectations of love and love poetry by demonstrating that love does not exist in a hermetically sealed, airbrushed realm. This association of love with the gothic is apparent in other poems apart from the Amelia sequence; "A Gothic Fragment near Warren Hills" and "Comrade Dracula Joins the Revolution: A Wedding of Minds?" both associate marriage with death, vampirism and politics in a postcolonial *liebestod* that shows the propinquity of love and death in a climate of political fear and killing. Marechera's innovation is a transculturation of the gothic imagery of Romantic love (a large number of Eurocentric texts from *Jane Eyre* to *Dracula* to Mills and Boon utilise such gothicism) into the abjectly political and local.

However, his concern with the difficulties of loving a culturally different other within an oppressively violent context is relativised by the nightmare that love can bring: disease. Too Dionysian an embrace of the other can lead to death, which it did in Marechera's case. Hence the terrible poignancy of his poem "The Declaration" (163) in which "I dare not love you any more/ I am sick like any other dreadful whore." This poem bares the horrific psychic torture of a body and self that has, in a sense, been killed by love. An even more horrific torture is that the self is condemned to a living death in which it may not reach out for love before it dies and must harbour both vengeful and self-slaughtering thoughts: "delighting in my own frightful foulness I would infect/the whole/World—and snap my heels in the air with glee!" To be at once in a state where love is death is to be in an abjection that is outside of identity, order and system; here AIDS has literalised the death of the self and the other through desire. In other words, the desire for otherness can be dangerous, even deadly. Sexual desire is a primal force that can lead to hell as well as heaven: "My hand, inflames my heart at once with love and sordid/horror—/ To clasp your lips to mine, to taste O your delicious fruit/ Would only condemn you to the dreadful hell in which I/ fry." Tragically, this is what happened, and the dual outcome of Marechera's death and Veit-Wild's survival has echoed the social history of AIDS in southern Africa.

Marechera's love poetry challenges the usual theorising of postcolonialism as sociohistorical revolt. Its revolution rather consists in taking postcolonialism into the arena of love and desire, into the poetic realm of the senses. Whilst Marechera is best known for the scabrous prose of *The House of Hunger*, his poetry is also deserving of attention. The black electricity of his nerves led to lightning-fast epiphanies that he was able to quickly transmute into poetic images, creating results that have retained a fresh immediacy. This is particularly appropriate to love poetry which can quickly grow stale given its long and popular heritage. Marechera's Romanticism in his love poetry was unprecedented in Zimbabwean poetry, perhaps in Zimbabwean literature generally. He infused dynamism into the realm of love and its poetry via an anti-racial social stance and his suggestion that love involves a curiosity about and exploration of otherness, a suggestion ahead of its time in many ways. Marechera's exploration of alterity was complex; it involved an exploration of sexual, gender, racial and cultural alterity, but also, crucially, a reflection upon his self in the process, so that love's promise of freedom was actualised, even though that actualisation involved suffering within a conservative context.

In conclusion, it should be obvious that relating to the other is vital today. This mandates not only a concern with issues of multiculturalism and tolerance, but also a careful exploration of desire and its limits, which in turn leads towards a complex hybridity whereby the reader/subject is invited to push further and further into alterity and other cultures. Thus we might surmise that the other may be as much to do with desire as responsibility. Love between others suggests, as Deleuze and Guattari point out in *Anti-Oedipus: Capitalism and Schizophrenia*, that "the classical conception of desire as a lack" (25) is partially erroneous. Desire is productive as well as a lack. So Deleuze and Guattari substitute the idea of "desiring-production" for desire as lack, which does not denigrate desire's fantasies as somehow unreal. This is the point that I am making about otherness in postcolonialism; even if the desire for alterity is narcissistic and produces only a phantasm of that alterity, this phantasm is not necessarily negative in itself (even though its colonial history is often negative). Moreover, because "The libido is indeed the essence of desire" (*Anti-Oedipus* 143), exoticism is the first stage of the involvement with the other. Its clichés are precisely those that must be there in the attraction stage of cross-pollination. Of course, if the interaction remains entirely within the realm of the exotic cliché, then only the self will be discovered in the face of the other, which will remain inscrutable and enigmatic, and thus less truly different or human. So postcolonialism both encourages an engagement with otherness via desire and exoticism, but also confirms the incommensurability of that otherness by foregrounding the mechanisms and history of exoticism. As Irigary has it: "Welcoming the new which comes from the other must replace enclosure in knowledge already acquired, learned, historically transmitted" (112). Marechera's love poetry actualised this theory, showing its practical mundanities as well poetic elements. Marechera was particularly good at manifesting desire and abjection in all their vicissitudes through a defamiliarising poetic and extra-rational language. He managed to both instantiate and extend the theory, in the process reinvigorating poetry and suggesting new ways forward for African writing, perhaps even paving the way for new writing like *African Love Stories: An Anthology* (2006). Marechera and postcolonialism are clear that exoticism is necessary, but it is only an avenue of approach to the other; there are varieties of alterity that are only audible in silence, a space free of projections.

Fuzzy Goo's Stories for Children
Literature for a "New" Zimbabwe?

Julie Cairnie

In recent years there has been a flurry of texts—some of them highly success-ful—about growing up white in Rhodesia. These include Alexandra Fuller's *Don't Let's Go to the Dogs Tonight* and Peter Godwin's *Mukiwa: A White Boy in Africa*. While these books have garnered a lot of press and some critical attention[1], there have also been a number of texts that tell the stories of contemporary black children's lives in Zimbabwe, such as Yvonne Vera's *Under the Tongue*, Shim-mer Chinodya's *Tale of Tamari* and Save the Children's *Our Broken Dreams*. In his review of *Tale of Tamari*, Memory Chirere offers a positive critical assess-ment of Southern African texts' treatment of childhood:

> I have always wanted to claim that Chinodya and a good number of other prominent Southern African writers have gradually perfected the art of describing childhood. I have in mind Ezekiel Mphahlele's *Down Second Avenue*, Luis Honwana's *We Killed Mangy Dog*, Dr. Charles Mungoshi's *Coming of the Dry Season* and many others.

Somewhat paradoxically, the publication of narratives of white and black child-hood in Zimbabwe has peaked at the moment of, what I will call, childhood's disappearance: most of the remaining white population is comprised of the eld-erly, and black children are increasingly handed adult responsibilities (as AIDS orphans, as border crossers).[2] White narratives of childhood tend to engage in various forms of nostalgia, while texts about black children tend to present a problematic that requires examination and even intervention *in the present*.

The expulsion and exodus of white Zimbabweans is a radical break with the

---

[1] See Ashleigh Harris's "Writing Home: Inscriptions of whiteness/descriptions of belonging in white Zimbabwean memoirs/autobiography" and Anthony Chennells's "Self-representation and national memory: white autobiographies in Zimbabwe."

[2] There are possibly as few as 20,000 whites remaining in Zimbabwe, a population that is disproportionately comprised of the elderly. According to UNICEF, "[t]he population of Zimbabwe is estimated at 12.2 million (Census 2002) with over 49% of this being children between 0-17 years" (http://www.unicef.org/zimbabwe/overview.html).

multiracial idealism that characterized the country at Independence in 1980, but the dire situation of most black children is a particularly shocking departure from the early ideals of Independence. Mugabe's new government set out to improve the lives of black children through improved healthcare, other social services, and most notably equalized educational access. The latter took the form of free primary education (to grade seven) and access to secondary school for O Levels (four years) and A Levels (two years). The result of this very successful program was the highest literacy rate on the continent—well over 90%. In a 1991 article on the state of Zimbabwe one decade after Independence, Andrew Nyanguru and Margaret Peil point out,

> Improvements in education and health care have touched the lives of most people; schools and clinics in villages across the country help to fulfill aspirations for a better quality and standard of life. The number of children in primary school went up from 820,000 in 1979 to 2.2 million in 1986 and the numbers in secondary schools from 66,000 to over 545,000; the university had 7,699 students in 1989, compared to only 1,931 just before independence. (607)

More recently, school registration figures have dropped significantly: UNICEF estimates that 39% of age-appropriate boys and 37% of age-appropriate girls were registered in secondary school between 2005-9. The collapsed economy and the impossibility of indexing teacher's salaries means that many schools are closed, or classes regularly interrupted, as teachers (and students) search out means of making money.[3] Moreover, UNICEF estimated in 2009 that there were one million AIDS orphans and one million four hundred thousand children (aged 0-17) who are orphaned due to all causes (http://www.unicef.org/ infobycountry/zimbabwe_statistics.html#74). This means that children are forced to earn a living, care for younger siblings, and deal with the vicissitudes of life in a much-changed Zimbabwe. In short, Zimbabwean children are the most vulnerable group and, as such, literature about and by children reflects and engages with this vulnerability.

Significantly, it was during the still-optimistic days of post-Independence—the 1980s—that Marechera unflinchingly interrogated the ideals of postcolonialism and, as I will demonstrate, childhood. In their introduction to *Emerging*

---

[3] Save the Children estimates that "[m]any children are going without education – around 75% of state schools are not functioning properly because the majority of state teachers are not working as they are not paid enough to survive and have to look for or work for food. Many poor families are being forced to send their children out to find work or wild foods and simply can no longer afford to send them to school." (http://www.savethechildren.net/alliance/what_we_do/emergencies/zimbabwe/)

Perspectives on Dambudzo Marechera, Flora Veit-Wild and Anthony Chennells discuss the iconoclastic writer's status as "the black heretic" (xii) and recount, "In 1978, at the height of the Zimbabwean liberation war, Marechera heckled when Robert Mugabe addressed his nationalist compatriots at the Africa Centre in London" (xi). Marechera "refused to adopt a one-dimensional and celebratory perspective on Africa" (xiii). One manifestation of this refusal is *Fuzzy Goo's Stories for Children*[4], dedicated to "all the children of Zimbabwe," and which explores the ways in which postcolonial violence, abuse and uncertainty permeate children's lives. The stories were produced in collaboration with six-year-old Max Wild, a white child whose father was a German diplomat and whose mother went on to become the executor of Marechera's literary estate and his biographer, Flora Veit-Wild. Marechera "was inspired by the 1987 Book Fair's theme of children's books" (*Source Book* 343), but the text was rejected as too mature for the Zimbabwe Book Fair. It was eventually published posthumously in *Scrapiron Blues* (1994).

Fuzzy Goo's Stories for Children points out that neither children nor the postcolonial nation thrive, even though the narrative of progress and benevolence functions as nationalism's (and childhood's) core myth. Marechera's twenty-five-year-old text speaks in compelling ways to Zimbabwe's current crisis of childhood, and conveys that neither childhood nor the postcolonial is neat and univocal. Instead, children have a range of experiences and perspectives, and these are captured through a range of genre. Marechera's children's text is comprised of four short pieces. Rather than read these pieces in order, which could perpetuate the narrative of progress that the text as a whole seeks to undermine, I prefer to examine the texts in loops; the text, and the problematic of postcolonialism and childhood is far more complex than a linear reading permits. I wish to point out that the four pieces unsettle the linear narrative of progress and continue to be deeply relevant in the "new" Zimbabwe. Rather than developing and thriving, Zimbabwe and its children are degenerating: the crisis has crippled basic services and the healthcare system has collapsed. Moreover, acute child malnutrition is on the rise. All of this takes its toll on the nation, local community, and the family; and, in many ways, Zimbabweans are responding: kubatana.net lists dozens of organizations in Zimbabwe servicing children and youth, and there have been many efforts (often from Weaver Press) to present accounts of children's lives in the "new" Zimbabwe.[5] In this essay I situate Marechera's children's stories as deeply relevant now and in a posthumous dialogue with a number of contemporary texts by and for children.

---

[4] Included in *Scrapiron Blues*, 211-47.
[5] I am thinking of Magosvongwe, Chirere and Zondo's *Children Writing Zimbabwe*; Michael Bourdillon's *Child Domestic Workers in Zimbabwe* and *Girls on the Street*; *ABC of all the questions we never dare to ask*; and Irene McCartney's *Children in our Midst*, as well as many others.

Before looking closely at *Fuzzy Goo's Stories for Children*, it is imperative to explore the confluence between ideas of postcoloniality and ideas of child-hood. A lot of research in the social sciences and humanities points to this con-fluence. Saul Dubow, in *Scientific Racism in Modern South Africa*, explains that "the adults of 'inferior' groups (often metaphorically referred to as "child races") could be compared to the children of 'superior' groups" (49). In *On Postcolo-nial Futures*, Bill Ashcroft explains that colonization involved "separating the 'adult' colonizing races from the 'childish' colonized" and underscoring a sense of responsibility towards both white children and subject races: both were *tabula rasa*, "amenable to inscription, despite its inherent menace" (39). In "What is a Child?," a key article that doesn't address postcolonialism or race at all, Tamar Schapiro points out the adult's "paternalistic responsibility" to the child (716). Her description of Kant's "categorical imperative" (718) bears striking resem-blance to the so-called "white man's burden." The white child is an especially pernicious problem in the colonies: for a start, he/she requires a lot of interven-tion and management in order to preserve him/her from contamination, a point Ann Stoler makes in *Carnal Knowledge and Imperial Power*.[6]

Moreover, the narratives of both postcolonialism and childhood are linear, and the emphasis is on the movement from immaturity to maturity, savagery to civilization, and underdevelopment to development. This is the kind of trajectory that Schapiro outlines in her discussion of "the child." Anne McClintock chal-lenges the linear narrative of postcolonialism as "prematurely celebratory" (13). While McClintock does not specifically discuss childhood, her questioning of the postcolonial arrival point or destination is deeply relevant to a critical exami-nation of childhood. Imperialism, not coincidentally, proliferated alongside the emergence of the child, and in the twentieth century several documents declaring children's distinct rights were promulgated. The assumption in documents such as the Declaration of the Rights of the Child (1959, 1989) is that children are not living their lives as children[7] should, and the expectation is that this problem can be corrected. These documents, while admirable in their objectives, are predi-cated on the expectation of progress. They are aspirational documents, however, rather than texts that are, as McClintock puts it, "prematurely celebratory." It is often viewed as shameful that many (postcolonial) countries—as diverse as Can-ada and Zimbabwe[8]—do not enable *all* children to thrive and, frankly, progress;

---

[6] For the colonized, white children signal permanency: in *Don't Let's Go to the Dogs Tonight* Alexandra Fuller conjectures that a lot of Africans would have been happy to see her die from the fever that beset her upon arrival in Cape Town: "one less madam."

[7] "For the purposes of the present Convention, a child means every human being below the age of 18 years unless, under the law applicable to the child, majority is attained earlier." (1989 Declaration)

[8] "Make Poverty History" is an international organization that underscores these international

and is often viewed as shocking that children can comprehend and narrativize violence. Marechera's *Fuzzy Goo's Stories for Children* challenge, then and now, these and other preconceptions about what it means to be a child.

***

Both "Fuzzy Goo's Guide (to the earth)" and "The Magic Cat" challenge a vital assumption of postcolonial nationalism: the inevitability of progress. While one child narrator is precocious and the other innocent, and while one text's criticism is blatant and the other more subtle, both texts unsettle the linear progress narrative. "Fuzzy Goo's Guide" initially strikes the reader as a rambling invective. The piece is divided into three sections: Blah, Pebble and Gah (all are "characters" in the narrative). Connections are established between the three parts: references recur, characters re-appear and Fuzzy Goo is always present. His view mediates events. The text ends with Gah's senseless death, but there is no sense of closure. Instead, the text is characterized by a great deal of critical insight and cultural knowledge, but a dire lack of certainty; there is no coherent sense of a future Zimbabwe without pervasive violence and death. "Fuzzy Goo's Guide" is, ultimately, a deeply cynical indictment of the nationalist postcolonial narrative of progress. Robert Muponde (2006), in his discussion of childhood and nationalism in "The House of Hunger," explains that Marechera "does not write within the nationalist framework which requires childhood to supply the optimism of an "unfinished genesis" […] of the nation, nor does he accept that adulthood is a common, desirable destiny for all" (530). The emphasis here is on lack of progress, even "degeneration," and Muponde points out that "Fuzzy Goo's Guide" demonstrates that "[g]rowing up is […] a sign of degeneration" (525) and that it is "dangerous for childhood to reach into adulthood, which represents symbolic degeneration of the body and spirit" (526). Children do not progress or thrive in Zimbabwe; rather, they are subject to systemic brutality (by teachers, police and health care workers). "Fuzzy Goo's Guide" poignantly gives the lie to the promises of Independence and the (albeit aspirational) promises/objectives of the Declaration of the Rights of the Child.

Children, such as Fuzzy Goo, are forced to be precocious. The text, though, raises questions about authenticity: is Fuzzy Goo believable as a child? Muponde (2006) argues that "Marechera is that character Fuzzy Goo" (525). The text blurs adult and child perspectives. The narrative is stream-of-consciousness, which seems to mimic a child's thought processes, but there are erudite and sophisticated references and allusions. It is unlikely that a child would have read so widely and processed the world in such a complex way, but Marechera himself has been characterized as a voracious reader and complex thinker. This is impressively

---

connections. (http://www.makepovertyhistory.ca/)

evident in his essay "The African Writer's Experience of European Literature,"[9] written in the same year as *Fuzzy Goo's Stories for Children*. It is unlikely that Fuzzy Goo is a child because few children, especially poor and vulnerable children, would have access to such an array of reading material. Few children, too, could process the world in such a complex way. Doris Lessing, in her Nobel Prize speech in 2007, draws a striking contrast between the voracious appetite for books in Mugabe's "new" Zimbabwe and the dust-gathering library collection in a private boys" school in London, but concludes that because that appetite is not fed there is little hope that young people in Zimbabwe will flourish as readers and writers. Muponde (1999) argues that the "lewdest things, though we may not suspect it, are said and written by children themselves" (253). Moreover, a realistic point of view and narrator may not be key to understanding the effects of "Fuzzy Goo's Guide." Childhood is not static and protected, and the point seems to be that children are far more experienced and astute than we adults might imagine. In a debate about realism, Alison Flood argues that children's fiction "needs to engage with the issues that concern and worry its readers, otherwise it becomes irrelevant to them. Sure, there's a need for happy endings and jolly jaunts, but there is also a need to address the darker side of life" (Flood).

While "Fuzzy Goo's Guide" is precocious (and this is putting it mildly), "The Magic Cat" *seems* innocently naïve. Arguably, this is the most difficult of the four texts because it is so deceptively simple. In an interview with Tinashe Mushakavanhu, Max Wild recalls, "'The Magic Cat' was less cynical, and I definitely related to it in a very childlike way" (Mushakavanhu). On the surface, "The Magic Cat" embraces Zimbabwe's nationalist narrative of progress. The child narrator (Fuzzy Goo) describes his cat visiting key national sites, including Great Zimbabwe and Heroes Acre, and rehearsing bland and cliché phrases: "It is ours. I am proud of Zimbabwe!" These sites are iconic and even ironic here, but how is this criticism of postcolonial nationalism subtly conveyed in "The Magic Cat"? In a general assessment of childhood in Marechera's oeuvre, Robert Muponde (2006) argues that "Marechera's childhoods are projects that are designed to do demolition work on the founding imaginaries of Zimbabwean cultural and political nationalism." Muponde further insists "that childhood cannot be used as a pliant tool of Zimbabwean political imaginaries" (529). "The Magic Cat" resists this role for childhood by attributing the text's jingoism to the cat; Fuzzy Goo mediates the cat's gushing nationalism for us. There is, then, a measure of critical distance. While the cat embraces the postcolonial "arrival point," the narrator is more skeptical. This is reflected in the occasional dark, uncertain moments in this bubbly narrative poem:

---

[9] This lecture is included on the DVD.

At midnight
in a dark room
my black Cat—a polished
black shape

This sentence fragment is at odds with the optimistic and seemingly unambiguous vehemence of the rest of the poem. The use of children's language, combined with a few interspersed dark lines/moments, serves to slyly undermine nationalism's progress narrative. Zimbabwe's nationalist narrative does not stand up to scrutiny; it is devoid of meaning and substance.

It is significant that Marechera collaborated with six-year-old Max Wild; the child provided the illustrations for "The Magic Cat," a piece that comingles the adult and child perspectives, precocity and naïveté. In her reflective essay "Hippo and Hyena" in this book, Flora Veit-Wild, Max's mother, recalls that she and Marechera devised "a creative writing workshop for children": "the first one went well, in the second, Dambudzo got drunk and obnoxious and the children, all still quite small, frightened and discouraged" (104). While Marechera made some children cry, he managed a close relationship with Max; and while he enjoyed intellectual companionship with adults he was also disconnected from many. Veit-Wild recalls,

> I once, and this was only a few weeks before he died, made the mistake to usher a very hesitant suggestion on how he could improve a story he was just writing and had asked me to read (he very seldom did that). It was the story "Fuzzy Goo's Guide to the Earth," dedicated to the 1987 International Book Fair in Harare, which had "Children" as theme. I said I liked it but suggested he should give it a bit more of a real plot, children would prefer that. Dambudzo did not look at the story again. It stayed incomplete. (105)

It is hard to miss the irony of "The Magic Cat" in Zimbabwe today, but Max Wild acknowledges that he did not fully comprehend *Fuzzy Goo's Stories for Children* and even a subsequent children's story that Marechera wrote: "After those two stories I remember Dambudzo talking about a new story about a boy and a bus or something. I think he finished it but I"m not sure if it was published. I think I wanted to illustrate that one too, but it was to complicated for me to understand, which I was a little disappointed about." Can children understand critical and complex texts? Can they understand irony? Is "The Magic Cat" a text for children? These are some of the questions Sue Walsh addresses in a related discussion. In "Irony? But Children Don't Get It, Do They?" she points out that, the trouble with reading irony in children's literature has to do with what appears as a necessarily uncomfortable relation between "irony" and the "child." [. . .] "Irony" requires a notion of language as that which does not necessarily mean what it says, whilst the "child" and its language are antithetically produced as meaning what they say in all "innocence" (33).

"The Magic Cat" nudges at the opposition between irony and the child, and thus points out that children and their lives are much more complex than many adults, and much of children's literature, permits. Children comprehend far more than is assumed.

The complexity of children's lives and postcolonial Zimbabwe is certainly evident in Save the Children's 2007 online text, *Our Broken Dreams: Child Migration in Southern Africa*, published twenty years after Marechera wrote *Fuzzy Goo's Stories for Children*. The London-based charity set out to examine and ultimately rectify the problem of children's border crossing, and this took the form of a collection of children's stories and drawings framed and mediated by adults with their "best interests" (Schapiro 735) in mind. The text, co-published by Save the Children and Weaver Press, is available both online (as a free download) and in print. There is a clear sense of collaboration, the comingling of adult and child perspectives, and a discernible benevolent objective. Facts and statistics are presented; children's life stories are told (directly, paraphrastically, and through bubbles emanating from drawn figures mouths); children's, often disturbing, drawings are included to elucidate the narratives; there are editorial notes, by Irene Staunton, general editor of Weaver Press, and Chris McIvor, director of Save the Children in Mozambique. In his introduction, McIvor highlights the importance of children expressing themselves and comments on children seizing the chance to speak out (xii). One child laments that "no one is interested in our story" (xiii). Irene Staunton explains,

> The primary objective behind: *Our Broken Dreams: Child Migration in Southern Africa* was to enable children who have decided (usually on their own) to find their way to South Africa in search of work, an income for their families, and a better life, to tell their stories in their own words. (xv)

The interpellated reader here is the sympathetic and benevolent adult with the means to help improve the lives of these most vulnerable children; despite the simple narratives, colourful and childlike fonts and images, readers of this accessible text are not children at all. This text highlights the complications evident in "Fuzzy Goo's Guide" and "The Magic Cat," and the irony of the text may be read, in part, through the discrepancy between the children's aspirations and the ways in which their lives actually unfold. The effect of the irony is not cynical invective, as we encounter in "Fuzzy Goo's Guide" and "The Magic Cat."

In the "new" Zimbabwe children cross borders—especially to South Africa—in order to realize the postcolonial dream of progress. Many of the children are optimistic about their potential success. This points to the tenacity of the narrative of progress, but the viability of progress is consistently challenged. The editors explain that a boy who is deported from South Africa plans to return, despite the risks and obstacles:

> Many of this youth's family are living illegally in South Africa. His expectations about what he—and they—can achieve is high, and he is outraged rather than pained when things don't work out as planned. The whisper at the Reception Centre was that despite having just been deported, he was planning to go straight back across the border. (16)

In his own words, the boy tells the interviewer,

> My brothers talk good about South. They said, "Man, there are many jobs there. This life of yours of just sitting at home when you are this old is not good." And I envied their bicycles and radios. Some have TVs at their homes. It was very painful to see others bringing their nice things from SA and we had nothing. (16)

The fact that he and others have to pursue this dream in a dangerous, hostile space challenges its viability. Indeed, the children's stories rarely unfold or end happily. There are not only tales of deportation, but of physical and sexual abuse. A team of interviewers set out to record these children's stories; sometimes they are recorded verbatim and sometimes they are paraphrased, but they are also contextualized and mediated by adults who have their "best interests" in mind. Progress and benevolence are circulating myths of postcolonialism and childhood, but the stories in *Our Broken Dreams* are nuanced, and occasionally mildly hopeful. One girl, crossing from Mozambique to South Africa recalls,

> If you are crossing, they can propose to you. One day I crossed with my aunt, and the guard said, "Ah […] today you have crossed with this girl. […] Me, I love her." But others who were there said, "Can't you see that she is still a child? It's not possible for you to say, 'I love this child.' It's not possible!" (68)

The children in *Our Broken Dreams*, similar to Marechera's children, have a complex and contradictory relationship to the narrative of postcolonial and childhood progress, but the former conveys a keener sense of the possibility of intervention; its irony is less cynical, in large part because of the benevolent and mindful interventions of adults.

***

Marechera's "Baboons of the Rainbow" and "Tony and the Rasta" highlight children's comprehension of postcolonial violence. The children's narratives and drawings in *Our Broken Dreams* corroborate this claim. Max Wild, too, appreciated the violence in "Baboons of the Rainbow," but in terms of its entertainment value: "'Baboons of the Rainbow' got a lot darker, especially as the story went on, I didn't think twice about the violence and thought it was very entertaining, as you can see from my drawings" (Mushakavanhu). Both of Marechera's texts point out that there may be a change of political leadership in Zimbabwe, but violence continues to be meted out: in "Baboons of the Rainbow" colonial and postcolonial violence inhabit the same conceptual space, and in "Tony and the Rasta," as Muponde (1999) insists, "there are resonances of a lived history, a remembered location—Vengere tangwenas (shanties) way back in the Rusape of the seventies" (256-7). The third piece in the sequence, "Baboons of the Rainbow," is a moral fable. Consistent with the fable, there are talking animals and a moral message. The moral message is not a general commentary on human social relations, but a cunning indictment of postcolonial hypocrisy. Muponde (1999) explains that,

> Marechera provides children with total expression where there is nothing sacred or beyond comment in the child's experience of reality. The idea, for him, is not to arrive at a conclusive definition of children's literature but to investigate its possibilities. This places him from the outset in the same ambiguous position as other serious writers who write for children. (255)

Moreover, "[c]onventional literature for children is seldom in step with immediate events or reality" and has "little relevance to children's lives" (258). Max Wild "remember[s] not understanding some of the adulty stuff towards the end, like the drinking, cigar smoking and listening/ playing music. For me it didn't really make sense or go with the story at the time and seemed a little irrelevant." Perhaps it would be difficult for black Zimbabwean children to understand fully, but they—then and now—would have a keener sense of the violence and hypocrisy of the allegorical baboons. After all, Max Wild describes his childhood as "very carefree."

The tale circulates around three hungry baboons: black, white and green. In the first section, black and white baboon fight each other because their hunger is feral. When Green Baboon arrives and implores them not to fight, they conspire to eat him. First they eat him simply and without restraint (like animals or "savages"), and then decide to eat him in a more "civilized" way, with wine, dessert and sophisticated conversation and music (sentences are punctuated with "what?" which clearly signifies the British colonial upper class). In the second part, post meal, white and black baboon sing songs, again drawn from a range of sources. The moral of Marechera's children's fable is clear: there is very little perceptual difference between the colonizer (white baboon) and the new postcolonial leadership (black baboon), as both brutalize and consume the average citizen (green baboon). This is a text that interpellates a young audience and which again utilizes a young illustrator; the drawings are gruesome and unsettling. Max Wild, though, explains that Marechera completed the drawings: "In fact, Dambudzo and I stayed up pretty late that night, finishing the illustrations, and I remember getting tired and him helping me with the drawings. The last couple of drawings he did himself, and I had gone to bed, which you can see if you look closely." *Our Broken Dreams* certainly contains this level of violence, but the form of a fable does not mediate or soften the violence. Moreover, children recreate their experiences of violence through their own drawings, just as (if not more) horrifying than those that accompany "Baboons of the Rainbow."

In "Tony and the Rasta" the child is able to comprehend the brutality of adults and their hypocrisy. Muponde (1999) reads this story biographically:

> Marechera here fictionalizes his own biography which demonstrates the problem of authorial invisibility. Ultimately, because Tony and the author share so much of their experiences—the memory of absolute loss and brutal dispossession—the narrator almost becomes Marechera. (257)

If Marechera "distrust[s . . .] the attempts of other voices or identities to tell his life, then it is his own way of recreating his empathy with children who inhabit similar nightmarish landscapes" (257), whether in Southern Rhodesia in the seventies or Zimbabwe in the eighties. Tony does not just read about violence and brutality, like the implied child reader in "Baboons of the Rainbow," but bears witness to it and is a victim of violence himself. He is Green Baboon. Muponde (1999) explains that Tony is confronted with "issues that are normally considered beyond the perceptions of children" (256). Unlike the other pieces in *Fuzzy Goo's Stories for Children*, "Tony and the Rasta" has a cautiously optimistic tone and trajectory. Rather than a fully realized *bildungsroman* (or narrative of progress), this text permits 'small" progress, the possibility of a different life for Tony. The focus here is on the child, in terms of language, perspective and context. As Muponde (1999) points out, "There is in Marechera and his children a paranoid distrust of growing up in an unreconstituted society and language" (261). Tony defies the stereotype of the brutalized, poor orphan: he is sensitive, intelligent and questioning. It is hard to overlook the text's grim realism; Tony is exposed to violence, rape and Shantytown's collective anxiety on a daily basis. Still, the most significant difference between Tony and Marechera's other children is that he has a responsible and loving adult to mediate on his behalf, his Rasta teacher. Despite his precocity, there is a strong sense in which Tony requires the intervention of a caring adult. Here we witness adult-child collaboration and intimacy. Significantly, the Rasta teacher is also a victim—he is beaten by thugs—and thus understands Tony's experience of victimization. There is profound empathy in this relationship. While the teacher only manages to offer Tony a fragment of peace and beauty—he takes him to Cleveland Dam on the outskirts of Harare—it is enough (for the moment) to sustain Tony.

Shimmer Chinodya's 2004 juvenile novel, *Tale of Tamari*, speaks in compelling ways to Marechera's study of children's comprehension of violence and hypocrisy, and the possibility of 'small" progress, in the form of benevolent and mindful adult intervention. Remarkably, Tamari is less damaged, traumatized than Tony; she loses both parents to AIDS, is dependent on an unscrupulous uncle and is close to being a victim of sexual abuse. *Tale of Tamari*, published by Weaver Press for the educational market, is directed toward young readers. In contrast, Robert Muponde (1999) argues that *Fuzzy Goo's Stories for Children* is "for adult children" (261). While *Tale of Tamari* exposes young readers to Tamari's experience of disenfranchisement and violence, its emphasis is, ultimately, on the people who protect and love her. In his review of the novel, Memory Chirere explains,

> This is, arguably, the first creative HIV/Aids story from Zimbabwe that does not harp endlessly on how to die or not to die of AIDS. The novella goes for Tamari and Kuda's refusal to pity themselves. Besides being Aids orphans, they insist on a near-normal teenage life-style notwithstanding the dwindling resources and the endless misfortunes.

The narration is third person, which is significant because Tamari's youthful optimism is (like Tony's) checked or qualified. This is a text for children and written by an adult, and while it is emphatic in its emphasis on the importance of sympathy towards AIDS orphans and argues for the reform of their lives, it is ultimately children's literature which engages, as Muponde (1999) would put it, in the "social control of children" (255) The children require the benevolent protection of an adult with their "best interests" in mind, and Tamari herself never challenges the authority of adult, whether they are benevolent or malevolent.

***

In early 2009, just before the Oxford Marechera Celebration, I taught a third-year undergraduate English course on the literature of childhood in Zimbabwe, and most of my (largely white and middle class) students were horrified by the ways in which children live and lived in Zimbabwe. Responding to a barely sub-limated missionary instinct, some of these students wanted to go to "Africa" and "make a difference." Other students took this material as an affront to their own understanding of childhood, complicated in North America (and in Europe) by the postponement of adulthood that seems to accompany a university education. I also found that my students had difficulty with texts, like Marechera's, which present children who are not necessarily recognizable as such. This signals a deeper problem about the universalizing of childhood, as well as the static rep-resentation of African children as victims, images on a television screen. It is the multifarious nature of childhood that needs to be underscored and explored. Dambudzo Marechera's *Fuzzy Goo's Stories for Children* supports the idea that children are not isolated from economic, political and social crisis, then or now, but they are fully engaged, emotionally, intellectually and viscerally. How do we, as adults, become fully engaged with the crisis of childhood in Zimbabwe? What is our role? How do we avoid the missionary ethic? How do we intervene, like Tony's Rasta, on behalf of disenfranchised children?

AFTERWORD
Me and Dambudzo
A Personal Essay*

Flora Veit-Wild

I have often been asked why I did not write a proper Dambudzo Marechera biography. My answer was that I did not want to collapse his multi-faceted personality into one authoritative narrative but rather let the diverse voices speak for themselves. But this is not the whole truth. I could not write his life story because my own life was so intricately entangled with his. While I have generally come to be known as "The Marechera Authority," there have always been two narrative strands behind this persona—the public and the private. While the public one has stood out as strong and clear, my private life has been interlaced with love and passion, loss and pain, with illness and the threat of death. Yet, what I have gained is so much more than what I have endured that I am filled with gratitude, and I might add, with laughter. My personal involvement with Dambudzo Marechera has affected my professional life in a way I would never have expected. The many ironic twists, the tricks that Dambudzo played on me even posthumously, make *our* story an immensely rich and funny one, one that I now, more than 25 years after I came to know him, want to tell.

***

I first met Dambudzo Marechera in Charles Mungoshi's office. They were drinking vodka. Mungoshi was then an editor with Zimbabwe Publishing House (ZPH), one of the new publishing houses established after Independence in 1980. I had started a correspondence course for journalistic writing before coming out to Zimbabwe and was gathering information for articles about the upcoming Zimbabwean literary scene. I had heard about the legendary writer who slept in doorways and on park benches. Lately, it was reported, he had slept on the ping-pong table of a German commune after they had thrown him out of their house.

I did not expect him there, on this bright October morning in 1983. While Harare's Avenues were sparkling blue with Jacaranda blossom on the east-west

---

* First published in *Wasafiri* 27.1 (March 2012): 1-7.

axis and blazing red where the Flamboyants lined the numbered streets going north to south, I stepped into a rather drab office; a desk with a telephone and a pile of manuscripts in the in-tray, some wooden chairs, and in a corner, a bulging plastic bag and a portable typewriter—Dambudzo's belongings, as I would learn later. He was using ZPH to freshen himself up after a night out in the streets.

"Hey, have a seat," he said, pulling a chair for me to Mungoshi's desk. His open face was looking at me expectantly, and Charles—not a natural speaker—gladly left his guest to his eloquent colleague. So that is *him*, I remember thinking, so accessible, charming and boyish, clad in denims and a faded light blue t-shirt—incredibly young. He was 31years old, I was 36. I was wearing sandals, a pink blouse, and wide, softly flowing trousers with a striking flower pattern. Looking me up and down, he said: "Oh, my lawd, your garments cannot be from here. You would rather expect them in a Bloomsbury setting than in prissy old Salisbury." His stilted Oxford accent and the exaggerated emphasis on some of his half mocking, half serious words made me smile. I was curious to know him better.

The Oasis Hotel and the UZ swimming pool

We arrange to meet soon again at the Oasis Hotel garden, a popular place for expats and locals. When I enter the poolside bar, I find him surrounded by people yelling: "Hey, Dambudzo, what are you writing about?" He has some copies of *The House of Hunger* under his arm, which he is trying to sell - a few dollars for the next beer. "Shit man," he says, when we sit down, "all they know about my writing is that it contains hot sex. But, between you and me, I learn all that from books." Which is true, as I will find out later. His own sexual behaviour was not at all outlandish.

We talk. I tell him about my life, my political activism in the 1970's, how we collected 100.000 Deutsch Marks for ZANU PF to buy four land rovers; the money then confiscated by the West German government because Mugabe was classified as a "terrorist." And now I find myself in a country ruled by this erstwhile terrorist, now lauded as the "pearl of Africa." The historical ironies crisscrossing my biography have just begun; so many more will follow. Dambudzo is a good listener and can relate to my experiences, as he lived with leftists of all sorts in the squatter communities in London, closely following the developments in Germany. The Baader-Meinhof group gave him ideas for his urban guerrillas in *Black Sunlight*. He tells me how alienated he feels in his home country. All his former fellow-students from the University of Rhodesia have become civil servants or university lecturers. Slogans about "building the new nation" wherever you go. Socialist realism is on the agenda, his own writing denigrated as Western modernist decadence, blah blah...

I am open to his views. After years of working with Maoist cadre organisations, I am wary of the so-called struggle of the workers and the peasants against capitalist oppression and international imperialism. I am excited to find a black intellectual who does not try to make me feel guilty for the crimes of colonialism but points his finger at his own leaders. In the years to follow, I develop an increasing allergy to the patronising stand of European ex-lefties towards the poor colonised souls. The Albert Schweitzers reborn. Dambudzo Marechera is becoming my mentor. His ruthless critique of all types of attitudinizing is utterly liberating. I feel at ease in his company, I feel no racial bias, no need to justify my presence in his country. His curiosity about my life and ambitions, paired with his wittily flirtatious manner work like a magic spell.

Our next date fails due to a misunderstanding. When we do meet again, he gives me his nicely typed poem "In the Gallery." We arrange further dates. I drive to town from our house in Highlands using our family car, a white left-hand drive VW Passat station wagon, and meet him in one of the bars. We talk. I pay for his Castle Lager. Sometimes it is Chateau Burgundy. I drink G & T's. We go dancing. He snatches kisses while I talk. During the daytime he "wanders through Hararean mazes."[1] He writes more poems, tears them up in fits of anger. Some of them survive. I will include them later in *Cemetery of Mind*[2]—traces of a burgeoning love for life.

One night he suggests that we drive to the UZ (University of Zimbabwe) campus, a couple of miles north of the city centre. It is his old hideout. After his return from London in 1982 and the aborted filming with Chris Austin,[3] he held readings and lectures there. The students venerated him. They let him sleep on the floor in their dormitory rooms. They called him Buddy. Albert Nyathi, now a well-known *imbongi*, was among them, as was Tendai Biti, right hand of Morgan Tsvangirai and minister of finance in the "Unity Government" of 2009.

We sit in the dark by the UZ swimming pool. We tumble about in the grass. It feels playful, joyful, frivolous. Yet back in the car, he starts pressurizing me. I want to drive home. He urges me to stay. He pulls my hand into his lap and, angrily, provocatively, he says: "You see what you are doing to me, you can't leave me like THIS."

But I do. I give him the picnic blanket from our car, and he sneaks into the lavatories of Manfred Hodson Hall—where he resided as a University of Rhodesia student in 1972/1973 until the "pots-and-pans" demonstration, during which he was expelled as one of the ringleaders (for details, see Veit-Wild, *Source Book*

---

[1] See epigram to his "Parkbench Journal" in *Mindblast*.

[2] See the section "A Writer's Diary" in *Cemetery of Mind*.

[3] He had a contract with the South African filmmaker, who wanted to film his return to Zimbabwe after eight years in the UK. The project collapsed within the first few days owing to a row between Marechera and Austin. For details see my *Dambudzo Marechera: A Source Book on his Life and Work*, 281-290 and Chris Austin's essay in this volume.

95-114; Veit-Wild, *Teachers* 205-213). Alfred Knottenbelt, who had famously defied Ian Smith's Unilateral Declaration of Independence in 1965, was his warden. 30-year old Terence Ranger, another prominent figure in the early days of the university, staged an anti-colour-bar protest and was pushed into the pool by an angry white Rhodesian, the very swimming pool where we almost made love.

On that night in October 1983, I was oblivious to the history of these places. I would learn about it only much later when I followed the writer's tracks from his birth in 1952 to his death in 1987. I would then also discover his play, "The Stimulus of Scholarship," serialized in the UZ students' magazine *Focus* in 1983-84—the very time when the campus vlei became *our* first hideout. Did he talk to me about it? I cannot recall.

Did I have any idea what I was getting into? I had always had a longing for the wondrous, the fantastic, the outlandish. Dambudzo appealed to the clownish, melancholic, poetic part of me, which was menacingly dark and colourfully bright at the same time. I had never suppressed it, lived it out in pantomime or in romance, but had always been pragmatic enough to know that for "real life," I had to make rational choices. Dambudzo more than anyone before embodied this "other" side in me, he led me through many closed doors, he fostered my infatuation with the mad side of life, the "Coin of Moonshine" (Marechera, *Cemetery* 27).

After those nightly tumblings at the pool and in the car, I consult with one of my German friends, an expat wife like me. A group of us meet regularly for gym, gossip and ranting about men. We are all in a state of excitement, stimulated by the beautiful country and the grand spirit of hope of unlimited possibilities that reign in Zimbabwe in those early 1980's. We are open to the new, ready to go beyond the boundaries of our lives as wives, mothers or teachers. I tell my friend that I am drawn to Dambudzo, but that I know it will be very complicated. Her laconic answer: "But you like it complicated."

Her words propel me forward. Like the skydiving I do around the same time, I jump. I go for the free fall. Similar to the sensation when I first jump from a plane, I feel a complete whirling of body and mind. Yet, as daring as it is, I have my safety net: my family, my social and economic infrastructure, my inner groundedness. I have always been a fearless person. But I have been able to afford the occasional jump only because of my protected childhood, my emotional and financial security. I always believed I would eventually land on safe ground.

What I do not know at the time is that my involvement with Dambudzo will be almost fatal; that for a very long time I will walk on shifting ground. Nor do I know that Dambudzo, the troublemaker,[4] will unwittingly make me into his

---

[4] "Dambudzo" means "causing trouble or pain" in Shona.

mouthpiece once his voice is gone and thus make me gain recognition I would never have dreamt of.

The Seven Miles Hotel

For the first night we will spend together, we drive out to the Seven Miles Hotel on the road to Masvingo. The manager in suit and tie greets us with a slight bow: "Good afternoon, Mr. Marechera." We sit under one of the thatched umbrellas. I feel awkward, the only white face among a raucous crowd of drinkers, mostly employees from the city meeting their girlfriends after work. I get strange looks, and Dambudzo obscene remarks, in Shona, about his "white chick."

Now it is I who is getting impatient, while he dithers. He needs another beer and a third or fourth, before we timidly ask for a room. Even more embarrassing: "For how long? Half or whole night?" Dambudzo keeps his eyes to the ground, while I stammer, "Well, maybe rather the whole night," thinking a night's sleep in a proper bed might do him good. "All right," says the manager stiffly, "That will be 40 dollars." I pay and take the key.

The room is a rondavel with a steep thatched roof. It is sombre inside. It is quiet. Now we are far from the noisy crowd, just me and him. When we lie on the bed, I see a dove rustling up from its nest. It escapes through the opening into the night sky. As I close my eyes, the roof starts spinning in my head. I hear a voice murmuring, "this is magic, this is pure magic." The voice is mine.

In the early hours of the morning, I disentangle myself from his arms and tell him I have to be home before my children wake up. He sits up, alarmed. His face, mellow and tender a few hours before, is tight with anger and suspicion. "So you are leaving me here, stranded. You have set all this up to get me into a trap. Who is behind this plot?" Baffled, I try to calm him. "You will easily find a lift into town in the morning." I leave with an anxious knot in my throat. It is a foreshadowing of the extreme shifts in mood that will mark the eighteen months of our relationship.

Boscobel Drive

After a few weeks, Dambudzo moves into our house. It feels too bad to leave him "stranded" in the streets after we made love in the car (I had never done that before) or at a friend's house. In the sordid city hotel, where we spend one night, all the black women stare at me. In the morning I find a window of my car smashed.

My husband agrees to let him stay for a while. He likes him and recognises his extraordinary literary style, a welcome exception to the rather boring middle-of-the road African writing. Like me and a few other friends, he hopes to stabilise him by getting him off the street.

This is, of course, a vain hope. Dambudzo refuses all attempts to get him therapeutic help, to reduce his drinking, or establish a healthier life style. He is afraid he would lose his distinct personality, the source of his art. Yet, for a little while, the shelter, a bed, clean clothes, regular meals and sharing in our family life revive his spirits. He sits in the garden typing the Kamikaze poems. He sits in the guest cottage with six-year-old-Max and types "The Magic Cat" and "Baboons of the Rainbow," with Max drawing the illustrations. He sits in the playroom with three-year old Franz and paints. We also take him to outings and on picnics, to our artist friends on a farm in Raffingora—which will appear in his poetry.

He stays with us for three to four months, interrupted by times when we have to "expel" him, as he puts it—friends or family are visiting, or the frictions grow too much to bear. After Christmas 1983, we take visiting friends to the Vumba Mountains, leaving him behind in the house. When we come back, he has written his poetic sequence, "My Arms Vanished Mountains" and asks us to record him reading it with Ravel's "Bolero" playing in the background. The recording is on the DVD included with this book: you can hear his voice swelling in sonority and bathos—he is helping himself to Chateau Burgundy while reading—his voice dramatically enhanced by Ravel's crescendo. It is quite hilarious to watch him set himself "in" scene. Yet his wish to have it recorded turns out to be provident, because a couple of days later he tears the manuscript up in one of his tantrums. Thanks to the recording, I will be able to transcribe the piece after his death, with transcription errors, as critics will remark.

The long poem itself is like a fiery concerto of overpowering imagery, resonating with the impetuous sounds and rhythms of the Brahms, Beethoven, Tchaikovsky, Smetana and Grieg symphonies that he listened to at our house while we were away. Bewildering to me, the listener then and later, how his verses convolute the traumas of his youth ("The Boulder, Father Boulder") with the antagonisms in our relationship. The "eaglets in Vumba" still swirl through my memory today, binding Stephanie (as he calls me in the poem)[5] to his lonely self in that "week a pang of desire." And I hear his drunken voice rolling the r in a way truly comical to German ears when he evokes images of Der Alte Kanal. This ancient waterway near Nuremberg, where we lived in the years before coming to Zimbabwe, picturesque in its tranquillity, with its quaint little lock keepers' houses—these images came from the photo book of the Kanal from our bookshelves (Liedel and Dollhopf). I had told him how we used to take the boys there, in a pram or on our bicycles. The "three country-men" in the poem he both envies and sneers at; his arms "flung wide open / out for you, Stephanie" who however has made him into "the place she staked out, pegged, registered."

---

[5] He had told me he would use this name when referring to me in his writing.

The poem says it all. It cannot last. Sharing me with my husband, his host and sponsor, fills him with increasing resentment. My husband, then director of the Zimbabwe German Society, organises a reading for Dambudzo in February 1984, his first public appearance for a long time. Two years later, he commissions Dambudzo to conceptualise a lecture series on African writers speaking about their craft. Dambudzo's own opening lecture "The African Writer's Experience of European Literature" will, when published posthumously, become one of the most quoted documents in the growing body of Marechera scholarship.[6] I use it often in my teaching. No better antidote to the p. c. induced attitudes about being "Eurocentric" blah, blah. "That Europe had, to say the least, a head start in written literature is an advantage for the African writer […]. I do not consider influences pernicious: they are a sort of apprenticeship." No wonder that the current generation of African writers see in Marechera the great liberator of the mind.

For his fellow writers, it wasn't always easy to handle the drunken rebel. Ama Ata Aidoo, who lived in Zimbabwe at the time, and was the second writer to present a lecture, began her talk with a tribute to Samora Machel. He had just died in a plane crash, allegedly by the hands of the South African regime. As Ama Ata was saying something in honour of "our fallen heroes," Dambudzo, a mug of beer in hand, brayed from the back of the packed lecture hall: "Fuck the heroes." Ama Ata, flabbergasted, shrieked, "Shut up, Dambudzo," and then resumed: "Our dead…" "Fuck the dead," came the drunken echo from the back, at which she closed her manuscript and made to leave, unless we, the organisers, removed Dambudzo from the room—which we did, by force of manpower.

February of 1984. Dambudzo is still staying at our house. He spends most of his earnings from the reading on drink. The combination of alcohol and his usual paranoia creates a series of unpleasant frictions and disasters—often a mixture of high-strung drama and absurd comedy. One evening, on his return from the bars, he feels threatened by my husband, who, Dambudzo hallucinates, is wielding a sword. Then he slips and cuts himself badly on a glass cabinet. Rejecting first aid from a neighbouring doctor, he insists instead on waiting for the police, blood pooling on the floor around him. When the police arrive, they drive him and my husband to the police station, where he files a charge of manslaughter against his alleged assailant. After being bandaged in a clinic, he is driven back home and put to bed, two policemen sitting with him, helping themselves to his vodka and reading parts of his manuscript of *Mindblast*. Only at that stage does he agree to withdraw the charge—and all is well again.

Our relationship grows increasingly difficult. After every painful argument I

---

[6] This lecture is included on the DVD.

swear to myself that this will be the last time. Then the longing and fretting start over again, and I go looking for him in the city bars.

Why could I not let him go despite the tremendous tensions, grudges, and pain on all sides? There was a deep bond between our bodies and our minds, which still needed time to unfold. It was an irrational force, which I can still feel today but not explain. He also disarmed me with his utter truthfulness, his loyalty, and—despite his obvious penchant for melodrama—his modesty. Having made a terrible scene the night before, he would apologize the next morning: "You know me, when I don't get what I want, I throw a tantrum. Just like Franz." He would rub his short-sighted eyes with the back of his slender hands, boyishly, bashfully—and I found myself loving and forgiving him.

Sloane Court and the Amelia poems

The happiest time of our love life begins when we manage to secure a bedsit for him in the Avenues. It is on the ground floor of Sloane Court on Sixth Street and the corner of (then) Rhodes Avenue. I have it cleaned and redecorated, give him furniture, put curtains up, this and that. As with each new beginning, he is in good spirits. He is writing. He also has a job for a couple of weeks, teaching literature at a private college.

I often sneak in through the French window of his flat, and we spend a few delirious hours before I go to teach German at the Zimbabwe German Society. At that time, he writes poems full of erotic images—when I read them years later or even teach them, I relive those moments. I remember stumbling into class, with his taste still in my mouth and his scent on my skin, the subtext to my public persona as literary scholar and university professor.

Next comes the period of the Amelia sonnets, written as he feels betrayed, left alone, discarded. Before travelling to Germany with my family in August 1984, I tell him that I will be back, but he feels just as abandoned as when I'd had to throw him out of my car during our first days together. To him, I am lost. Amelia turns into a ghost, she is dead, she haunts him in his dreams. Reading those poems, I sometimes wonder whether there was more to it, whether there was already an intimation of tragedy that lay ahead.

When I return from Germany in September 1984, Dambudzo is distant. He believed I would never come back. He has another girl, a blond woman. Soon she is gone, teaching somewhere in the rural areas.

We are close again, as close as we can be, the usual ups and down, fury and frenzy, passion and panic. I have bouts of deep depression. Our love seems elusive. In between there are moments of elation.

He shows me the Amelia poems. I have never written poetry myself nor have I read much of it but more than anything else, his poems allow me to see how it is through his writing that he wards off the "incompatibilities, which over-whelm, harass and threaten to crush him," as I write in my first published piece about him, an essay that I had to compose as the final assignment in my jour-nalism course (Veit-Wild, "Schreiben," trans. as "Write or Go Mad"). Through Dambudzo I start to understand the "terrifying beauty" of true art. Henceforth I will be more receptive where I find it and more critical where it is missing. The irony at this point in my life is that I am the inspiration or catalyst for some of his most beautiful writing.

I interview him as part of the series of conversations with Zimbabwean po-ets, which would later be published in my "baby-book": *Patterns of Poetry in Zimbabwe*. This is where my split identity begins. His poems are about our love, but I talk about the work with him as a literary scholar. The interview will later become another much quoted source. He possessed great lucidity in looking at his own work.

Repeatedly, he complains that I always leave him; that we never have much time together. One day he denigrates me and my work; the next, he makes plans for us writing a book together. That is my hope: that we will transform all the pre-cious and precarious ties and conflicts between us into working together. Naïve thinking on my part. Our creative collaboration will only come once he is gone.

Lake McIlwaine and after[7]
Urged by his laments that we never have enough time together, I arrange for a three-day outing to Lake McIlwaine. It is January 1985.

A horrendous disaster. I swear: Never, ever, again.

Yet, two or three weeks later I crawl under his sheets again. How often? One, two or three times?

Then, finally, I feel that I will be able to let go.

In April I am ill with some kind of virus infection. Fever, a rash, swollen glands. Similar symptoms to Pfeiffer's glandular fever, though not really identifi-able. Two years later I would know.

September 1985. Again I am back from a family holiday. I find D. in bed, in his fortress of sheets and blankets, reading. Everything is dirty. The fridge and the stove have stopped functioning. He lives like a caveman. Late in the day he goes out to get drunk.

Now that we are no longer lovers, we are more relaxed with each other. He seems happy to see me back. "I am always worried when you are outside the country. I always think you can't take care of yourself." How sweetly ironic.

---

[7] The Lake McIlwaine episode is reconstructed by Flora Veit-Wild in the short story "Lake McIlwaine" included in section 1 of this book.

While I was away, he had another car accident, riding with drunken guys. All of his front teeth were knocked out. They have been replaced courtesy of the Canadian Embassy.

One day in February 1986, D. tells me that he has been to a clinic for a test of his semen. There was blood mixed with his sperm. He says it was hilarious. The female nurses were very embarrassed. The legendary writer in for a semen test. They got a male colleague to show him where and how to collect the specimen. When he comes out of the cubicle with his vial, the nurses don't know where to look.

Twenty-five years later, I was looking through notes and papers of the time, when I found a receipt by Montagu Clinic dated 25/2/1986 for testicular surgery. I looked after him when he was not well and paid the bills. Is it already HIV–related? In 1986, HIV was beginning to be part of public consciousness. Did they test him? If so, what was the result? Did anyone tell him he was HIV-positive?

1987

This will prove to be a bad year. Especially for Mrs. Marechera, Dambudzo's mother, who will lose three of her nine children within five months.

On one of my usual "rounds" to D.'s flat, I find him in a very poor state. He is coughing badly and has a high fever. I take him to our family G.P., Nick C., who has seen D. before. "You are not looking good today, Dambudzo," he says, and, after listening to the rattling in his lungs, tells me: "Take him straight into Parirenyatwa."

A couple of days later, Nick asks me to come and see him. He knows that Dambudzo does not want to have anything to do with his relatives, so he discloses the news to me, whom he regards as his closest friend. "Dambudzo has AIDS," he tells me, "HIV-related pneumonia. One cannot tell how long he is going to live."

The news set me into a state of panic. Three weeks later I get my test results: I am HIV-positive.

I do not speak to D. about it. The load is too heavy. I don't want him to feel guilty. He once mentions that the hospital doctors have found a "strange virus." Does he know which one and what it means? I do not know.

When I come to see him in hospital, he tells me that his mother and other female relatives have been for a visit. News has spread that he is dying. As always he is utterly dismissive. "All they want is my money," he says.

Out of hospital after a couple of weeks, he is frail. He appears at an African literature conference at the University. Colleagues and students are happy to have him around. He is there, he speaks, he "behaves." He seems subdued, not his usual angry self.

In April, his eldest brother Lovemore dies of liver cirrhosis. D. goes to Mar-
ondera, where family members gather but returns already a day later, before the
funeral takes place. He is disgruntled, feels maltreated and excluded by his relatives, especially by his brother Michael, now the head of the family.

In June, his sister Tsitsi is "bombed to heaven."[8] I read about it at breakfast on
the first page of *The Herald*. Half an hour later, D. phones, shaken. I drive with
him to the site of destruction. Later Michael appears, other relatives. Then Mugabe and four of his ministers arrive and pay their condolences. Though she was
the only one among his brothers and sisters for whom he felt affection, he would
not attend her funeral. They are making her into a "national hero" and bury her at
Heroes Acre. He refuses to be a part of this.

On 15 August, I find him in his flat, feverish, dehydrated, out of breath. I take
him straight to the hospital. His lungs are damaged to an extent that he hardly
gets enough oxygen. Yet, when I come the next day, I find him upright in his bed,
smoking. His wish, muttered in between drags on his cigarette: I should bring him
something to write with, he wants to make a will.

I don't seem to realise how critical the situation is. I should have gone right
away to get pen and paper. When I return the next day, I find him unconscious.
He dies in the early hours of the next day.

What would have been different if he had written a will?

"Which one of you bastards is Death?"

*Dambudzo, I am sitting by your bed watching you die. I have never seen anyone
die before, so I don't know whether it will happen within the next hour, day or
week. I have asked the nurses who glide in out of the room at long intervals, ignoring my presence. Dying is shameful and nobody wants to be implicated. I feel
like an intruder, white in a black hospital, encroaching on a foreign culture at
one of its most secretive moments. The nurses tell me one cannot tell, it can be
very soon, but can also take its time.*

*When did you write the "Bastard Death" poems? Days or weeks or months
ago? You did not show them to me, I will find them tomorrow when I clear out
your flat. You are in conversation with this bastard now, not arguing anymore,
silently acknowledging his presence as he lets you draw your last wafts of breath.
You seem far away, your mouth and nose under the oxygen mask. The mask is
all they can provide to relieve your struggle. Antibiotics won't help, not with one
side of your lung already gone and the other near collapse. It is only a matter*

---

[8] Her Zambian husband worked for the ANC. He had brought a TV home from Mozambique into
which South African agents had planted a bomb. When Tsitsi wanted to switch it on, it went off,
tearing her to pieces and destroying the flat. See *Source Book*, 375-377. DM alludes to it in his
poem "I Used to Like Tomatoes," *Cemetery of Mind* 207.

of time. I am sitting here, helpless, watching you breathe in, ever so slowly, as deeply as your corroded lungs allow you, wheezing as your chest heaves up and then rattles down. There is a pause after each breath, and I listen anxiously, waiting for the next. The pauses seem longer and longer. Each time I wonder, is this the last one?

But while you are going to join your ancestors—oh, how you will howl at them to leave you alone! —let me tell you how the Bastard is threatening to get me—is hovering above my house, too—because this is also part of our story.
For many years I will live full of joy about every new day that I will be in good health. But, unlike you, I will be lucky. I will survive.

The After-Life

After Dambudzo's death, there was talk among publishers and friends about what to do with his unpublished work. I did not want to do it. I wanted to focus on my PhD research, which I had started in 1986, and also, I did not feel sufficiently qualified. I did *not* say that my life was too closely interwoven with Dambudzo's to be the one to select and edit poems that had been inspired by our relationship. How could I work on his biography without mentioning his love life and the real causes for his death? Yet, in the end, Irene Staunton and Hugh Lewin, my main consultants—who had just founded Baobab Books and published the tribute collection *Dambudzo Marechera 1952-1987*—persuaded me that I was the best person to take on this task.

So I did. I took on what was to become a deeply gratifying labour of love. In a way I have been in constant conversation with him, safe from his invectives, free to do with "him" what I deem proper.

Ironically, Dambudzo, out of his grave, "paid me back." To my great surprise, seven years after his death, I found myself appointed Professor of African Literature by Berlin's distinguished Humboldt University. I would enter a career that I had never planned or expected.

Yet there has also been the dark side, the menace. Dambudzo haunted my dreams. Once, not long after his death, I dreamed he was throwing little poison darts at me from across the street. They stuck in my skin, but I pulled them out and walked away, safe. When he appears to me now, the threat is gone. He seems calm, composed, almost serene.

During my family's remaining years in Zimbabwe, I worked concurrently on my PhD and on the posthumous publications and the biography of Marechera. Both, my dissertation, *Teachers, Preachers, Non-Believers,* and my *Source Book* appeared in 1992. I attended conferences and published articles.

In 1993 we returned to a re-unified Germany. East German universities were being restructured, so also Humboldt. A chair for African Literatures and Cultures had been created. Although I had only passed my PhD at Frankfurt University in 1991 and did not have the usual prerequisite for such a post, the German Habilitation, other work can be recognised as an equivalent. In my case, this other work consisted of my Marechera oeuvre.

Yet another historical irony came into play. In 1974, the West German government had not admitted me as a high school teacher because of my adherence to Maoist organisations. I was a victim of what was called "Radikalenerlass."[9] Twenty years later, I was ordained as "Beamter auf Lebenszeit" (civil servant for life). And this not only thanks to Dambudzo, the troublemaker and the most anti-authoritarian spirit I have ever known, but also thanks to the changed political environment in my country. The academic committee at Humboldt University had shortlisted an Africanist from an East German University as number one for the position. However, he had been implicated with the GDR regime and therefore lost his job. That is why the government authorities did not accept his candidature at Humboldt, thus making way for number two on the list, the erstwhile Radical, which was me.

***

This is, in outline, *my* story of Dambudzo Marechera.

He unlocked many doors for me and let me peek into the marvellous world beyond. He gave me intimations of hell but also the strength to resist.

He, who said he had never met an "African" but only human beings, made me into an "Africanist." What a prank, Dambudzo.

---

[9] Decree of 1972 prohibiting members of extremist organisations from becoming civil servants or teachers.

Top: Marechera Celebration, Oxford, May 15-17, 2009. Bottom: Drew Shaw, James Currey, Gerald Gaylard, Anopa Makaka, Memory Chirere, Lizzy Attree, Tolu Ogunlesi, Tinashe Mushakavanhu

Jennifer Armstrong, Julie Cairnie

Carolyn Hart

Comrade Fatso as the ghost of Dambudzo

Heeten Bhagat

Drew Shaw, Brendon Nicholls

204

N. Vance, R. Fraser, A. Niven, F. Veit-Wild

Norman Vance

James Currey

Robert Fraser

Alastair Niven

Flora Veit-Wild

Brian Chikwava reads from *Harare North*

Jane Bryce

Elleke Boehmer

Memory Chirere, Tinashe Mushakavanhu, Brian Chikwava

Zoë Norridge and Dobrota Pucherova

Memory Chirere, David Caute

M. Chirere, G. Gaylard, D. Pucherova, T. Sebina, H. Bhagat   Nana Oforiatta-Ayim

Flora Veit-Wild with students   James Currey, Dobrota Pucherova, Robert Fraser

David Pattison   Jane Bryce, Brendon Nicholls

i'm
standing
by you
O Toilet
a black
Hamlet
soliloquising
the dread
hours away.

SERVANTS' BALL - BLITZKRIEG
Adapted from **Dambudzo Marechera**
11th - 15th May (3rd week)
7.30 Moser Theatre, Wadham   **wegottickets.com**

Sophie Lewis (director of *Servants' Ball*), Jeneece Bernard

Matthew Waksman, director of *Blitzkrieg*

Simon Bright, Dumi Senda, Anopa Makaka

New College tour

BIBLIOGRAPHY

ABC of all the questions we never dare to ask. Cape Town and Harare: Kwela Books and Weaver Press, 2003.

Aidoo, Ama Ata, ed. *African Love Stories: An Anthology*. Banbury: Ayebia, 2006.

Albert, Richard N. *An Annotated Bibliography of Jazz Fiction and Jazz Criticism*. Westport, Connecticut: Greenwood Press, 1996.

Armah, Ayi Kwei. *The Beautyful Ones Are Not Yet Born*. London: Heinemann, 1969.

Armstrong, Jennifer. "Is Marechera a Modernist?"<http://unsafe.blogspot.com/2006/08/is-marechera-modernist.html>

Attridge, Derek. *J.M. Coetzee and the Ethics of Reading: Literature in the Event*. Pietermaritzburg: University of Kwazulu-Natal Press, 2005.

Awoonor, Kofi. *This Earth, My Brother*. London: Heinemann, 1972.

Bakhtin, Mikhail. *Rabelais and His World*. Trans. Helene Iswolsky. Cambridge, Massachusetts: MIT, 1965.

Balogun, Odun. "Taban lo Liyong's *The Uniformed Man*: A Reconstructivist and Metafictional Parody of Modernism." *The Language of African Literature*. Ed. by Edmund L. Epstein and Robert Kole. Trenton, NJ: Africa World Press, 1996. 251-63.

Baudrillard, Jean. "Beyond the Unconscious: The Symbolic." *Discourse* 3 (1981): 60-87.

Baudrillard, Jean & Marc Guillaume. *Radical Alterity*. Los Angeles:Semiotext(e), 2008.

Bauman, Zygmunt. *Liquid Love: On the Frailty of Human Bonds*. Cambridge: Polity, 2003.

Bethlehem, Louise. "'A Primary Need as Strong as Hunger': The Rhetoric of Urgency in South African Literary Culture under Apartheid." *Poetics Today* 22. 2 (Summer 2001): 365-389.

Boehmer, Elleke. *Stories of Women: Gender and Narrative in the Postcolonial Nation*. Manchester: Manchester University Press, 2005.

---. "Tropes of Yearning and Dissent: The Troping of Desire in Yvonne Vera and Tsitsi Dangarembga." *Journal of Commonwealth Literature* 38. 1 (2003): 135-148.

Bourdillon, Michael. *Child Domestic Workers in Zimbabwe.* Harare: Weaver Press and Save the Children, Norway, 2006.

Bourdillon, Michael and Rumbidzai Rurevo. *Girls on the Street.* Harare: Weaver Press, 2003.

Bryce, Jane. "Inside/out: Body and Sexuality in Marechera's Fiction."*Emerging Perspectives on Dambudzo Marechera.* Ed. by Flora Veit-Wild and Anthony Chennells. Trenton, NJ: Africa World Press, 1999. 221-234.

Carter, Angela. "A witness, a prophet". *The Guardian* 21 June 1979.

Carpenter, Humphrey. *Robert Runcie: the Reluctant Archbishop.* London: Hodder and Stoughton, 1996.

Caute, David. *Marechera and the Colonel.* London: Totterdown, 2009.

---."Marechera in Black and White." *Cultural Struggle and Development in Southern Africa.* Ed. by Preben Kaarsholm. London: James Currey, 1991. 95-111.

Chennells, Anthony. "Self-Representation and National Memory: White Autobiographies in Zimbabwe." *Versions of Zimbabwe: New Approaches to Literature and Culture.* Ed. by Robert Muponde and Ranka Primorac. Harare: Weaver Press, 2005. 131-144.

--- and Flora Veit-Wild. "Introduction: The Man Who Betrayed Africa?" *Emerging Perspectives on Dambudzo Marechera.* Ed. by Flora Veit-Wild and Anthony Chennells. Trenton, NJ: Africa World Press, 1999. xi-xix.

Chikwava, Brian. "Seventh Street Alchemy." *Writing Still: New Stories from Zimbabwe.* Ed. by Irene Staunton. Harare: Weaver, 2003. 17-30.

---. "The Jazz Goblin and His Rhythm." *Short Writings from Bulawayo 3.* Ed. by Jane Morris. Bulawayo: Amabooks, 2006. 132-139.

Chinodya, Shimmer. *Tale of Tamari.* Harare: Weaver Press, 2004.

Chirere, Memory. "Ignatius Mabasa's *Mapenzi* and the Innovation of the Shona Novel." *Beyond the Language Issue: The Production, Mediation and Reception of Creative Writing in African Languages.* Ed. by Anja Oed and Uta Reuster-Jahn. Köln: Köppe, 2008. 221-25.

---. "*Mapenzi*: Leaving the Centre in Order to Get to It." *The Southern Times* 28 November 2003: C4.

---. Review of *Tale of Tamari.* <http://www.weaverpresszimbabwe.com/latest-reviews/ 78-tale-of-tamari/300-review-of-tale-of-tamari-memory-chirere.html>

Chirere, Memory, R. Magosvongwe, and J. Zondo, eds. *Children Writing Zimbabwe: Selected Stories from Cover to Cover.* Harare: Culture Fund, 2008.

Coetzee, J.M. *Disgrace.* London: Vintage, 2000.

---. "What is a Classic?" (1991). *Stranger Shores: Essays 1986-1999.* London: Vintage, 2001. 1-19.

Covino, William A. *Magic, Rhetoric, and Literacy: An Eccentric History of the*

Composing Imagination. Albany: SUNY Press, 1995.

Currey, James. "Publishing Dambudzo Marechera." *Africa Writes Back: The African Writers Series and the Launch of African Literature*. Oxford: James Currey, 2008. 278-95.

Declaration of the Rights of the Child (1959) <http://www.un.org/cyberschoolbus/humanrights/resources/child.asp>

Declaration of the Rights of the Child (1989) <http://www.unesco.org/education/pdf/CHILD_E.PDF>

Deleuze, Gilles & Felix Guattari. *Anti-Oedipus: Capitalism and Schizophrenia*. Trans. by Robert Hurley, Mark Seem & Helen Lane. London: Athlone, 1984.

Deshell, Jeffrey, et al. "The Fiction Collective Story." <http://www.fc2.org/about_us.aspx>

DuBois, W.E.B. *The Souls of Black Folk*. Oxford: Oxford University Press, 2008.

Dubow, Saul. *Scientific Racism in Modern South Africa*. Cambridge: Cambridge University Press, 1995.

Eagleton, Terry. *Heathcliff and the Great Hunger: Studies in Irish Culture*. London: Verso, 1996.

Fanon, Frantz. *Black Skin, White Masks*. Trans. Charles Markmann. London: Pluto, 1967.

Flood, Alison. "Children can handle much more realism than Anne Fine thinks." *Guardian* (online), 26 August 2009. <http://www.guardian.co.uk/books/booksblog/2009/aug/26/children-realism-anne-fine. 30/8/2009>

Foster, Kevin. "Soul-Food for the Starving: Dambudzo Marechera's *The House of Hunger*." *Journal of Commonwealth Literature* 27.1 (1992): 58-70.

Foucault, Michel. *Madness and Civilization: A History of Insanity in the Age of Reason*. [1961]. Trans. Richard Howard. London: Tavistock, 1967.

Fraser, Robert. *God's Good Englishman: Samuel Johnson Bicentenary Production, 1784-1984*. Directed by Ian Watt-Smith. Oxford Playhouse, Cambridge Arts Theatre, King's Lynn Festival, Opera House, Belfast, 1984.

Fuller, Alexandra. *Don't Let's Go to the Dogs Tonight: An African Childhood*. New York: Random House, 2001.

Gagiano, Annie. "Marecheran Postmodernism: Mocking the Bad Joke of 'African modernity'." Annie Gagiano, *Dealing with Evils: Essays on Writing from Africa*. Stuttgart: Ibidem-Verlag, 2008. 21-43.

---. "Marechera's Wordhorde and the Scrapiron of War." *Versions of Zimbabwe: New Approaches to Literature and Culture*. Ed. by Robert Muponde & Ranka Primorac. Harare: Weaver, 2005. 41-54.

Gaylard, Gerald. *After Colonialism: African Postmodernism and Magical Realism*. Johannesburg: Wits University Press, 2005.

Godwin, Peter. *Mukiwa: A White Boy in Africa*. New York: Grove Press, 1996.

Gray, Nancy. *Language Unbound: On Experimental Writing by Women*. Urbana: University of Illinois Press, 1992.

Grazier, Julie M. and Misty Farrell. "Voices from the Gaps: Gayl Jones," 23 May 2001. <http://voices.cla.umn.edu/authors/GaylJones.html>

Harris, Ashleigh. "Writing Home: Inscriptions of Whiteness/Descriptions of Belonging in White Zimbabwean Memoirs/Autobiography." *Versions of Zimbabwe: New Approaches to Literature and Culture*. Ed. by Robert Muponde and Ranka Primorac. Harare: Weaver Press, 2005. 103-17.

Hart, Carolyn. "In Search of African Literary Aesthetics: Production and Reception of the Texts of Amos Tutuola and Yvonne Vera." *Journal of African Cultural Studies*. Vol. 21, No. 2. December 2009: 177-195.

Helgesson, Stefan. *Writing in Crisis: Ethics and History in Gordimer, Ndebele and Coetzee*. Pietermaritzburg: University of Kwazulu-Natal Press, 2004.

Hurston, Zora Neale. "How It Feels to Be Colored Me." [1928]. *I Love Myself When I Am Laughing ... And Then Again: A Zora Neale Hurston Reader*. Ed. by Alice Walker. New York: Feminist Press, 1979. 152-155.

Irele, Abiola. *The African Imagination: Literature in Africa and the Black Diaspora*. Oxford; New York: Oxford University Press, 2001.

Irigaray, Luce. *The Way of Love*. London: Continuum, 2002.

Jones, Gayl. *Corregidora*. Boston: Beacon Press, 1975.

---. *Eva's Man*. Boston: Beacon Press, 1976.

---. *The Healing*. Boston: Beacon Press, 1998.

Katz, Steve. *Kisssss, a Miscelany*. Tuscaloosa: FC2/University of Alabama Press, 2007.

Kristeva, Julia. *Desire in Language: A Semiotic Approach to Literature and Art*. New York: Columbia University Press, 1980.

---. *The Powers of Horror: An Essay on Abjection*. New York; Columbia University Press, 1982.

Laing, R. D. *The Politics of Experience*. Hamondsworth: Penguin, 1967.

Lessing, Doris. *African Laughter: Four Visits to Zimbabwe*. New York: Perennial, 1993.

---. "A Cultural Tug-of-War." *Books and Bookmen* XXIV.ix (June 1979): 62-3.

---. *The Grass is Singing*. London: Flamingo, 1994. (1950).

---. "On not winning the Nobel Prize." 7 December 2007. <http://nobelprize.org/ nobel_prizes/literature/laureates/2007/lessing-lecture_en.pdf>

Levinas, Emmanuel. *Totality and Infinity: An Essay on Exteriority*. Trans. Alphonso Lingis. Pittsburgh: Duquesne University Press, 1969.

Liedel, Herbert and Helmut Dollhopf, eds. *Der alte Kanal damals und heute. Ludwig-Donau-Main-Kanal*. Würzburg: Stürtz, 1981.

Loomba, Ania. *Colonialism/Postcolonialism*. London: Routledge, 2005.

Mabasa, Ignatius. *Fools*. Trans. Joyce Mutiti. Unpublished, 2011.

---. *Mapenzi*. Harare: College Press, 1999.

---. "Why I Write in Shona." <http://pamabasa.com/?Why_I_Write_in_Shona>

Mafuba, Dick. "Ideology and Dambudzo Marechera's 'Throne of Bayonets.'" *English Studies in Africa* 54: 1 (2011): 105-118.

Marechera, Dambudzo. "The African Writer's Experience of European Literature." *Zambezia* 14. 2 (1987): 99-105.

---. "The African Writer's Experience of European Literature." [1987]. *Dambudzo Marechera: A Source Book on his Life and Work*. By Flora Veit-Wild. London: Hans Zell, 1992. Trenton, NJ: Africa World Press, 2004. 361-368.

---. "The African Writer's Experience of European Literature." [1987]. *African Literature: An Anthology of Criticism and Theory*. Ed. by Tejumola Olaniyan and Ato Quayson. Oxford: Blackwell, 2007. 186-91.

---. *The Black Insider*. Comp. and ed. by Flora Veit-Wild. Harare: Baobab, 1990.

---. *Black Sunlight*. London: Heinemann, 1980, 2010.

---. *Cemetery of Mind*. Comp. and ed. by Flora Veit-Wild. Harare: Baobab, 1992.

---. *The House of Hunger*. London: Heinemann, 1978, 2009.

---. *Mindblast*. Harare: College Press, 1984.

---. *Scrapiron Blues*. Comp. and ed. by Flora Veit-Wild. Harare: Baobab, 1994.

Martin, Reginald. "An Interview with Ishmael Reed." 1983. <http://www.dalkeyarchive.com/catalog/show_comment/213>

McCartney, Irene, ed. *Children in our Midst: Voices of Farmworkers' Children*. Harare: Weaver and Save the Children, UK, 2000.

McClintock, Anne. *Imperial Leather: Race, Gender and Sexuality in the Imperial Contest*. New York: Routledge, 1995.

McLoughlin, Tim. "Conflict and Instability in Marechera's *Cemetery of Mind*." *Commonwealth* 19.2 (1997): 42-50.

Muchemwa, Kizito and Musaemura Zimunya. "An Overview of Post-Independence Zimbabwean Poetry." 3 October 2008. <http://www.poetryinternational.org/piw_cms/cms/cms_module/index.php?obj_id=13089>

Muhwati, Itai. "Mass Neurosis, Entrapment, Closure and the Race's Race of Life in *Masango Mavi* (1998) and *Mapenzi* (1999)." 2006. Institutional Repository, University of Zimbabwe. <http://ir.uz.zw:8080/jspui/handle/10646/515>.

Mupfudza, Ruzvidzo Stanley. "The Eyes of a Walk." *A Roof to Repair*. Harare: College Press, 2001. 52-59.

---. "Mermaid out of the Rain." *Writing Still: New Stories from Zimbabwe*. Ed. by Irene Staunton. Harare: Weaver, 2003. 161-167.

---. "A Picture of Madness." *Moto Magazine* (July 1993): 11.

---. "Who is Afraid of Marechera?" *The Herald* 2 May 2001: 7.

Muponde, Robert. "At the Window." *No More Plastic Balls and Other Stories.* Ed. by Robert Muponde and Clement Chihota. Harare: College Press, 2000. 224-233.

---. "The Fury of Futility." Unpublished.

---. "Reconstructing Childhood: Social Banditry in Marechera's Children's Stories." *Emerging Perspectives on Dambudzo Marechera.* Ed. by Flora Veit-Wild and Anthony Chennells. Trenton, New Jersey: Africa World Press, 1999. 253-63.

---. "The Storm." *No More Plastic Balls and Other Stories.* Ed. by Robert Muponde and Clement Chihota. Harare: College Press, 2000. 194-200.

---. "Touched." *No More Plastic Balls and Other Stories.* Ed. by Robert Muponde and Clement Chihota. Harare: College Press, 2000. 201-215.

---. "Unhappy Family, Unhappy Children and the End of Childhood in Dambudzo Marechera's *The House of Hunger.*" *Childhood* 13.4 (2006): 519-32.

Musengezi, Chiedza. "Notes by Chiedza Musengezi on *Mapenzi.*" Unpublished, 2009.

Mushakavanhu, Tinashe. "Max Wild recalls a childhood with Dambudzo Marechera." *Mazwi: Zimbabwean Literary Journal* (2009). <http://www.mazwi.net/interviews/max-wild-recalls-a-childhood-with-dambudzo-marechera>.

Mutasa, David. E. and Itai Muhwati. "A Philosophical Interpretation of the Significance of Oral Forms in I. Mabasa's Novel *Mapenzi* (1999)." *Literator: Journal of Literary Criticism, Comparative Linguistics and Literary Studies* 29.3 (2008): 157-179.

Nyamfukudza, Stanley. *The Non-Believer's Journey.* London: Heinemann, 1980.

Pape, John. "Black and White: The 'Perils of Sex' in Colonial Zimbabwe." *Journal of Southern African Studies* 16.4 (December 1990): 699-720.

Pattison, David. "The Search for the Primordial I in the Novels *Black Sunlight* and *The Black Insider.*" *Emerging Perspectives on Dambudzo Marechera.* Ed. by Flora Veit-Wild and Anthony Chennells. Trenton, NJ: Africa World Press, 1999. 193-208.

Pelton, Ted. "Steve Katz: Experimental Fiction Writer at Medaille." April 16, 2009. <http://artvoice.com/issues/v8n16/literary_buffalo/steve_katz>

Priebe, Richard. *Ghanaian Literatures.* New York: Greenwood Press, 1988.

Quayson, Ato. *Calibrations: Reading for the Social.* Minneapolis: University of Minnesota Press, 2003.

Ranger, Terence. "Nationalist Historiography, Patriotic History and the History of the Nation: The Struggle over the Past in Zimbabwe." *Journal of Southern African Studies* 30. 2 (2004): 215-234.

Reed, Ishmael. *Mumbo Jumbo.* Garden City, NY: Doubleday, 1972.

---. *The Last Days of Louisiana Red.* New York: Random House, 1974.

---. *Yellow Back Radio Broke-Down.* Garden City, NY: Doubleday, 1969.

Rettová, Alena. *Afrophone Philosophies: Reality and Challenge.* Stredokluky: Zdeněk Susa, 2007.

Rowell, Charles. "An Interview with Gayl Jones." *Callaloo* 16 (1982): 32-53.

Save the Children. *Our Broken Dreams: Child Migration in Southern Africa.* <http://www.savethechildren.org.uk/en/54_5434.htm>

Schapiro, Tamar. "What is a Child?" *Ethics* 109.4 (July 1999): 715-38.

Shange, Ntozake. *For colored girls who have considered suicide / when the rainbow is enuf.* Alexandria, Virginia: Alexander Street Press, 2003.

---. *See No Evil.* San Franciso: Momo's Press, 1984.

Shaw, Drew. "Transgressing Traditional Narrative Form." *Emerging Perspectives on Dambudzo Marechera.* Ed. by Flora Veit-Wild and Anthony Chennells. Trenton, NJ: Africa World Press, 1999. 3-22.

Stoler, Ann Laura, *Carnal Knowledge and Imperial Power: Race and the Intimate in Colonial Rule.* Berkeley: University of California Press, 2002.

Sweetman, David. "Interview with Dambudzo Marechera." *Arts and Africa*, no. 288P, BBC African Service transcript [London], 8 July 1979, 3-4.

Taitz, Laurice and Melissa Levin. "Fictional Autobiographies or Autobiographical Fictions?" *Emerging Perspectives on Dambudzo Marechera.* Ed. by Flora Veit-Wild and Anthony Chennells. Trenton, New Jersey: Africa World Press, 1999. 163-176.

Vambe, Maurice. "The Instabilities of National Allegory: The Case of Dambudzo Marechera's *The House of Hunger* and *Black Sunlight*." *Current Writing* 13.1 (2001): 70-86.

Veit-Wild, Flora. "Carnival and Hybridity in Marechera and Lesego Rampolokeng." *Emerging Perspectives on Dambudzo Marechera.* Ed. by Flora Veit-Wild & Anthony Chennells. Trenton NJ: Africa World Press, 1999. 93-104.

---. *Dambudzo Marechera: A Source Book on his Life and Work.* London: Hans Zell, 1992. Trenton, NJ: Africa World Press, 2004.

---. "De-Silencing the Past—Challenging 'Patriotic History': New Books on Zimbabwean literature." *Research in African Literature* 37.3 (2006): 195-204.

---. and Anthony Chennells, eds. *Emerging Perspectives on Dambudzo Marechera.* Trenton NJ: Africa World Press, 1999.

---. *Karneval und Kakerlaken: Postkolonialismus in der afrikanischen Literatur.* Berlin: Öffentliche Vorlesungen an der Humboldt-Universität zu Berlin, Philosophische Fakultät III, 1995.

---. "Lake McIlwaine." *Wasafiri* 27. 1 (March 2012): 8-10.

---. "Me and Dambudzo: A Personal Essay." *Wasafiri* 27. 1 (March 2012): 1-7.

---. *Patterns of Poetry in Zimbabwe*. Gweru: Mambo Press, 1988.

---. "Schreiben gegen den Wahnsinn: Der zimbabwische Schriftsteller Dambudzo Marechera." *Tageszeitung*, 4 December 1987, 16; also published in: *Englisch Amerikanische Studien*, March 1988, 147-150.

---. *Survey of Zimbabwean Writers: Educational and Literary Careers*. Bayreuth: Bayreuth African Studies, 1992.

---. *Teachers, Preachers, Non-Believers: A Social History of Zimbabwean Literature*. London: Hans Zell, 1992.

---. "Write or Go Mad." *Africa Events*, March 1986, 58-59; also published in *Dambudzo Marechera – 1952-1983*, ed. by Ernst Schade & Flora Veit-Wild. Harare: Baobab Books, 1988, 28-29.

---, ed. *Writing Madness: Borderlines of the Body in African Literature*. Oxford: James Currey, 2006.

---. "'Zimbolicious'—The Creative Potential of Linguistic Innovation: The Case of Shona-English in Zimbabwe." *Journal of Southern African Studies* 35.3 (2009): 683-697.

Vera, Yvonne. *Under the Tongue*. Harare: Baobab, 1996.

Walsh Sue. " 'Irony? But Children Don't Get It, Do They?': The Idea of Appropriate Language in Narratives for Children." *Children's Literature Association Quarterly* 28.1 (Spring 2003): 26-36.